The
Performer's
Tale

Freema
1953

VANESSA MORTON

The Performer's Tale

Nine Lives of Patience Collier

Foreword by
Dame Penelope Wilton

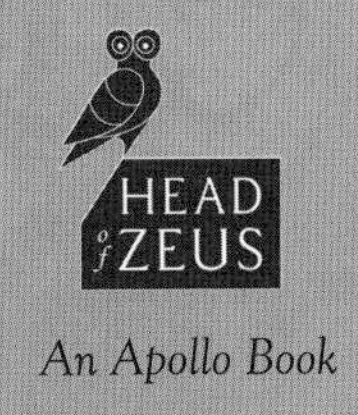

An Apollo Book

An Apollo Book
First published in the UK in 2021 by Head of Zeus Ltd

1 3 5 7 9 10 8 6 4 2

Editor: Sue Lascelles
Designed by Alastair Campbell
Indexer: Cliff Murphy

A CPI catalogue record for this book
is available from the British Library

ISBN (HB) 9781800245150
ISBN (E) 9781800245136

Printed and bound in Spain
by Graficas Estella

Head of Zeus Ltd
5–8 Hardwick Street
London EC1R 4RG
WWW.HEADOFZEUS.COM

In tribute to an extraordinary woman, and to all those who worked with her during this golden period of performance.

CONTENTS

AUTHOR'S NOTE

It was back in 2010 that I first heard about the actress Patience Collier's archive. Her daughters Susan and Sarah were discussing what to do with her vast array of boxes, held in attics and in expensive storage pods. It was valuable stuff, fifty years of performance and personal history. But what about the diaries, they wondered? – and here they giggled. Wouldn't the collection need to be censored before it could be offered to a theatre archive?

Listening in vaguely to their conversation, I turned up the volume. A large, untapped, revealing archive? Belonging to Patience Collier – whom I remembered from my teens: loud, fearsome, eccentric and always unpredictable? An actress whose perfectionism shone through in her every performance, and who appeared with every starry director and actor of her time? Though her name has faded from public consciousness – she died in 1987 – it still conjures cool memories of iconic television and film from the 1970s and 80s – *Sapphire and Steel, Who Pays the Ferryman, Fiddler on the Roof* and *The French Lieutenant's Woman* – and startles with recognition in repeats of radio and television classics.

I jumped at the chance to explore the material. Sarah brought over box after box. Gradually, other bundles of letters and additional material turned up in family lofts and cupboards, or were brought out diffidently as my project got underway. Here in the collection were prolific scrapbooks of every production – packages of stills – green-inked and sometimes coded diaries – gold-embossed albums from the early years of the twentieth century, a Central European world in London's Bayswater – startling letters, frank and pithy exchanges.

It soon became clear that here was a significant story – of some fifty years of changing tastes, styles, culture and popular media from the 1930s to the 1980s: of a woman weaving her way through the twentieth century, mixing with the great and the good, the artists, the leftists, the world of entertainment. Of a woman with a late-blooming career in unsupportive times, constantly reshaping her presentation of herself to the world as the political mood and spirit of the times changed: of a thoroughly difficult and combative yet vulnerable person, drawing love and admiration, but also fear and dismay. Of a brilliant character actress who increasingly behaved like a grande dame. Why and how did she become this larger than life person?

A key if small part of the archive were the notes of Patience's great friend, the former radio producer Audrey Postgate. In the late 1970s and 1980s, she had worked with Patience on a potential memoir: when Patience died, Audrey's whirlwind notes recording cogent memories and observations were added to the collection. Though needing to be pieced together from scraps of paper and notecards, these read as though one were in the room, providing a rich source of Patience's direct speech.

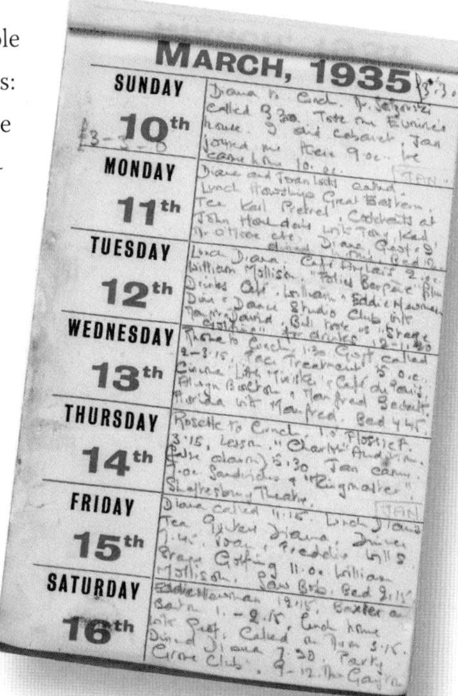

Crucial again were the interviews I was able to hold with dozens of her contemporaries: actors, directors, wig-makers and costume designers, stage-managers, children, grandchildren, friends and even enemies. Through them I was able to circle round the Patience I was getting to know so pithily from her diaries and recollections, gathering memories so vivid it was as if she had died only yesterday.

A performer through and through, from a tiny child to her last days, this then is her tale.

Vanessa Morton, *December 2020*

FOREWORD

BY DAME PENELOPE WILTON

I FIRST MET Patience Collier in Alec McCowen's dressing room, after a performance of *The Philanthropist* at the Royal Court Theatre in 1971. This was my first play in London and only my second job. It was a fleeting meeting and not a particularly warm one. I think she was rather put out that this young thing should be having a drink in the Star's dressing room, so I didn't stay long.

It wasn't until some years later when I married Daniel Massey that I really got to know her. Dan and she had worked in a revue together – *Living for Pleasure* – and he was devoted to her. On his own admission he was quite a volatile young actor, impatient and at times not easy to work with. But Patience seemed to understand him, and finally, under her instruction, got him to visit every dressing room before the show and say good evening. This apparently went some way to making a more serene atmosphere backstage!

I worked with Patience in Karel Reisz's film of John Fowles' novel, *The French Lieutenant's Woman* in 1980, in which she played Mrs Poulteney, a puritanical waspish old woman who employs the heroine – played by Meryl Streep – as a companion. That was just one of her creations. With the help of a good design team, whether in film or theatre, Patience herself would disappear and a totally different character would emerge. She had a reputation for being very exacting, but designers loved working with her, and she appreciated their skill. Acting is all about being very specific.

My own relationship with Patience was entirely separate from Dan's or so it became. Perhaps the truth is I was easier to manage than Dan, and Patience liked things to be on her terms. So if she was coming for lunch she would ring and ask what we were having? I never knew a week in advance, so she would order what she wanted. Lamb chops were a favourite. This used to make me very annoyed and I'd grumble and say I won't put up with this behaviour. But the day would come, the lunch would be prepared, Patience would arrive, and we would spend an afternoon of the best conversation. My lunch would be praised to the sky. I would be left feeling I was the most marvellous hostess, and my lamb chops a *succès fou*!

Lunches at her home at Campden Hill Road were a rather more formal affair. The kitchen was presided over by Alice, Patience's cook housekeeper. You would catch a glimpse of her through the hatch from the kitchen to the dining room. After what was always a very good meal the guests would be sent down to the kitchen to thank her. I once made the mistake of asking if Alice had had her lunch as a chicken was passed through the hatch and Patience shut the doors. She turned to me and said, "Alice always gets served first and she gets the best!"

What I remember most about Patience was her interest in other people. She very rarely spoke about herself and she gave you her full attention while you were together. I only once saw her drop her guard with me and that was when her husband Harry died. They had been living very separate lives for a long time, but she missed him and had a few tears as I sat holding her hand. "'Nobody will look after me now like Harry did". She was, of course, a wonderful actress who cared so much about her craft. But I will remember her as an example of what friendships can be.

PROLOGUE

THE ROLE OF Mrs Poulteney in the film of John Fowles's novel, *The French Lieutenant's Woman*, has come at a decidedly down period in actor Patience Collier's life. It is 1980; she is feeling old and worn. She has had only one television role in a year. Her feet, her legs, her back, her bowels, are all playing up. She has been consulting dieticians, trying special diets of apple purée, having periods of boring bed-rest and 'house-coat' days to ease her legs, screaming down the stairs for Alice Lytton, her eighty-year-old housekeeper, who toils up with her bad hip, muttering.

But the offer of the sour-faced tyrant Mrs Poulteney re-energises Patience. After a highly satisfactory interview in April at Twickenham studios with Karel Reisz, the film's director, everything seems to proceed in exactly the right way. Reisz visits her at home at 23 Campden Hill Road in Kensington, astutely bringing with him the very person she would wish to see first, the costume designer. The stars of the film, Meryl Streep and Jeremy Irons, come to tea. The entire production seems to have a sense of finesse and quality about it: make-up artists and hairdressers are top of the range, and two theatrical firms are employed which Patience considers the very best, Cosprop and Wig Creations. Building up the look of Mrs Poulteney goes without a hitch; her own wardrobe is raided for her outfit in the 'reality' party scenes in which the actors appear as 'themselves'.

The whole affair, running over the summer, is wonderfully 'spoily': her ego is 'in a joy', as she later puts it. The strange demands of film, the taking scenes out of sequence, the close-ups, the dubbing long after everything else is over, all seem of no consequence compared with the fuss that is made of her, 'the powdering, patting, combing, pinning, minding', all in the pursuit of perfection.[1] Reisz, working with scriptwriter Harold Pinter, she thoroughly admires: he is 'a wonderful leader of a TEAM', she writes in her diary, 'in control absolutely'. He has a careful, thoughtful perfectionism of which she thoroughly approves.

It is not easy to get the voice of Mrs Poulteney as she wants it. She works hard on the script at home as usual, bringing in friends and coaches to assist, building up what *The Financial Times* reviewer will call her 'fishwife bark and Biblical bromides' in a part which shows her at the peak of her powers.[2] It is a furiously busy time – planning for her catered seventieth birthday lunch for forty-one people, including 'the Timothy Wests', the 'Dan Masseys', Janet Suzman, Trevor Nunn and Peter Hall; reacting to her daughters' marriage problems; reading the scripts for the role that is to immediately follow in ATV's cult sci-fi series *Sapphire and Steel*; recoiling with shock from the news of the suicide of a former lover. She has no time to go to his funeral.

Among the friends and assistants who come to the house to hear Patience's lines during this period is former radio producer Audrey Postgate. They have known each other well for years, since Patience's days in radio after the war, when Audrey – then Jones – worked in the BBC's Features department. Though far from uncritical of Patience's ways, Audrey is at ease with her, enjoys her company, finds her fascinating, listens with empathy to her stories – and now is collecting her memories of an extraordinary life for a book about her. For months now they have been working away in between social and professional appointments: 'Good "Book" talk', Patience records in her diary. 'Book jottings on the 27 bus.'

These sessions become less frequent during the busy summer of 1980, but they are still finding some time to 'DO THE BOOK'. Patience is reading her old friend Alec McCowen's own theatrical memoir with special interest, discussing Audrey's ideas with her, deciding that 'it has to be HER book'. She is absorbed in revisiting her diaries of a past self – sometimes verbose, at others the briefest of appointment listings, occasionally coded, but usually frank – and recording her reactions in her contemporary journal: 'started to read my 1933 Diary! Peculiar.' With Audrey, she leafs through volume upon volume of family albums, photo-

Patience's longtime friend, Audrey Postgate at the BBC, where she worked in the Features department.

graphs, letters and the large scrapbooks she has always compiled for every production, with their good luck cards and telegrams, programmes, reviews and even small props, sellotaped and glued in. She has given Audrey stuff to borrow, while telling her about her life.

In Patience's mind, these sessions have been proceeding in an orderly fashion: 'Audrey, to do notes on my 1931–35 period', she would write in her diary: 'Excitingly satisfactory.' But in Audrey Postgate's reporter's notebooks, the records of these conversations are anything but methodical. Notes of Patience's stories, scrawled in haste to keep up with her talk and record her pithy remarks are written on the back of Audrey's own domestic jottings. These are sessions where Patience will suddenly spring surprises, come out with gems which have to be got down on the nearest piece of paper to hand. Observations and memories of particular periods – RADA in the 1930s, left-wing politics in pre-war Cambridge, Belfast and Manchester, the arrival of independent television in the 1950s, the Royal Shakespeare Company in the '60s – are interspersed with Patience's revelations about her love life. Thoughts about Joan Littlewood or Peter Hall are interleaved with the most vivid of pictures from childhood, images repeated hypnotically about an extraordinary, extravagant and volatile past. Audrey, her old producer's skills sharpened, seizes on the best stories, the most cryptic of pronouncements; Patience relishes Audrey's absorbed attention. But she also finds herself trying to convey quite another world, a sense of herself before she adopted her name at the age of twenty-six for both her public and private life: a time when she was not Patience Collier as everyone knows her now, but Rene Ritcher.

The book is never completed. The sessions peter out as Patience becomes more vulnerable to ill health. Audrey's opening paragraphs are abandoned, notes left unsorted, file cards crystallising the most striking stories are tucked away in a small green box. In time, the scrapbooks and packets of photographs will be piled into attics and storage bins; the diaries in blue, red and green ink will become vulnerable to water damage in containers tucked under London viaducts. The story of Patience Collier, a performer in life as on stage and screen, dancing, striding, tottering across the twentieth century, is waiting to be told.

BRAND
by Henrik Ibsen
in a version by Geoffrey Hill
NT
NATIONAL THEATRE
23. 4. 78
I'm so pleased you are here, & so proud of your performance.
Much love,
FEBRUARY 1950
SEPTEMBER 1955
FOR YOUR EVERY FLORA
Floral Presentations
Floral Specialist
IN THE HEART OF THE
No. 1.
JANUARY 18th,

DURRANT'S PRESS CUTTINGS
Worcester Evening News
DURRANT'S PRESS CUTTINGS
Stage
JANUARY, 1935
SUNDAY
MONDAY
TUESDAY 1st
WEDNESDAY 2nd
THURSDAY 3rd
FRIDAY 4th
SATURDAY 5th
DURRANT'S PRESS CUTTINGS
The Daily Telegraph
27 FEB 1963
'KING LEAR' TO VISIT PARIS IN MAY
LONDON CAST
STRATFORD SEASON
DURRANT'S PRESS
WYNDHAM'S THEATRE
Special Performance
BY THE STUDENTS OF THE
Royal Academy of Dramatic Art
TUESDAY, 22nd MARCH, 1932
Floral Decorations

Rene Ritcher, c1932, launching herself as an actress, in a RADA sketch.

PART ONE

THE ACTRESS, THE MARXIST AND CHURCHILL'S DAUGHTER

THE ACTRESS

Rene Ritcher, the young woman who will become Patience Collier, is not conventionally beautiful perhaps. But she is striking, stylish, vivid and assured, a woman who is fun to be with and who draws people to her. Twenty-five years old in 1935, she is an actress – brilliant at comic roles as sparky young women, or characters far older than herself. At the moment she is 'resting', working as a clerk letting fashionable new flats in Chelsea. She has a wide social circle, is loyal to her women friends, and is both friends and lovers with a revolving group of young men. Her pink covered appointments diary is packed with social engagements in between domestic chores at her Hallam Street bedsit: shopping, hair, a part in a film crowd scene, modelling, West End shows, dinner at the Café Royal. Yet within a year, she will take on quite another life.

It would never have happened but for her friend Diana Churchill, the eldest daughter of the future prime minister. It is all down to Diana – the chain of events and young men that lead to Harry Collier.

It is a September afternoon in 1935, only a few days after Diana Churchill has married Conservative MP Duncan Sandys. Rene Ritcher and Diana are sitting on the Sandys' large marital bed, chatting and joking with Diana's nineteen-year-old cousin, Giles Romilly. Things have become pleasantly flirtatious between Rene and him; 'I've rather taken a fancy to you!' he says. Won't she join them at a party being given that evening?[1]

The party – for Diana's younger sister Sarah – is to be held at the Pimlico Road home of the Churchill girls' aunt, Nellie Romilly. It is a world with which

With Love Diana. June the 12th 1935.

Diana Churchill, eldest daughter of Winston,
whose friendship leads Rene to Harry Collier.

Vivien Hartley – Vivien Leigh to be – one of Rene's RADA friends.

Rene is thoroughly at ease thanks to Diana and her circles, a blend of aristocracy and bohemianism, and of opposing political allegiances. There are names always in the gossip columns, and people not yet famous who will become well-known, or infamous. The Mitford girls drift in and out – 'all the Mitford girls', Rene will later recount: Diana Mitford, living openly with Oswald Mosley and eighteen-year-old 'red' Jessica drawn to her rebel cousin Esmond; he and his older brother Giles have distributed peace pamphlets at their public school, run away and published their own manifesto. There are writers and performers, intellectuals and journalists: the young critic Philip Hope-Wallace, and Guy Burgess and Donald Maclean, who have recently made a show of renouncing their Cambridge Marxism. Rene swims easily through it all.

Rene Ritcher had first met Diana Churchill in 1930 at the Royal Academy of Dramatic Art, when the college was something of a construction site with work underway to replace the Gower Street buildings. There had been a makeshift feel to it, problems with noise, space and timetabling: classes were taking place in the college's theatre block on Malet Street. In fact, there was an air of change about this whole area of Bloomsbury. The massive London School of Hygiene and Tropical Medicine building on the corner of Keppel Street and Gower Street had been formally opened only the previous year: London University was set to develop a huge site further down Malet Street for its ambitious Senate Building. RADA's new modernist premises would complete the trio as a tribute to youth and education, an emblem of excellence and modernity.

Rene had already been two terms at the college when Diana arrived: soon they would form part of a crowd – with Vivien Hartley (soon to be Vivien Leigh), Gwyneth Lloyd and Griffith Jones – sharing the relentless schedules of mime, voice, dance, lectures, the competitions, the multiple termly productions, the rehearsals of plays by Beaumarchais in the optional French drama classes. In Diana, Rene saw a pale, pretty, red-haired but somehow inward-looking young woman, self-contained. She seemed surprisingly shy given her familiarity with the social and public worlds of her family, accompanying her mother to every glittering occasion since her coming out in 1928, and photographed with her father as he walked with the red budget box from 11 Downing Street to the

House of Commons. In Rene, on the other hand, Diana noted a young woman with dark good looks, energy and charisma, someone who made people laugh, who could mimic others to a 'T' and who was fixated on this acting business. They became friends.

For Diana, RADA represented the possibility of stepping outside her world, a romantic idea of going on the stage, popped into her head by her more ambitious younger sister, Sarah. Earlier, she had fancied being a nurse. Now that she was here, she was not altogether sure she enjoyed the experience of being taught and directed; perhaps, too, there was some truth in her mother's judgement that she had neither the talent nor the looks for the stage.[2] But for Rene, the compulsion to succeed, to prove herself, was paramount: she had quarrelled with her father and grown ill in the attempt to get to RADA. On her first day she had been elated when tutor Norman Page, a former silent movie actor, took new students through their improvisation paces and pronounced that she would 'do'. Here, skills had to be learned – in mime, creating a part, learning lines. Soon she was competing in acting, dance, fencing and verse-speaking, earning a 'commended' from the judges, appearing in four productions at the end of her first term, getting her share of challenging, leading or characterful, eccentric and comic parts.[3] She was fascinated by the intricate arts of character construction and voice production, did her homework, flying to Bertorelli's, the restaurant on Charlotte Street, to get the cloakroom woman to teach her how to pronounce her words for the part of an Italian. She was chosen to star at the royal opening of RADA's new Gower Street building before an audience packed with celebrities and grandees from the literary, theatrical and political worlds – celebrated novelist and playwright, Somerset Maugham: Director-General of the BBC, Sir John Reith: Shakespeare critic, Granville Barker: Chairman of the Shakespeare Memorial Theatre at Stratford, Archibald Flower, and Winston Churchill himself. She drew the highest praise for her performance: in fashionable Ashley Duke's *The Dumb Wife of Cheapside*, said the critics of her, 'Miss Rene Ritcher was most amusing as the lady who recovers her tongue and uses it to devastating effect.'[4]

Socialising, Rene and Diana swapped stories of their finishing schools in Paris, where the excitement of the city lurked just beyond their range. But it soon

Rene Ritcher, far left, in *Ten Cents a Dance*, sketch, RADA.

Rene Ritcher as a debutante, June 1929,
inscribed "To my darling Daddy, Rene".

became clear that whereas Rene's school had provided an intriguing interval, where she and the other English girls were taught drama and philosophy, and taken about the city to shops, museums and the Comédie Française,[5] Diana's school had been run by Protestant nuns who were determined to shelter their girls from temptation. They recalled being debutantes, their seasons only a year apart, the boredom of it all, the lines of cars full of girls waiting to be presented in the Mall outside the Palace, while inside a row of chamber pots was placed behind screens for those caught short during the long wait. Rene felt she had been 'trained up for the presentation, like a circus horse', paraded with feathers in her hair and an 'orf-white satin dress' cut on the bias.[6] Then there were the endless balls and parties where mothers watched anxiously to ensure their daughters had dancing partners, the debutantes themselves exchanging coded warnings about the attributes of the young men on offer. But while for Diana her debutante season had been part of an inevitable progression leading to yet more tedious parties, charity events and country house weekends, Rene's coming out had been at the hands of her pushy mother and resented as a waste of money by her father. There had been no aristocratic relative to introduce her at court: instead the services of a society lady had to be bought for a fee and some dresses. She had felt on the edge of things, not quite in control, only too conscious that she and her mother could never make it into the inner circles of smart society.

What brought Rene and Diana together particularly was the need to escape from their families. For Diana, RADA brought release from her critical mother, the huge shadow of her father and her adored but troublesome brother, Randolph. For Rene, it meant freedom from 'stupid mum's', from her mother Eva Ritcher's flaunting of her looks and personality, in recent years claiming a stage and gossip column presence as a singer. It brought relief from her quarrelsome and now separated parents, and from her doting father, just a little too free with his kisses. At home, Rene was used to people behaving badly, with both parents having a string of lovers, yet applying different rules to her. Now RADA gave her sexiness, encouraged her to be ostentatious, exhibitionist and extrovert. It gave Diana sophistication and poise, and greater ease with herself. It gave them friendships with both sexes and boyfriends, put them at ease with gay colleagues, taught them to enjoy theatrical camp, and brought them together with people they would not otherwise have known. At RADA, Rene later reflected – rather exaggerating the college's social inclusiveness – 'they were poor, they were rich, and no one cared a damn.'[7] It was that liberating sense of putting aside the boundaries and codes with which they had been brought up that enabled these two young women to become good friends: Diana, the aristocrat, and Rene, the Jewish girl of Central European extraction, daughter of a stockbroker.

Rene got her share of teasing for her Jewishness in this world where looks – and a critical self-awareness of them – were everything, and at a period where blonde prettiness was most likely to advance an actress's career. In a list of notional Christmas gifts to the college's favourite personalities, student-run *RADA News* offered Rene Ritcher '*a Grecian profile*', a pointed reference to the shape and size of her nose. She had got into the habit of making the put-downs of her childhood and teens – 'What a pity you have inherited your father's nose, like Byron's!' – into a self-deprecating joke, a comical 'story' which she would tell first, before others could make a catty reference. Diana had been brought up with the casual anti-Semitism of her class and time: 'I now understand American anti-Semitic prejudice', her mother had once written to Winston, remarking on the 'most porcine' behaviour of German American Jews she met on her travels.[8] But for Diana herself, Rene's origins never seemed to be an issue: she enjoyed Rene's parents as their daughter could not and she adored her handsome younger brother, Geoff, as did all her friends.

Both women left RADA in 1932, Rene with her diploma, prizes for 'Dramatic Recitation' and 'Versatility', and commendations from her tutors. She had, they said, been a 'real credit to her training': she needed only 'to control her vitality so as to make... best use of it' wrote stage and screen star Athene Seyler. 'I thought you came along splendidly', added principal, Kenneth Barnes. 'You know I hope you will get your chance.'[9]

Diana, however, left without completing the course. Accompanying her mother on a tour of the States, she seemed to be resuming her destiny: by the autumn she was engaged to John Milner Bailey, the son of a baronet and millionaire owner of South African mines, nine years her senior and someone she had

Rene and Geoffrey Ritcher at Diana Churchill's wedding, St. Margaret's Church, Westminster, 12 December 1932.

known for years as a friend of the family. Among their three hundred wedding presents, *The Times* listed a dressing-table set of jade green enamel and gilt in a case from the King and Queen.

Rene and her brother, Geoff, dressed particularly sharply for the wedding, to which Diana had invited the whole Ritcher family. The church of St Margaret's, Westminster was heady with white lilies, lilac and heather, the guest list studded with famous faces. Later, they caught the show again as it was replayed on Pathé News at cinemas round the country as the 'society wedding of the year'. They watched Winston Churchill pause for the cameras with Diana on the steps of their London house, a well-known, affable figure with his cigar, though out of office for three years now. Diana, carrying her white bridal prayer book, turned to fix the satin folds of her dress, which seemed to cocoon her. She seemed self-possessed, almost self-absorbed and older than her twenty-three years, in a kind of concentrated trance. Afterwards, coming out of the church, her new husband had steered her round to escape the hordes of people trying to break through the police cordon, followed by the train of bridesmaids, her two sisters among them. The crowds had jostled, boys climbed lamp-posts, people joshed with an elderly Lloyd George among the crush. In the West End, another 'Diana Churchill', destined to be a well-known actress, was appearing to good reviews in a succession of light comedies, like a strange alter ego. But Rene was pursuing a different path.

In January, 1933, the show *Strange Orchestra* gave Rene Ritcher her first speaking role and her first experience of being on tour. She marked the occasion by buying two large, hard-backed notebooks to write up her observations.

Rodney Ackland's drama was a play for the time, likely to challenge provincial audiences with its openness about sex and contemporary living and its sense of foreboding about the future. Producers Charles Buckmaster and H. Trevor Jones were taking a chance on it, though only a year earlier, young actor John Gielgud had declared it the first modern play he had wanted to direct. In this three-month touring production, Rene, now twenty-two, was set to play Freda, described by the author as 'ordinarily attractive, with a slightly common voice'. Observing her colleagues as they gossiped their way down to Bournemouth where the run was

SEVEN PERFORMANCES

FRIDAY, JANUARY 1st, to FRIDAY, JANUARY 8th
(Sunday, January 3rd excepted)
From 5.15 p.m. to 6.45 p.m.

THE ARTS THEATRE CLUB

begs to announce

A CHRISTMAS REVUE FOR CHILDREN

presented by

THE PLAYROOM THEATRE CLUB

Directed by Susan Salaman

The Programme will include:—

FEED MY COW
by A. A. Milne
THE THREE SILLIES
CUPID'S GARDEN
LAMB AND DUMPLINGS
WILLIKINS AND HIS DINAH
THE JOLLY WATERMAN
LORD ULLEN'S DAUGHTER
A CAROLS SCENE

BETTY PECHERON

JEAN MANSON
JULIET O'RORKE
DORA PICHON
RENE RITCHER

ERIC BERRY
GAVIN GORDON
ANTHONY JAYNES
JOHN MacNAIR

HAROLD TURNER (by kind permission of Murray Anderson)

At the piano: Norah P. Stevenson

PRICES,	Loges.	Stalls.	Circle.
Including Tax	£1 3 0	5/9, 3/6, & 2/4	5/9, 3/6 & 2/4

BOX OFFICE (Miss Collins) TEMPLE BAR 7544
Weekdays 10 a.m. to 10 p.m. Sundays 6.30 p.m. to 10 p.m.

The playbill for *A Christmas Revue for Children* at the Arts Theatre Club, January 1932

to begin, Rene drew up a dramatis personae capturing the characteristics of each member of the company in a few, scathing, Cowardesque words. Landlady Vera would be played by a 'platinum blonde...who lost her nerve and so brought her mother with her', the role of Esther by a 'pure virgin of twenty-two. Perfect in her part.' With herself, playing the frothy, histrionic, bit-part film actress Freda, she took a rather less caustic tone. 'Rene Ritcher', she wrote, 'a Jewish girl with vitality and the will to go ahead and get somewhere'.

She had already gained some professional experience since leaving RADA. With an allowance from her father, she had the luxury of being able to follow the friendly advice of theatre magnate Maurice Browne – she had had an introduction while still at RADA – and cut her first acting teeth in alternative theatre. In October, 1932, she appeared in two theatre club productions designed to avoid the attentions of the censor, both short-lived plays on serious subjects: capital punishment and the Treaty of Versailles. These were walk-on parts only, but the second play, by Emil Ludwig, had the attraction of being directed by none other than Theodore Komisarjevsky, the much-fêted Russian director, about whom still hung the air of revolutionary theatre. With *Strange Orchestra* she saw greater opportunity, but in fact it was a shambles almost from start to finish: under-rehearsed, the pay terrible, the producer foul-tempered, the actors often intoxicated and quarrelling. The production limped financially from city to city. Yet it brought her a measure of critical success and a growing ease with self-promotion: soon it was her photograph that appeared in the advance publicity.

This was her first time away from home on her own (her father insisting she avoided theatrical digs), an experience she self-consciously recorded in her notebooks: her first time in the provinces, in industrial cities, and her first experience of being an independent woman in strange hotels and boarding houses. She relished the attention she got as a 'theatrical person' from kind and curious hotel proprietors. She observed English manners minutely as she entered the hotel dining room alone – 'not a sound, save for the clicking of knives and forks, and the shuffle of the waitresses' feet'. She partied with friends and family down from London, took occasional Sunday breaks at the Knightsbridge flat she shared with her father, but also caught sight of an utterly foreign world of northern poverty

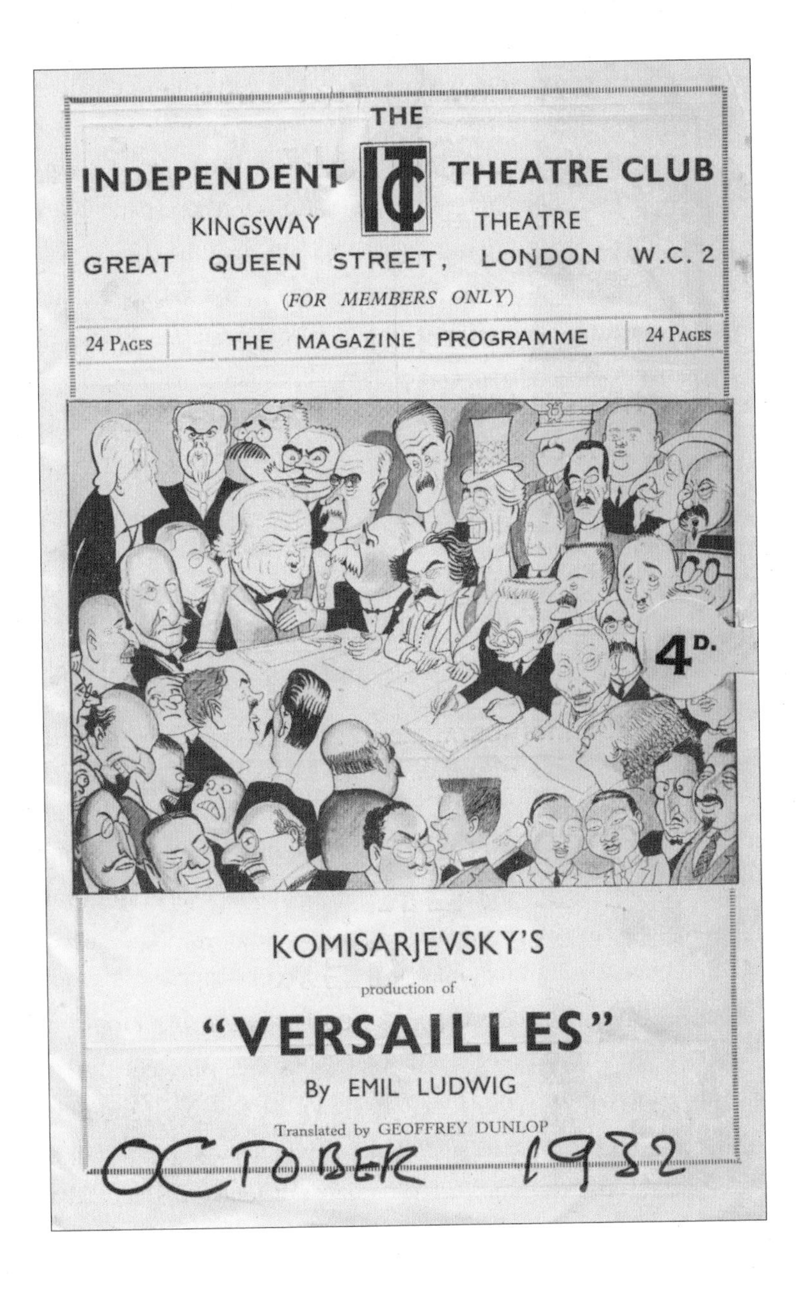
THE
INDEPENDENT ITC THEATRE CLUB
KINGSWAY THEATRE
GREAT QUEEN STREET, LONDON W.C. 2
(FOR MEMBERS ONLY)
24 PAGES THE MAGAZINE PROGRAMME 24 PAGES
4D.
KOMISARJEVSKY'S
production of
"VERSAILLES"
By EMIL LUDWIG
Translated by GEOFFREY DUNLOP
OCTOBER 1932

Programme cover for Theodore Komisarjevsky's production of *Versailles* at the Kingsway Theatre, Great Queen Street.

through train and car windows. Liverpool seemed huge, filthy, overpowering: 'We drove through cobble-streeted slums, where women in red berets carried children in dirty white shawls.' At night she painted her nails 'deep blood-red in front of the gasfire' of her hotel room, but also wanted desperately to learn, pasting sheets of information about Liverpool Cathedral into the diary, touring a knife factory and steel works in Sheffield – 'one of the most interesting and thrilling mornings of my life.' Her avid reading was self-improving, serious, contemporary, leftist even. In hotel rooms and even between waits at the theatre, she was deep into Julian Huxley's *A Scientist Among the Soviets*. In Glasgow, she visited the art galleries twice and made copious notes about her favourite paintings.

The tour also advanced her experience of men. She was drawn intellectually and personally to the playwright Rodney Ackland – 'I love his brain' – but when they kissed, noted that 'we completely lost our sense of humour.' She was embarrassed and annoyed by the puppy love of George, son of her hotel proprietors in Liverpool, who followed her tour with sad letters in schoolboy handwriting. With Barry Storri, the production's camel-coated stage manager, aged twenty-eight and estranged from his blonde wife, she had at first been repelled, then deeply physically attracted. Her family berated her – she must be mad to 'allow a *stage manager* to kiss [her].' But by Bristol, she and Barry had become a steady item; by Blackpool, they were sure they were in love, but knew they had no prospects. Soon, she had learnt 'what it is like to have a lover.'

Rene continued to see Barry for a few weeks in London after the production closed in June, but then they agreed to end the relationship. Just as she had predicted to her family, it had become a tour romance. She was back living at her father's lavishly antique-furnished flat, cosseted by his staff. She was soon seeing other men – nothing serious, lunching with girlfriends, Diana, Gwyneth, her cousin, Margot, feeling a little smug that she was free and unattached while so many of her friends were already caught and settled.

A month later, on Saturday, 12 August, 1933, Rene was boarding the Golden Arrow with her father at Victoria Station. She and Paul Ritcher had had a serious falling out and had only just made it up. Now she was accompanying him on

Paul and Rene Ritcher, c1933.

one of his gambling weekends to fashionable Le Touquet, she, coiffed and dressed to look older than her twenty-two years, he plump, sleek and affable. 'Daddy always sat with his back to the engine', she later recalled; 'he said he would only board Feet First in his coffin'. They arrived at the white, stucco Hermitage Hotel for a late lunch, unpacked and sunbathed by the pool, taking their time before going on to the casino.[10]

Paul's gambling chips.

Did Paul play *vingt-et-un* or *baccarat chemin de fer* that evening? Some details she would later find hard to recall. Wearing a striped evening dress, she sat behind him on his right to watch him play: 'I never wanted to gamble – it frightened me.' He was enjoying himself, turning from the table to chaff an acquaintance from the City, and flirting a little with the French film star Lili Damita, with whom he was sharing the bank. They had been winning a lot of money.

Following the game closely, Rene watched as her father picked up a card. For some reason, he seemed to be holding it just too long before he made a bid, 'keeping the table waiting'. She became embarrassed for him, touching his arm gently to suggest that he made his move. But suddenly, he fell across the table, fell forwards, and started to die. Attendants rushed forward, lowering him to the ground away from the table, loosening his tie. There were bank notes everywhere – 'the people round the table were handing [them] to me... [they] fell on top of my father. I held his hand and breathed his last breaths with him.'

People were looking, whispering: 'It's the father of the girl in the striped dress.' Time slowed, then accelerated; 'Jewish people from all over the Casino' crowded in on her to ask if they could help; the ambulance men took Paul away. Rene seemed to assume control, but as if she were someone else: in a clear penetrating voice, she said, 'I want a double brandy and the Paris telephone directory, please.' Her first call was to her Tante Irene Ritscher in Paris, who promised to be in Le Touquet the next day; the next to her godfather, Arthur Davis in London,

Paul's great friend: he also would be with her within hours. Her mother she could not reach: she was travelling somewhere on the continent. Casino officials put hundreds of francs in a bag into her arms and took her back to the Hermitage in a taxi. Somehow she got to bed.

Paul's death made headlines in the London Sunday papers the next day, the 'well-known City financier', with his daughter 'prominent in society', the witness to the tragedy. Back in London, though dozens of friends and relations sent her condolence letters, Rene felt anaesthetised for weeks, months. It was some time afterwards, when she was about to cross a road, that she realised suddenly she could not breathe: 'I must be the wickedest person in the world. I haven't shed a tear.' She did not even note her father's death in her diary until October of that year. She folded away the dark pink silk belt she had been wearing at the casino, placed it in an envelope, and buried it among her things. This part of Rene's life now closed in on her.

The event altered the very geography of Ritcher family relationships. Since her parents' separation in 1928, Rene's brother had attached himself more to their mother's camp, she to Paul's. There were family quarrels over Paul's estate, debt calls on it from his extravagant lifestyle: his most valuable effects were put into an auction at Christie's. Part of Rene and Geoff's share went to make up a substantial income for their mother: there seemed to be 'nothing, no money'. There was petty squabbling over things, bitterness never to be forgotten: my mother 'took my diamond bracelet and brooch when my father died', Rene would say. Diana, practical and generous in the face of disaster, stepped in when Rene was about to become homeless from her father's flat, installing her in a house in Pimlico along with their RADA friend Gwyneth.

March, 1934, and the huge cast of *Magnolia Street* were mounting an exuberant first-night party on stage at the Adelphi Theatre. The crowd players, ninety of them, mingled with the producer, Charles Cochran, and vied for the attention of their famous director – already Rene's idol – Theodore Komisarjevsky.

Rene seemed to be taking hold of things again after the shock of her

Sketch made by Rene Ritcher of Anthony Quayle, who played Benny Edelman, for Louis Golding's *Magnolia Street*, directed by Komisarjevsky, 1934.

father's death and the family quarrels. 'I remember feeling good,' she would later recall, 'now I can earn my own living.' She and her brother had buried the hatchet and were sharing a flat together – and after months without the will, energy or opportunity for work, she had positively stalked a role with Komisarjevsky in *Magnolia Street*, sneaking into rehearsals, sketching the main characters, studying the parts 'until I knew them by heart,' even designing costumes and make-up for each character before finally waylaying the great man at the stage door and securing both a crowd and an understudy role. She was gaining far more publicity than might have seemed possible: 'Rene Ritcher is appearing with great success,' the *Star* captioned her picture in a feature about the production. There had been the build-up to the opening, the telegrams, and now the first-night party joined by all her friends. Afterwards Maurice Browne, the theatre producer who had taken her under his wing, sent her an affectionate note and flowers, thanking her for the 'ripping party': 'if I trod on the corns of the daughter of the most reverend monseigneur, cardinal, pope, dictator Winston Churchill, I make NO apologies!'[11]

But the play closed after a run of only four weeks. Life seemed to resume a desultory pattern over the spring and summer – a few days of crowd work for the film *Oh, Daddy!* at the Gainsborough Picture Studios, the usual parties. She was seeing a number of men, no one serious, and lunching with her women friends; she 'got fed up with everybody' and took refuge with Diana. It was not until the autumn that she secured more work, with the Croydon Repertory Company, touring on the south coast. It was her first experience of rep – three modern plays with performances and rehearsals running in parallel. Rene liked the plays, relished the tour away, enjoyed sharing cheap digs with other members of the cast, got excellent character parts and good reviews, but the contract was for only two months. Her next role – as the brash, plump and elderly wife of an American gambler in *Roulette* – lasted longer, but while she was praised, the play itself was slated.

Geoff, meanwhile, was proving a drain on her. He was drinking too much, gambling, getting into debt. At the end of August, 1934, less than two months after turning twenty-one, he contracted what was almost certainly gonorrhoea (Rene cited it as 'G' in her diary), becoming feverish, developing 'complications', having to be nursed and following her to her lodgings when she began her repertory contract. By the spring, the drifting situation had become a crisis: Geoff was 'behaving badly to everyone, losing any sense of decency and pride'. Attempts to pay off the debts were making serious inroads on their income, and they were living too extravagantly. Rene took on a regular job to try and stabilise their position, the £2.10s-a-week post of lettings clerk for a new block of flats in Chelsea. But on 8 May, 1935, Geoffrey left suddenly for New York, telling no one, including his employer: now she had to deal alone with the debts, solicitors and landlord's agents, pack up their belongings and find somewhere cheap to live. Angry and despairing, she took on a bedsit at 105 Hallam Street near Great Portland Street in the West End, at a rent of £1 a week.

All through this period, Rene and Diana were lunching, shopping and dining together several times a week, their easy friendship a source of comfort to them both. Diana was dealing with the fall-out from what had proved to be a disastrous marriage: she and Bailey had separated barely a year after their glamorous wedding, and the Churchill solicitors had been instructed to sue for divorce. During August, 1934, the strange charade of her husband's act of adultery had been orchestrated in a Kensington hotel, with the staff paid to discover it. In February, the case came before the divorce courts; Diana attended with her old nanny, visiting Rene almost daily for support. [12]

Politics seemed to be offering both of them a kind of distraction. Rene was assisting her current boyfriend, Bob Newton, with his idealistic Shilling

Rene Ritcher as the plump and elderly wife of
an American gambler in *Roulette*.

Theatre project: she and her Communist cousin Margot even took Diana along to a Party meeting. But following the granting of the decree nisi, Diana threw herself into assisting her brother Randolph in a by-election campaign at Norwood, Lambeth, in which he was sponsoring an independent pro-Empire candidate against the official Conservative. Even their imperialist father was calling it a crackpot scheme – Randolph's candidate had until recently been a member of the British Union of Fascists. Diana was no longer the 'rather pop-eyed', shy girl of her youth, cynical companions of her brother commented, but a sophisticated observer of the scene, drinking champagne cocktails while the men talked; she gamely played her part in the election organisation, joined by her sisters.[13] But, as Winston Churchill predicted, the whole affair proved a fiasco: the Labour peace candidate came near to winning, the Conservative majority was drastically reduced, and Randolph's deposit was lost.

At Nellie Romilly's that September, 1935, the party is in full swing, the laughter growing louder. Rene Ritcher watches Diana at ease with her new husband, Duncan Sandys: good-looking, a career diplomat, an Eton man. Diana had confided in her back in May about Duncan, the last person anyone had suspected her of fancying since he had been the official Conservative candidate at Norwood: they had kept it secret for months for fear of jeopardising the decree absolute. Now Diana seems to find it amusing that her husband and father are clashing in the House of Commons over Germany's re-armament.

Rene's own life, in contrast, is difficult, living in her tiny bedsit, with uncertain career prospects and no steady boyfriend. The deep rift between her, her mother and Geoffrey persists, and she is saddled with debt problems they have at least in part caused. The landlords of the flat she had shared with her brother are threatening bankruptcy proceedings against her. She and her cousin have had a falling out about her apparent aimlessness, prompting Margot to tell her some home truths – 'there are many things about you that annoy me to death.'[14]

But that night it is with the young left-wing poet Gavin Ewart that she steps

Left-wing poet Gavin Ewart.

up a gear, sparking instant admiration: 'I say, what do you do – you're a wow! Let's drive around London.' Ewart, a second-year undergraduate at Christ's College, Cambridge, with a reputation for sexually outrageous and anti-establishment poetry, is fun: 'Dear Mrs Bath,' he later writes to her on the back of a picture postcard of an elderly, surprised looking King George V in full military regalia, 'Was he ever one of your boy friends?'

A few weeks later, on Saturday, 30 November, Rene travels to Cambridge for a weekend with Gavin. He meets her at the station, and introduces her to his left-wing, scientist friend, Harry Collier. They show her round Cambridge and spend the evening at an undergraduate party in Gavin's rooms. But it is Harry who later takes her back to his digs at Pembroke Street. Harry is 'beautiful and intelligent,' she notes in her diary.

This is, however, a different kind of relationship from her former liaisons, passionately physical and hypnotic from the start. 'HARRY' in pencilled capitals – her record of sex – begins to appear regularly in the bottom right-hand corner of her diary entries. Soon her journeys to Cambridge, his to London, begin to settle into a pattern. He travels up for scientific meetings and political events – a Marxist meeting, a demonstration against Mosley – then stays for the weekend. They socialise, tea at Lyons, spaghetti at Bertorelli's, evenings with the Sandys or with Rene's cousin Margot; then make love, rising only for lunch, or tea the next day. Friends speculate at the unlikely pairing of Rene Ritcher and Harry Collier, so magnetically attracted when they meet 'tousled…in our room in Cambridge'.[15] After all, she is a former debutante, a struggling actress, in debt, still living beyond her means, but a woman of skill, charm and energy for life; he is a scholar, a scientist, a Marxist and a serious-minded intellectual.

❧

THE MARXIST

HARRY COLLIER WAS twenty-three to Rene's twenty-five when they met that November day in Cambridge. He was a brilliant young postgraduate student at Trinity Hall, working in the University's Department of Experimental Zoology, living on research studentships and maintenance allowances, his research focussed on the physiology of the earthworm – how its movements were co-ordinated, what were the properties of its nervous system.

As a former grammar school boy among a sea of ex-public school students, Harry was keen to join the world of clubs and sport when he came up in 1930, and rowed for his college. But he also embraced the enthusiasm for poetry current among Cambridge intellectuals – the love of the metaphysical poets, the scorning of T. S. Eliot and Ezra Pound, the writing of verse heavy with sexual and surrealist imagery – becoming president of his college's literary society, and joining the circles of Gavin Ewart, Julian Bell and Hugh Sykes Davies.

Alongside the absorption with poetry soon came political conversion. Harry became politically active, a Marxist in a highly politicised Cambridge: 'we are all Marxists now,' Julian Bell wrote in *The New Statesman* at the end of 1933. In the spring of 1934, Trinity Hall's student magazine, *The Silver Crescent,* until now conjuring a strange but comforting world of Bertie Woosterish humour and heavy irony, was suddenly taken over by a savage analysis of the arms race. In its editorial, Harry collaborated with fellow Marxist Donald Maclean to argue for the alignment of students with workers against war, fascism and capitalism: 'England is in the throes of a capitalist crisis. Students cannot ignore the struggle.' His own poems sounded the note of doom:

Scientist Harry Collier in Cambridge, where he was deeply committed to the prevailing Marxist politics.

Unsafe from draught or drop, this mortal world
By minute nears millennium.
These bleached bones of flowers are the skulls
Of spring and dainty deathshead for mnemonic.[1]

Harry Collier was now deeply committed to the University's Socialist Society, to the town's anti-war movement, and to the support of the Hunger Marchers who stopped in Cambridge in the spring of 1934. That year he was sounded out for, and became, a member of the Apostles, the élite secretive society of brilliant young men which now, like other Cambridge organisations, had become a target for Marxists and socialists. He joined the discussion group that met weekly at Trinity or King's, among them Guy Burgess, Victor Rothschild and Hugh Sykes Davies. Anthony Blunt and Julian Bell had recently left active membership – 'taken wings' in the Apostle jargon – and would appear occasionally. This was Harry's world, a serious world, where the major objective was to contribute to the movement against war and fascism, and where it was expected that all one's friends, girlfriends or boyfriends, would think likewise. Beneath the surface within the Communist Party was the clandestine process of recruitment of spies for the Soviet Union: there was a widespread sense of betrayal in Harry's circles when Guy Burgess and Donald Maclean appeared to strenuously renounce their beliefs and alliances, even joining the Anglo-German Fellowship, on the secret instructions of the Soviets' interior ministry, the NKVD.

But science was the key to Harry. It was a prestigious field to be part of in Cambridge at this time: J.B.S. Haldane and J.D. Bernal were pioneering approaches to physiology, genetics and molecular biology. They also gave science a fundamentally political dimension, were among the University's leading Marxists, and as dons, were particularly influential. Harry was mentored by crystallographer 'Sage' Bernal, whose conversion to Marxism had been inspired by Soviet scientists' arguments that capitalism distorted the role of science: in a planned society, it would serve the common good. Bernal also believed that science should be wide-ranging, unboxed: one specialism should be able to draw on another to solve crucial problems. It was in this fluid atmosphere that Harry Collier's appar-

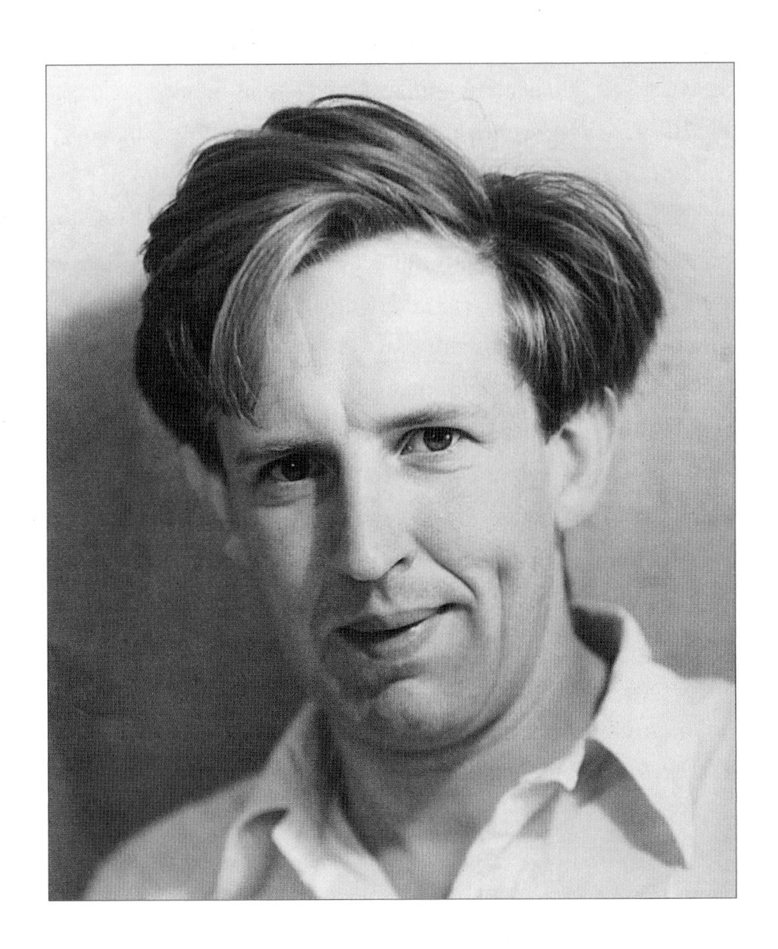

Crystallographer 'Sage' Bernal, who was inspired to convert to Marxism by Soviet scientists' arguments that science would serve the common good in a planned society.

ently highly specialist work was developing, while his politics were bringing him, he would complain to his tutor, into conflict with his departmental professor.

Into this intense world of work and politics came this most unlikely of lovers, Rene Ritcher: yet she and Harry seem to have been drawn to one another *because* they were complex opposites. Her exotic, extrovert qualities, her unabashed sexuality, her 'vitality, humour, intuition and humanity' he found powerfully attractive: she took him into circles way beyond his own, making her both exciting and not a little dangerous. She for her part found him handsome and physically attractive (a 'plain face' but a 'good body', she would later comment), but she was also magnetised by his intellectualism, his idealism, the clarity and sureness of his perspective. He was widening her horizons – she had never had a lover who quoted Donne at the drop of a hat, or who was deep into the merits of Surrealist art and who would tell her tales of staying with the Ernsts in Paris while Roland Penrose, Hugh Sykes Davies and he collected pieces for the international exhibition they were planning in London. They were fired by their differences: 'I had never met people who stuttered', she later reflected, or people who were shy, chaotic and 'covered in safety pins'. And for Harry, she knew, she was simply quite unlike the run of 'Cambridge girls... perspiring under the arms... wearing awful sandals'.[2]

On Monday, 13 January, 1936, they stayed in bed all day at Rene's London bedsit; she had performed the night before in a Sunday theatre club production of the Richmal Crompton story *Charity Begins.* At five, she got up to collect her things from the Aldwych Theatre and buy the papers. The reviews of the production were lukewarm, but praise was high for Rene's performance as the 'earnest churchworker... great gossip, and... complete muddler', Miss Case. Rene Ritcher was 'the most amusing person in the play... always an entertaining object of contemplation' wrote *The Stage*: she had a 'riotous time' commented *The Evening News.* She had had three weeks of rehearsal schedules, fitting dates with Harry around them – only on New Year's Day had she been late for rehearsal, recovering from their night at the Chelsea Arts Ball. For the moment, she could relax and try to put the bankruptcy proceedings now underway to the back of her mind. The focus was all on Harry, on the to-ing and fro-ing between London and Cambridge, the socialising, the lovemaking, the passionate love letters – and the quarrels. During those first weeks together, they had been fighting almost as much as making love.

Quite soon after their first meeting, Harry had seemed to recoil from Rene's 'admirable harlotry'. He was magnetically drawn to her differentness, yet also seemed to be irritated by it. They lost themselves in each other when they made love, he had written on Christmas Eve, quoting Donne, only to realise, as they dressed and parted, that they were a couple with 'misfitting interests...with fears disguisable only for a short period'. When they first met, he had seen her as 'dark, sensitive and wild', but 'with a touch of stageyness. A lovely machine with boomerang purposes'. Now he could be 'surprised and repelled by [her] streak of vulgarity'.[3]

He worried about her impact on his ideals: 'I shall try to be your lover', he wrote. 'Possibly as a fly to the fire. Possibly you won't stand the smash and batter of my concentration... I must take you up like a pair of spectacles. I shall see a lot of new things I've been like the blind about, through you; you'll blur some of my old good visions...'[4]

Soon his letters were becoming preachy, lecturing at length about ideas – 'he was mad about dialectical materialism', she would later recall – and though he would then apologise for his 'totalitarian earnestness', he would insist on monitoring her reading. He was drawn irresistibly by her style and appearance, yet would then criticise her make-up and wanted her to wear glasses if she needed them: 'I like you in tweed skirt, black jumper and low heeled shoes, with only powder on your face...' He soon began to lay into her 'unbridled emotion', her background and *milieu*, her debutante past, and what he brutally called the 'family tradition of illiteracy'. He resented the sheer obsessiveness of their relationship and the power of her attraction over him. The fights, sex and domesticity were becoming increasingly intertwined: 'He's a negative boy; you're a positive girl,' a friend tellingly remarked.

Harry seemed to want to bring her over to his world, seeing little to respect in hers. He began to try to teach her how to live, wanted to her to grow up, be her 'own' woman. 'You've got an alert mind, but it really is very undeveloped and incapable of sustained action,' he wrote, comparing her unfavourably with Diana Churchill, who was entirely at ease with political discussion as Rene was not. 'Why shouldn't you have a grown-up intellect, why shouldn't you handle abstract themes and argue about other things as well as you argue for what you want for yourself?' he asked.[5] The tussles between them would break out, be made up, break out again.

Yet by February, 1936, they were already talking of marriage and on the seventeenth of that month – the day after another bitter quarrel – they decided to get engaged. That Rene handled it the way she did, immediately arranging an announcement in *The Times*, drawing a shower of cheques and congratulations from friends and family, was a mark of her naivety and background. But to him, it showed gross insensitivity to his values, allegiances and reputation, and suggested that she was trying to control him. He was deeply embarrassed by her public, high society-style announcement of what he had assumed was a private arrangement, and made her send the cheques back.

A month later, on 22 March, Rene found she was pregnant. They had had scares before, but this time there was no doubt. Despite this personal crisis, she and Harry kept to their plans to go to Paris and then Cannes that week, but were evidently in turmoil over what to do. It had all come too soon: it was too 'forcing'. Yet it was another month before she put arrangements in place to terminate the pregnancy. Neither of them had the ready cash to pay for a safe abortion, nor apparently knew the ropes, even though poorly disguised nursing homes were as commonly accessed by wealthier women as backstreet abortionists were by the poor. They turned to Diana, herself now happily pregnant with her first child. She took Rene to her own doctor 'in vain', then pursued the issue to Harley Street, where arrangements were made with a doctor well known among actresses and upper-class young women for her specialisation in 'women's complaints'. Diana also agreed to lend them the £60 fee for an abortion.

Things had to carry on as normal, meanwhile: only Diana, Margot and another close friend of Rene's from childhood, Erica Marx, were in the know. On Friday, 24 April, the day that plans for the termination were finalised, Harry was due to take Rene to meet his mother at her home in Swanage for the first time since their engagement. They spent the weekend with her, the three of them going for a walk on the Sunday with a picnic. Rene liked Mrs Collier immediately: 'she is grand.' But on Monday, back in London, Diana supplied them with the cash, and Rene and Harry travelled to the Bayfield Health Resort, Bookham, Surrey. 'Little Collier', as Rene referred to the foetus in her diary, was 'taken away' the next day in the bathroom that Bayfield's proprietor, Dr Laura Bliss, had converted into an operating theatre. Rene 'sewed, read, wrote letters and slept' at the nursing home for the rest of the week, making no note of how she felt in her diary, either physically or emotionally. Harry, writing briefly and practically, had rung round her friends – Diana, very solicitous; Margot, pleased it was over. He had also spoken to Rene's mother who, completely ignorant of what was happening, had complained of waiting in all day for her: 'A freezing mix of snobbery, said in a voice like you at your wickedest, which made me cold', he wrote.[6] Visiting Eva on her discharge from the nursing home, Rene found her crowing about Geoffrey's engagement to a Jewess. So different to *her* engagement, was the clear message: 'You do know you'll revoke your share of your grandfather's will if you marry a *goy*.'[7]

It was a long, warm, and disturbing summer, that summer of 1936, when the British press was full of the Berlin Olympics but stayed tight-lipped about the new king's relationship with Wallis Simpson. With the outbreak of the Spanish Civil War in mid July, the Cambridge Left's focus would shift dramatically. No longer could anti-fascism and anti-war go hand in hand: this would clearly be an international fight against fascism. Soon it would become a question for all comrades of 'What will you do to aid Spain?'

For Harry's circles, the summer began on 11 June with the opening of the International Surrealist Exhibition at the New Burlington Galleries, London; they had been preparing for it for well over a year. It was launched with great publicity, the police keeping at bay the crowds eager to see this new weird art. The papers were full of the playful stunts being pulled off to capture the spirit of Surrealism: Salvador Dali lecturing in a diving suit, Dylan Thomas serving

Poster for the Internationalist Surrealist Exhibition in London, 1936, designed by Max Ernst.

boiled green string to the spectators, Sheila Legge parading in Trafalgar Square as the 'Surrealist Phantom of Sex Appeal'. Works by a wide spectrum of artists – Brancusi, Picasso, Man Ray, Henry Moore, Paul Nash – were shown alongside the Max Ernsts Harry had helped bring back from Paris; different art forms and media were juxtaposed, the organisers photographed among the exhibits as part of the event they called 'revolutionary'. They expected, indeed courted, the torrent of abuse from the capitalist press – Lord Rothermere's *Daily Mail* called the exhibition 'disgusting and decadent'. Less palatable were the attacks on Surrealism as 'anti-rationalist' from other strands of the Left, influenced by the Soviet line of socialist realism.[8]

As it happened, Rene visited the exhibition more often than Harry, trying her hardest to like the works, and to match the intellectual cool of the leading Surrealist women. Harry himself was deeply absorbed in advancing his own research, and applying for lectureships and research posts: he hardly needed the Party's exhortation, 'a Communist student is a good student'.[9] That spring, following the abortion, Rene had again stayed with him for long weekends, and things had seemed relatively peaceful between them. She worked with him in the lab, learning to cut sections of the worm's nerve cord; she socialised with the comrades and walked with him in the country. They borrowed money from her father's old partner to repay Diana and to help out Rene, going to see him together so as to enable their engagement to override his concerns over her threatened bankruptcy. In London, she was leading a more serious life, going to peace meetings, lectures at Marx House with Margot, and hearing prominent Labour and Socialist Medical Association campaigner Dr Edith Summerskill speak. She wrote happily of their settled engagement to his mother, who, despite her own tough independence, replied benignly, 'You are honoured to be learning about the worm's bits and pieces – a real collaborator...To feel that through anyone, you can become a satisfied woman is certainly to live up to all that one can hope for, in life – how much you will be able to accomplish!'[10]

But then, in mid-June, the comparative calm was dramatically shattered. On the rebound from another row, they decided to wait no longer but to marry immediately. Rene wrote to Mrs Collier with the news: they would keep it all very quiet until the rush of Harry's work was over, she said, adding that she was so looking forward to 'leading an ordered, everyday life' in place of the strain of conducting a relationship between London and Cambridge. But Harry's mother reacted furiously, pointing out that they would have nothing to live on but Rene's tiny income from her father's legacy. She blamed her entirely: 'I am afraid I shall not believe in your "love" for Harry if you want to force him into a move which may ruin his future.'[11] Harry now also recoiled. On Friday, 19 June, when Rene was due to meet him at King's Cross station, having spent the whole afternoon with a bankruptcy court official, she received his 'fatal wire': he was not coming, would NOT marry her, and would not be *forced* by her.

Rene now experienced a kind of madness of despair. She travelled to Cambridge 'distracted.' Harry was not there but she sat outside his rooms at 6A Pembroke Street for hours, before being let in at the side door. She did the unthinkable, opening the two letters from his mother lying on the doormat, reading Mrs Collier's warnings to Harry in shock. Rene learned that she was the kind of woman who would trick him into marriage by becoming pregnant, or would find a way to damage him if he finished with her: she would be unfaithful to him if they married. Eventually she returned to London to be comforted by Diana, staying overnight with her and Duncan.

She wrote repeatedly to Harry over the next few days:

> *At last I am forced to realise that my great need and love for you is not sufficient reason for your wanting to marry me. I realise, also, that your unkindnesses, challenges, broken promises and detailed criticisms of me, after our times of happiness together, are brought about only by your fear of them bringing us closer to a marriage you do not want. [But] may we continue being lovers? It would be a comfort and you need no longer be frightened of intimidation.*[12]

She tried to continue her life, collecting together information on her debts for the Court, visiting the Surrealist Exhibition again, ceasing to use lipstick, wearing glasses, trying every way she knew to demonstrate that she was a serious person who could fulfil his ideals. But she heard nothing from him all week: 'I am having a horrible time...this dramatic silence...is causing such an agony of mind as to sweep away any reasonableness I may have been trying to gather up', she wrote.[13]

Then other news broke. On 26 June came reports of the opening of the trial of Dr Bliss, the doctor who had performed Rene's abortion. She and her nurse were charged with 'conspiring together, and with other persons unknown, to unlawfully use an instrument or some other unknown means with intent to procure the miscarriage of five women', an offence liable to penal servitude. [14]

The police – exhorted to be vigilant in the face of widespread contravention of the abortion law and a spirited campaign to reform it – had raided Bayfield House only weeks after Rene's termination and found an operation in progress. Suddenly the private actions of Rene and Harry and thousands like them had become a matter of public censure and debate; she and Diana must have been fearful that somehow her own medical records would be discovered, rendering them liable to prosecution. On Saturday, 27 June, Rene travelled to Cambridge in a state of hysteria, and, down by the river, threatened to commit suicide.

Harry was still away from Cambridge and hearing the news of her actions from a distance, saw her behaviour not as desperate, but as a *performance*, as tactics, designed to control him. It had been a 'fundamental exhibition of personality', he wrote, bringing humiliation on him amongst his friends, colleagues and comrades. He forbade her from ever risking his career again by coming to stay at Pembroke Street: 'As you know, I do not want to marry you, & my only concern is to stop you being too much hurt.' To his mother, he wrote, 'I'm delaying breaking off the engagement, in case she becomes desperate, until all my professors [and tutors] are away in the country or abroad.'[15] Yet he remained deeply ambivalent about her and undecided about his own intentions. His next extraordinary step – the drawing up of a series of demands and conditions on her in a kind of one-way contract which he called 'Magna Carta' and 'Parva Carta' – seems to have been intended as an elaborate means of pushing her away, a test which she could not pass. But for Rene it presented a challenge which she accepted. The clauses were drafted and re-drafted, and written out repeatedly: she appeared to be making all the concessions:

> *I promise never to do anything so ridiculous as to commit suicide or try in any way to be damaged... I promise never to force you to stay engaged to me and never to try and make you marry me...*[16]

To Harry's anger, she must now respond with surrender. There was more than a whiff of masochism about Rene's reaction to his fury: she longed for their love-making when he would cup her breasts and whisper, 'There, little girl.'[17]

❧

BECOMING PATIENCE

On the basis of their 'Magna Carta', they seemed to reach some kind of ceasefire, and Harry left for a holiday in Bristol, for a cooling-off period. But now Rene asserted herself, taking a quite different step which Harry would come to label a crafty game: 'There is certainly something of the adventurer in her,' he confided to his mother. 'I suspect she's a very dogged character.'[1]

Rene had had only temporary acting engagements since *Charity Begins* in January, 1936 – a day or two on a film set here, another bit of modelling there. Her lack of work was, Margot recognised, contributing to her overwhelming feelings of abandonment and despair. She already knew Alfred Huxley, the producer at the Cambridge Festival Theatre, and on Saturday, 11 July, with Harry away, she travelled to Cambridge to see him about joining the company. The next day she was making arrangements to move out of her London bedsit to a room 'over the shop' at the theatre. She had got the job, she wrote to Harry, would have a salary of £1 a week at the start and pay 10/- for her room: she would be doing nothing against him, and would be fulfilling all the terms of the two Cartas. Countering his apparent lack of appreciation for her ambitions and talents, she now looked forward to his 'knowing me as a woman with a lot to do.'[2]

In 1936, the Cambridge Festival Theatre was well past its days as one of the leading experimental theatres in the country. Terence Gray, who had founded it in 1926, had radically redesigned the former regency theatre building, installed modern lighting, pioneered an open stage space, and experimented with the 'holistic' production ideas of Gordon Craig. He had introduced Cambridge audiences to energising and creative theatre productions, which had helped launch the careers of a number of future greats, drawing on some of the best theatre, design and choreographic talents around.

But since his departure in 1933, the theatre had staggered. A new rival theatre, the Cambridge Arts, financed largely by J. M. Keynes, had opened to great fanfare in February, 1936, and now appealed more successfully to University audiences. In contrast, the Festival's current directors were relying on plays that had proved a success in London, or been made into hit films. Nevertheless, the Cambridge Repertory Players were a serious company, putting on popular but contemporary plays. Rene was quickly absorbed with the practicalities, starting rehearsals for her first play only four days after her engagement by Huxley, organising the removal of her furniture, and painting her room. She liked the company, and had met up with an old friend from RADA: 'It's very good to be working again', she wrote to Harry.[3]

Though her first part was small – in A.A. Milne's *Mr Pim Passes By* – absorption in acting once again seemed to revive her confidence, and put her on the attack against Harry's increasingly devastating charges.

> *I have been thinking a great deal about your character and career as a person apart from me. You, as well as I, have many things undeveloped, and as you can help me grow in new and better ways, so I can help you. I think we both possess complementary assets and defects and ought to be able to give a lot now that there is no ongoing terror in our relationship...*
>
> [Rene to Harry, 14 July 1936]

> *You have not said a kind word since you left. However much I try to be normal, hardworking, sane and carry out my promises, you, in your turn, do everything to make things even more difficult for me ... You have had to make no promises of how you'd behave. Think for a moment about someone else's life. I think all the time about yours.*
>
> [Rene to Harry, 16 July 1936]

For the next play, Clemence Dane's *A Bill of Divorcement*, Rene took the role of Sydney Fairfield, in which Katherine Hepburn had made her Hollywood debut in 1932 – a woman meant, the author directed, to be 'very sure of herself, but when she loses her temper, as she often does, she loses her aplomb'. *The Cambridge Evening News* was ecstatic: the play was deemed one of the best performed by the company, and Rene was applauded as 'a distinct asset to the Company's ranks'. She has 'personality, her attack is good...her diction quick and clear' and there was a likeable 'vigour and pleasantness about her acting as a modern girl of the forceful type'. The tough repertory system – daytime rehearsals for the next play back to back with evening performances of the current production – was giving her a sequence of opportunities as she rapidly became one of the company's main draws. 'You won't know me when you get back,' Rene told Harry, 'I'm such a new girl.'[4]

Harry appears to have maintained a grim silence for two weeks, until he suddenly turned on her again in three extraordinary letters. When apart from her, his anger and frustration seemed to balloon. He was unimpressed by her acting job – the Festival was a commercial has-been compared with the more fashionable Arts, and it all went to prove her supreme talent for *pretence*. He was furious at what he saw once again as her forcing tactics in installing herself in Cambridge, still more incandescent at her staying in Pembroke Street for a few days before her room at the Festival was available. She had stopped him working, from entering for grants, made life so deeply unpleasant for him that he now dreaded coming back to Cambridge. He felt unable to be either a successful scientist or a committed comrade, and saw her as the sole cause. Had she no consideration for his reputation, he wrote on 22 July: where was her response to his additional 'very necessary clauses to *Parva Carta*?' If no agreement came soon, he would 'fight with every ounce of energy I've got, with the gloves off, as they used not to be'. Henceforth the engagement was definitely off, not just privately between them, but to their friends.[5]

Yet as always, there was still sufficient ambiguity about his intentions as to give Rene some hope. She must not come to Pembroke Street on his first night back on Friday, 24 July, he wrote, but if she obeyed *this* requirement, she could come on Saturday evening. 'I'm sorry to be harsh, but I take a serious view of this.' She telegrammed back to him at his mother's house: 'ARRANGEMENT ACCEPTED TOTAL RESPONSIBILITY.' That weekend, they renewed their sexual relationship.

On Monday, Harry came to the first night of *A Bill of Divorcement*. On Tuesday, 28 July, she travelled to London for her Public Examination at the High Court as Miss Rene Ritcher, spinster, of Hallam St., London, returning to Cambridge for the evening performance. But by the start of September, the terrible rows had re-erupted. 'Miserable, wanted to die at his not seeing his power over me', she wrote in her diary on 1 September. In despair too at the Festival's failure to give her a promised pay rise, she walked out of the theatre.

Friends no doubt waited for the next turnabout, and sure enough, within days their relationship was on again. On 4 September, Rene noted in her diary that Harry was concentrating on completing his entry for the prestigious Gedge prize, the theatre management had settled with her, and she was back performing. Harry, who had been applying for academic openings, heard that he had won the Musgrave studentship in biology at Queen's University, Belfast, for the forthcoming academic year, putting a new cast on their position. On Sunday, 6 September, she cooked chicken at his digs, lounged all day – and Harry finished his Gedge submission. On the 7th, she moved out of her little room at the theatre and into 6A Pembroke Street with him – and on Tuesday, 8 September, they were married.

It was an utterly simple, quickly arranged Registry Office affair at the Shire Hall: no friends of Harry's attended, no comrades, not even his mother who, no doubt, was deeply disturbed by the event. There were no friends of Rene's either, not Diana, Gwyneth , Erica nor Margot, no school friends, nor her brother. Only Rene's mother attended, resigning herself to what she had already declared an unsuitable marriage.

At 11.30, Henry Oswald Jackson Collier, twenty-four, research scientist, and Irene Marjorie Ritcher, twenty-six, (of 'no occupation'), both of 6A Pembroke Street, Cambridge, said their vows. Afterwards, Eva Ritcher drank their health at their lunch together at the Bull Hotel on Trumpington Street. That afternoon,

Portrait of Rene Ritcher by her cousin,
Margot Lewis.

Goodbye to her past: Rene modelling for photographer Jack Teller in 1935/6.

she waved goodbye to them from her train window as she returned to London. It was done. Harry and Rene now took a walk together in the Botanical Gardens, and turned in to Pembroke Street for an early night.

Why had they married? Had Harry somehow been tricked by her wiles, as he would later be inclined to claim? Rene was certainly not pregnant, nor did she pretend that she was. It seemed that after all their fighting, all the reconciliations, they had bounced, finally, into commitment, as though the magnetism between them had finally overcome the repulsion. But friends worried: Rene took care to go and see Diana the day after the wedding to confide everything.

Now Rene was determined to shape herself into the wife Harry wanted, to begin again, 'stripped of nearly all [her] old habits.'[6] She agreed even to the last of his conditions that he would NOT marry someone called 'Rene Ritcher' with all that name's associations – to him – with frivolity, superficiality, the West End and bankruptcy. Henceforth she would take on the name they concocted together – a teasing play on that of an older actress, Constance Collier. '*Patience* Collier' was a name not just for the stage (would she even pursue her career? friends wondered) but for everyday, for always: a name that sounded so sensible, so English, so serious – and so decidedly not Jewish.

Harry had accepted the scholarship at Queen's, and the Colliers now prepared for their departure for Belfast. During the rest of the month, they caught up with friends, visited Harry's mother in Swanage and his grandparents in Folkestone, all making the best of it. They partied in London, and said their farewells to her mother, and to Diana. On 8 October, 1936, they took the train up to Liverpool and caught the boat to Northern Ireland, to a new life.

Rene, now the new, serious Patience Collier, 1936

PART TWO

COMRADES

THE LEFT

Harry and Rene – Patience Collier now – stepped into fresh lives. Belfast could not have been more different from Cambridge or indeed London: gritty and characterful, but also a gloomy and dismal metropolis where economic depression seemed like a way of life, with 'gaunt and malnourished men...standing idly on street corners'. It was a Victorian industrial city in decline, divided by religion and inequality, with baffling politics, and a plethora of tribal, smoky, ornate bars, where sharp-accented people seemed to speak volubly but in code. There had been sectarian riots only the year before they arrived.[1]

Though parted from his old political and intellectual circles, settling in was easier for Harry. He was soon absorbed in academic life in the Zoology department at Queen's, in the grand, castellated buildings next to the Botanic Gardens. The Musgrave was the most prestigious scholarship of the University, enabling him to undertake demonstrations, give one-to-one tuition and even plan a short course of lectures on comparative physiology. His research was progressing towards a doctorate, though he planned to publish his findings ahead of that. He was working under the congenial Australian Professor T. T. Flynn.[2] Patience, on the other hand, had no obvious entrée into local circles: she had left her many friends and the Festival Theatre job behind her. Yet she seemed to embrace the city's challenges enthusiastically, as well as the opportunity to prove herself in her new role, as the partner Harry seemed to want.

With her birth name abandoned, she was assuming another character. She was even developing the role of diligent and thrifty housewife. Patience and Harry had found decent digs near the University with a Mrs Stuart on

Shaftesbury Avenue off the Ormeau Road, and now Patience managed their rooms, popping over to the Ormeau laundry with their washing. She was learning to cook: Harry had bought her *The Scientific Cookery Book* – partly as a joke – but she was soon compiling recipes in order to acquire the skills denied her at her father's flat 'with his caviar bill and two servants'.[3] The savage rows and recriminations seem to have died, and they were developing mutual interests besides sex. They set about exploring urban Belfast, taking walks beyond the city, to the ancient Giant's Ring monument at Ballynahatty, to Stormont, and Strangford Lough ('fell in the bog', she noted in her diary). They would go to the cinema at least twice a week, and to the theatre, seeing O'Casey's *Juno and the Paycock* performed by the touring Abbey Theatre company against the red and gold of the Grand Opera House.

Soon they gravitated together for their social and political life to the comrades at Sherlock's Bar and the Left Book Club at 17 Union Street in the city centre. Patience, determined to demonstrate that she was now Harry's committed comrade as well as his lover, fell in with these new circles completely. The Left Book Club – LBC – had been fermenting political debate across the UK for some months now, with its radical publications and meetings particularly centred on Spain. Friends of Harry's had already joined the International Brigades: some would die, including John Cornford in December and Julian Bell the following year.

The LBC was proving an attractive focus for a wide spectrum of left and liberal opinion, crossing and blurring party lines; a significant organisation too for the Communist Party with its strategy of building a Popular Front against fascism. It was particularly alluring in Belfast, where mainland party politics were unlikely to appeal across the sectarian divide. It drew in artists and writers such as John Hewitt and Sam Hanna Bell, who linked their politics back to late eighteenth-century United Irishmen traditions, and used both the popular media and socialist press to spread their ideals.[4] At meetings like these, Harry began asking whether there was not some useful work they could do for the few months they were likely to be in the city.

They lighted on social research. Walking the streets, you could see the stark contrasts in housing and living standards between neighbourhoods: more than one in four of the insured workforce in Ulster were unemployed. Newspaper articles highlighted cases of appalling poverty and ill-housing: a family had been found living in a cave-like cellar; children were going to school without breakfast and warm clothes; there was high incidence of tuberculosis in the province. In England, Sir John Boyd Orr had demonstrated the links between poverty, poor diet and health in seminal public health studies.[5] Could not something similar be done for Belfast, exploring the links between locality and disease in a precise, scientific and thus hard-hitting manner?

The Colliers began collecting cuttings and statistics – Harry wrote a letter to *The Belfast Telegraph* – and to raise the issues at the LBC. They called a special meeting, and on Monday, 16 November, 1936, the Ulster Society for Economic Research (USER) was formed. The group aimed to survey conditions in Belfast, and obtain 'authentic facts and figures on the conditions of the poorer classes', particularly with regard to nutrition and housing. The project would contribute to a patchwork of studies now available in mainland Britain, with USER modelling the research on Orr's in order to facilitate comparisons. Harry would lead the project, but Patience would be its organising secretary and a key contributor to the work.

The small group of USER members – friends, comrades and researchers – began to meet weekly, and Patience, finding talents in herself she had never before recognised, recorded their objectives, deliberations and findings. The group immediately came up against a raft of problems: housing standards were difficult to define; authorities collected statistics in different ways and over different time periods; there was no coherence on neighbourhood boundaries. How exactly could they calculate income levels per head? How should they deal with unsatisfactory official statistics and changing rules regarding the dole? All these issues Patience fully reflected in her notes. But despite the difficulties, the research began rapidly to reveal the dramatic collusion between levels of poverty and the incidence of tuberculosis, ward by ward. Levels of infant mortality in the Falls areas, they identified, were three to four times those in what locals jibed as the 'Malone Road' area near the University, where the Colliers themselves lived.

Their partnership on the project worked surprisingly well. Harry ferreted away at the statistics, determined to use them carefully and scientifically and communicate their findings in a logical manner. Patience, for her part, could put her finger on the issues when they got into a mess of statistical problems and was proving to be a brilliant organiser. She was good at appealing for help, designing posters, understanding how organisations worked, getting to the right people. Largely through her, USER soon secured the interest of a wide range of key officials and agencies, from the Medical Officer, to the baby clinics, the Unemployment Assistance Board, the churches, the Co-operative Women's Guild, and the University's Faculty of Economics. She found that she was a highly effective 'hustler': apparently unsympathetic officials, approached in the right way, became willing to share statistics, allow access to schools and clinics, discuss findings, make enquiries and follow up. When the group put its initial conclusions together in the early spring of 1937, she so thoroughly convinced the Head of Economics at Queen's of their significance that he held a special tea party to enable distinguished guests – the Vice-Chancellor, the Registrar-General and a brace of academics – to hear the USER findings from Mr and Mrs Collier. As a result, the University offered help with additional statistics and analysis.

Patience was also finding that she could contribute to the 'primary' research, conducting many of the personal interviews that would elicit information on income and diet, sitting with the mothers in the clinic and going into people's homes. Strangely, people did not seem to be deterred by her 'ladylike English voice': she would go to clinics, sit and talk to mothers, find out how much their husbands earned. 'I was never questioned...nobody seemed to resent it', she would later reflect. There was something about her direct interest in the details of other people – 'I was so interested in the sandwiches they made' and how to make a good stew – which made people accept her presence. She found the work surprisingly easy; it was so different from anything she had done before. It was 'nothing to do with acting, nothing to do with praise', and it was important.[6]

'Health and Poverty in Belfast' was published in *The Ulster Medical Journal* on 1 April, 1937 – mostly Harry's work, but written up with Patience and appearing above her name. Scholarly and careful, it mapped mortality and TB rates

THE
ULSTER MEDICAL JOURNAL

PUBLISHED QUARTERLY ON BEHALF OF THE ULSTER MEDICAL SOCIETY

Vol. VI 1st APRIL, 1937 No. 2

HEALTH AND POVERTY IN BELFAST

Report by the Ulster Society of Economic Research

M'Gonigle and Kirby[1] have recently shown that, in the normal circumstances of a large proportion of the population of Great Britain, income may be one of the main factors which determines death-rate. Examining, for example, a series of income groups, rising step by step from a group at 25/- to 35/- per family weekly, to a group at 75/- and over per family per week, they found an astonishing difference in death-rates. Mortality in the 25/- to 35/- group was 25.96 per thousand. It fell regularly, as income rose, to 19.23 per thousand in the 45/- to 55/- group. In the group living on 75/- a week or more, the death-rate had fallen to 11.52 per thousand. These results are derived from too small a total sample (3,196 persons) to be regarded as conclusive, and they relate only to the town of Stockton-on-Tees. But the field opened up by these authors is a very significant one; fresh surveys elsewhere may be of the greatest value.

In addition to the main results indicated by this example, a very important principle is demonstrated. It is that causes, which are not to be discovered from a broad average, emerge when a lump is split into proper groups, and handled as a series. It was with the object of confirming or

that the work, of which the

Belfast divided into four Blocks according to the Percentage of Applications for Transitional Payments in each Ward, November, 1931—September, 1933

The number of fresh Cases of Tuberculosis in each Block, 1932, 1933. Each ▮ represents one case per thousand population

Windsor 5.6%
Cromac 7.4%
Under 8°/o
2·7

Clifton 8.2%
Woodvale 9.8%
St. George's 9.3%
Duncairn 10%
8.1°/o–10°/o
4·5

Falls 10.8%
Ormeau 10.1%
Smithfield 10.9%
Dock 10.4%
Shankill 11.5%
10.1°/o–12°/o
5·8

St. Anne's 12.1%
Pottinger 13.2%
Court 12.2%
Victoria 14.3%
12.1°/o and over
6·8

The Ulster Society of Economic Research (USER) research article, 'Health and Poverty in Belfast' – the Colliers' joint work – published under Patience's name, April 1st, 1937.

across the city, showing through neatly drawn graphs and diagrams the correlation between poor health and low income. Patience now conducted a campaign to publicise the findings, within Ulster and beyond, while survey and statistics squads continued their work. During May, she was receiving letters from across the country, including correspondence from Sir John Boyd Orr himself. But that month, Patience's USER meeting book petered out. Harry's studentship would soon be up, and they were already planning their departure. Others would take on the research work in due course.[7]

Harry's applications for jobs had in fact begun almost as soon as they had arrived in Belfast. Would they be moving to Edinburgh, Nottingham, London, back to Cambridge, or perhaps staying put? Without a completed PhD, or a medical degree, posts in physiology were at best difficult if not impossible to obtain. But he was finally successful with an application for the post of Demonstrator in Comparative Physiology at the University of Manchester.

They left Belfast that autumn with some reluctance. They had liked the city, and their comrades and colleagues at the LBC and at Queen's had liked them. 'Kindest regards to your wife for whom we both (my wife and I) have a strong regard', wrote the Dean of Science in a generous letter to Harry. Patience particularly had some cause to regret the timing of their departure. She had had no theatre work while in Belfast, but efforts to wedge her way into the BBC there had at last paid off with small parts in two radio plays scheduled for September, and she had secured a promising contract to play the lead in a forthcoming radio production. Manchester was going to have to be good. Patience noted in her diary that one of the few fights she and Harry had had during their time in Belfast was 'about her acting'.

When the Colliers arrived in Manchester in September, 1937, they expected to be there for at least three years: Harry's new job would give him teaching experience with medical students, and time to progress and hopefully complete his own research. They settled in Wythenshawe, a vast housing estate originally planned as a garden city in the 1920s, but with few amenities as yet built: 'we lived in the longest road – miles of working class houses', Patience would later recollect. They had to travel by bus to the city centre and money was tight.

Almost immediately they were involved in Manchester's strong array of left-wing and anti-fascist politics. The British Union of Fascists had based their northern headquarters in Salford only a few years previously: it had grown prodigiously in Manchester and the surrounding area until the organisation was made illegal in 1937, and there had been a sequence of sharp clashes between Mosley's supporters, police and Jewish and left-wing demonstrators in the city. Now the Colliers found a city with a strong and growing Communist Party and an enthusiastic drive for uniting anti-fascist groups in a Popular Front, causing division within and between the Labour Party and Independent Labour Party. Support for the Republican cause in Spain was huge: there was an active Left Book Club, and dynamic, local campaigns attacking poverty and ill-health.[8] Patience was soon applying the skills and commitment she had learned in Belfast, becoming involved in the Manchester Maternal Mortality Committee, led by the Co-operative Women's Guild and officially all-party, but heavily supported by the Communists. She was recognised as an experienced organiser, keen to work: 'it suited me deep down – the condition of the babies and the filth.' Pregnant herself by the spring of 1937, she found the work to improve conditions energising, and was soon encouraged to join the Party: 'you're so efficient and strong-minded.'[9]

Manchester was a large world, unto itself, scornful of London. Olive Shapley, working at BBC North at the time, and before long a friend of the Colliers, would later recall a North of 'tightly knit communities', where everyone knew each other's business – a 'warm and courageous place [though]...a restricted one.'[10] She and other BBC colleagues 'exiled' to Manchester relished another life: left-wing, intellectual, liberated, with groups drawn to the city's different clubs – including the Salon Club, the Unnamed Society and the Film Society – and arts events: the Hallé Orchestra, the pre-West End theatre runs. The Colliers were part of these arts networks, Labour and Communist, Jewish and non-Jewish, left, intellectual, professional and bohemian groupings. As members of the University community they also mixed with the younger and more progressive medics and scientists.

It was through these circles of the left that the Colliers met Harold Lever – then a twenty-two-year-old, left-wing barrister on the North-West circuit and

Olive Shapley, left, interviewing for the BBC Radio North documentary, *Coal*, 1939.

already actively seeking a parliamentary seat. And it was as a comrade with professional theatre experience that he introduced Patience to the newly re-named Theatre Union group, knowing she would be interested in their political objectives, as well as their artistic ideas. She had almost certainly come across the group already through their performances for social causes – for the Maternal Mortality Committee, trade unions, trades council and political meetings.

Late in 1937, just a few months after Patience's arrival in Manchester, Harold Lever took her along to watch a rehearsal of the group at the Lesser Free Trade Hall. Over thirty years later, she would tell Howard Goorney – one of the new young actors in the group at the time – of that extraordinary encounter. She and Lever climbed the back staircase, went through a small door at the top, and then looked down through 'a brilliant light, very very far down', straining to see. Out of the dazzle came what Patience would describe as 'the most wonderful voice', that of the twenty-four-year-old Joan Littlewood in the Spanish classic *Fuente Ovejuna* or *The Sheepwell*.[11] The play was being adapted by the group as part of its support for the Republican side in the Civil War.

When Patience Collier first encountered Littlewood, the theatre group was being re-formed and re-launched. The original 'agitprop' Red Megaphones – formed by Joan's partner Jimmie Miller, and one of a number of Lancashire agitprop theatre groups in the late 1920s and early 1930s – had already been re-invented once as Theatre of Action. Now, following the successful staging of the anti-war play *Miracle at Verdun* with the Peace Pledge Union, the group was struggling to find the blend of theatre they wanted: 'the vitality of...street theatre and some of the acting technique of the legitimate theatre'. The *Verdun* production had drawn in dozens of amateurs: publicity for their new Theatre Union actively encouraged 'unspoiled' amateur participation as well as co-operation between organisations, while continuing to produce plays 'dealing with international social problems' for trade union and like-minded groups.[12]

Littlewood and Miller were re-inventing Lope de Vega's classic play, developing an expressionist, 'anti-curtain theatre' style which drew on German and Russian radical theatre on the one hand, and British and American music hall, documentary and movie on the other. As Theatre of Action, the group had

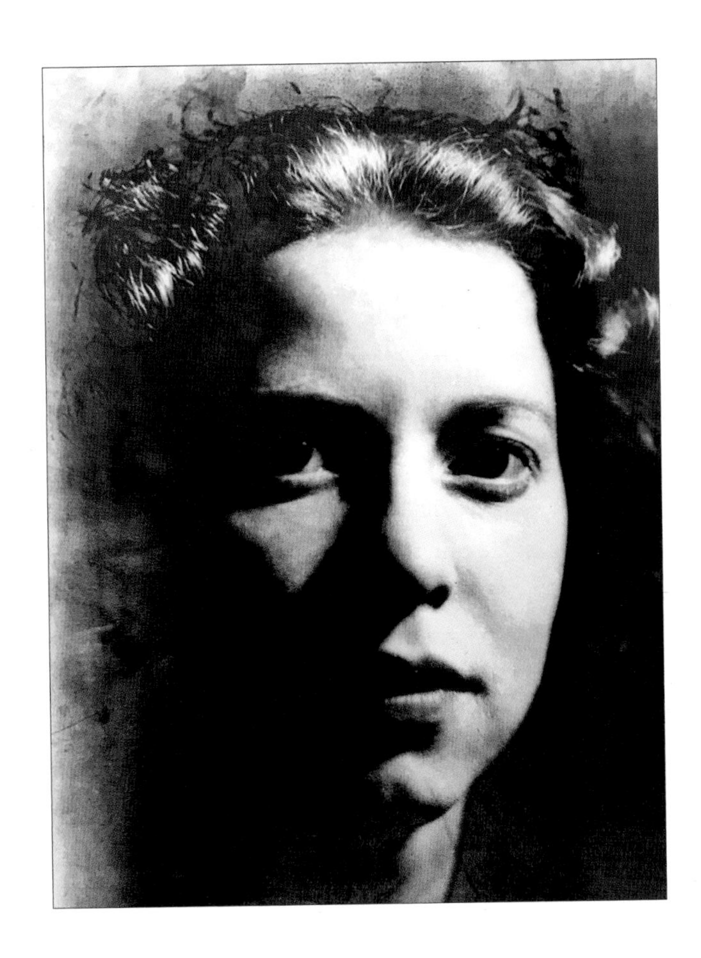

Joan Littlewood, performing in *Fuente Ovejuna – The Sheepwell* – and inspiring Patience with "her most wonderful voice," ideals and production methods.

performed contemporary left-wing plays – Clifford Odets's *Waiting for Lefty*, Ernst Toller's *Requiem*. They would transform others and create their own, most notably what they called a 'satirical ballet', the anti-war production *John Bullion*. Meanwhile Littlewood and Jimmie Miller (later to rename himself Ewan MacColl) were earning their bread and butter from the BBC in Manchester, contributing to Archie Harding and Olive Shapley's ground-breaking radio documentaries about life and work in the North: *Steel*, 1937, *Cotton*, 1938 and *The Classic Soil*, 1939. Joan's voice was also familiar to northern audiences as a frequent reader for regional radio.

Patience Collier and Joan Littlewood had some surprising things in common.[13] One was RADA, where their studies had briefly overlapped: Joan remembered Patience from her last-term performance, though the memory did not appear to have been reciprocated. Their view of their time at the Academy could not have been more different, however. Joan, a scholarship girl at sixteen, had hated everything RADA stood for: the other girls 'all debs or rich Americans – wriggling into their rubber girdles, comparing lipsticks and making bee-sting lips at the mirrors'; she had eaten her sandwiches in the toilets to avoid them. She would recount with relish the story of the RADA doorman giving Patience's friend, Diana Churchill, a good piece of backchat.[14] Nevertheless, she had taken from RADA the skills she valued: like Patience, she had particularly loved the dance and movement classes, drawing from them the life-changing ideas of Rudolf Laban. She had excelled where she chose, winning first prize for verse-speaking from the BBC adjudicator for the occasion, Archie Harding. Later, as director of BBC North, he would promote her talents.

It was Joan Littlewood's professional acting skills that Patience Collier particularly noted on that first encounter with her: 'Why isn't this woman playing leading parts in the West End?' she asked Lever. Patience knew outstanding quality and perfectionism when she saw them but would always relish Littlewood's unorthodox ways of pursuing them. And she admired Joan's outspokenness and sheer bloody-mindedness: Joan and Jimmie Miller were always falling out with other groups, quarrelling with the Communist Party; indeed thrown out from it for their deviation from realist theatre. Patience, too, felt no inclination to be

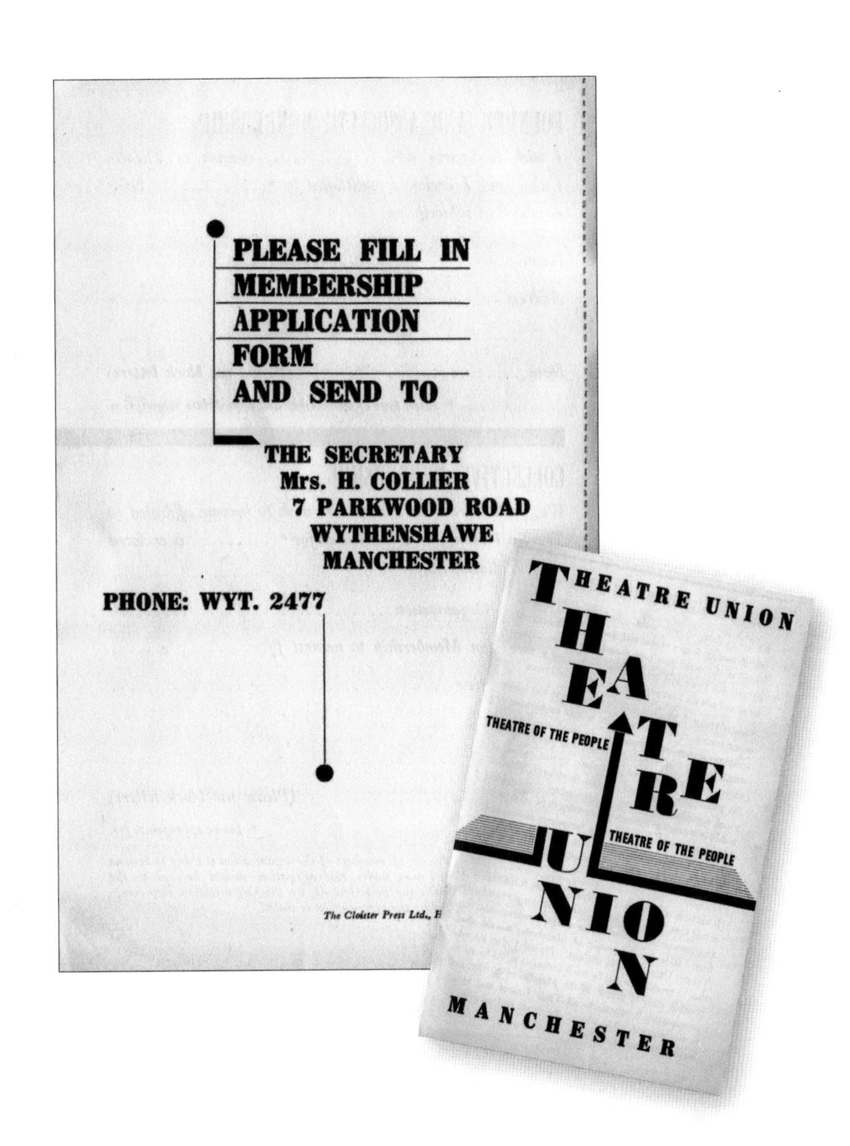

Cover of the Theatre Union manifesto, launched with Patience as its secretary.

boxed by the Party despite her left-wing commitments and the Manchester CP's keenness to have her. 'I hated their dreadful slogans,' she would later comment. 'I'm not a Communist. I'm a me-ist!'

Harold Lever, eager to back Littlewood and Miller but only if they were better organised, followed up that first encounter by arranging a meeting between Patience and the group. She met them all at a 'glorious, muddly evening' in the flat of left-wing painter Barbara Niven. A structure began to emerge for the new Theatre Union: a Production Committee on the one hand and a Business Committee on the other. Harold Lever was to be their business manager, and recommended Patience as their new organising secretary, who could bring the skills she had acquired and demonstrated with USER. Reluctantly – and somewhat suspiciously – the group agreed to the new arrangements.[15] Theatre Union's manifesto was now re-launched over the name of 'Mrs H. Collier, of 7 Parkwood Road, Wythenshawe':

> *All that is most vital in the repertoire of the world's theatre will find expression on the stage of Theatre Union...[It] intends that its productions will be made accessible to the broadest mass of people in the Manchester district...*

In the coming months Patience would cope with the difficult personalities of the group, the complexities of its democratic structures, the organisation and notification of meetings, and publicity for its ambitious programme of productions; she would also be the group's contact point for both individual and collective memberships as it gathered itself a growing reputation.

Harold Lever visited Patience at home in Wythenshawe over a year later, early in 1939, where he found her deftly changing her small baby's nappy, quite the *hausfrau* but feeling cut off from friends, activity and work. It was a strange time, heightened by international events. Preparations for war and home defence were accelerating around the Colliers and their comrades even while the government was attempting appeasement. The anti-fascist but also anti-theatre union

THE GOOD
SOLDIER
SCHWEIK

adapted from the novel of
yaroslav hasek by irwin
piscator · english version
by theatre union

LESSER FREE TRADE HALL
MAY 12TH TO 20TH 1939

programme

Programme cover for Theatre Union's production of *The Good Soldier Schweik*.

Patience with daughter Susan Jane, October 1938, the first child of 'a scientist and an actress'.

war efforts of Theatre Union were continuing, with another production of *The Sheepwell* planned for February and an ambitious programme of plays to follow, including works by O'Neill and Buchner, expressionist German theatre banned in Nazi Germany and a 'living newspaper' of contemporary Northern lives and conditions. Patience was still TU's organising secretary, but acting opportunities had been limited during her advancing pregnancy. She had been disappointed in her quest for work with the regional BBC, despite the Colliers' friendship with some of the key Manchester staff. Repeated applications had yielded only small parts and they had been brought to an end in the autumn as she felt increasingly unwell. On 12 October, 1938, she had given birth to Susan Jane, the first child of 'a scientist and an actress'.

So when Harold Lever reminded her of forthcoming auditions for a new Theatre Union production, *The Good Soldier Schweik*, she was definitely interested. Joan Littlewood would cast her in the role of the elderly, blimpish, Austrian Baroness von Botzenheim, who visits the 'malingerer' Schweik in prison to revive him for the front.

Though she had been working with Theatre Union for a year or more, this was the twenty-eight-year-old Patience's first actual production with the group, her first practical taste of Brechtian ideas, of Joan Littlewood's dynamic concepts of the relationship between audience and performers, and between actors and play. It was also her first appearance on stage as *Patience Collier.*

Jaroslav Hašek's satirical novel of the Great War – available in English from the Czech since 1930, with Joseph Lada's trenchant cartoons: anti-war, anti-imperialist, stabbing with large, grotesque humour – was quintessential Theatre Union material. Littlewood and Miller and the team of designers, technicians and actors tackled it holistically, adapting and translating Erwin Piscator's

Brechtian version for the stage, back projecting huge cartoons behind the action, enlarging its comic effects with music, dance and a revolving stage. Joan Littlewood prepared the cast with voice and movement classes and Stanislavski-based exercises, analysing 'everything in great detail, dissecting right down to the bone and then building up again.'[16] Running from 12 to 20 May, 1939, at the Lesser Free Trade Hall, it was an extraordinary production at an extraordinary juncture, Hašek's Czechoslovakia now having been overrun by the Nazis. *The Manchester Guardian*, fascinated, reckoned that the production by a 'movement with big ideas and limited resources' was over-ambitious and 'frankly a failure – but…almost a glorious failure.' And 'no archduchess could have entered with such pomp as was displayed by the Baroness von Botzenheim.'[17]

WAR

MANCHESTER EXPERIENCED ITS first air raids in the late summer of 1940 – persistent incendiary attacks, scattered over the sprawl of the city and suburbs. Life rapidly became a strange routine of air raid warnings, scrambles to the shelters, and of discovering the damage next day. The Colliers listened to Diana's father Winston Churchill's sonorous broadcasts to the nation, Harry frequently muttering insults at this arch imperialist and strike-breaker, now the hero of the hour.

The older Patience would remember the everyday life of the war as something almost to relish, the first time she had seen life to be fair – people living on a par, in contrast to her childhood, when her mother had 'sixty pairs of little satin shoes.' War brought a temporary equality, the 'first ordinariness': there were 'ration books and raids for everyone.' Like everyone else, she became adept at managing on potatoes and tea, targeting those shops where supplies suddenly appeared, queuing: 'There's no point in your pushing, madam.' They made their air raid shelter a game for Susan – like a 'little cottage down the bottom of the garden...' If they died, they had done all that they could.

The Blitz of Christmas, 1940, was the most terrifying. Preliminary incendiary attacks were quickly followed by high explosive bombs, then heavy bombardment over the two nights before Christmas. The whole of Manchester city centre was affected, more than three thousand people killed or injured, its major landmarks in ruins. Patience, needing to shop not only for her own family but for refugee neighbours, went into the city while they minded Susan. She would always remember the devastation – 'everything broken ...glass ...everywhere' – but also that despite everything, she had managed to join the longest turkey queue.[1]

Enduring their own Blitz, the Colliers were relatively isolated from what people were dealing with elsewhere, from the experience of family and friends in London, and her mother worrying about Geoffrey, a pilot in the Battle of Britain: the coldness between Patience and her family remained. It was impossible to know how distant and scattered Spitzel and Ritscher relatives still in Europe might be faring. But her old school friend Erica Marx had managed to escape from the German occupation of Paris with her lover, the artist Mariette Lydis, while a friend from Villa St Monique, Bice Wilson, also living in Paris, had got back to Britain with her children on the last boat, only five days before the Germans marched in.[2] Patience wrote anxiously to her beloved uncle and aunt in France, Marcel and Irene Ritscher, via the Red Cross, but there was no news.

At home, their neighbourhood was now full of Jewish refugees, bringing with them the voices and customs from Central Europe, which recalled Patience's childhood. Little Susan was petted by them, and fascinated by the small treasures of vivid embroideries they had managed to bring out with them. The Colliers and their new neighbours, the Freisingers, became friends. But other friendships and contacts diminished as people were conscripted, directed to other operations, their organisations moved or re-organised. Social circles contracted: travel and social life was restricted, particularly during the periods of the worst bombing; people were preoccupied with managing daily life.

Harry was also now far busier at work; his department had introduced a fourth term as part of the effort to get scientists and doctors qualified more quickly. But the Colliers' political circles had also fractured with the outbreak of war. There had been division within the Left, particularly among Communist supporters over the Stalin–Hitler non-aggression pact. Joan Littlewood and Jimmie Miller, producing their documentary revue, *Last Edition*, in March, 1940, were charged with mounting an unlicensed public performance, and were subsequently blacklisted by BBC North for the rest of the war.[3]

Bizarrely, others from their pasts turned up, exiled by war to the North from their usual *milieux*. Patience's old friend and mentor, Maurice Browne, down on his luck and bereft of his theatres, had joined a new repertory company based at

Harry during their Manchester period.

the Garrick Playhouse, Altrincham near Manchester and now invited Patience to act in the theatre's 1940 summer season, as people flocked to shows after the initial lock-down at the start of the war. That summer, Patience got Harry and Mrs Freisinger to share the babysitting, and joined Browne at the Playhouse in three plays. Air raids began, but the shows continued.

Working again gave her an appetite for more. The whole of the BBC Drama department had been evacuated from London to Manchester, so there might be new opportunities after her dismal experience of radio before the war. She wrote to the only contact at the BBC she still knew, was redirected to the Programme Contracts Executive in London, and even wrote to the Director-General. But the reply was frosty: all auditions had been 'suspended for the duration'; indeed, it was really 'impossible to consider married ladies with no microphone experience'.[4]

In 1941, the Garrick company extended its shows over two seasons, but the second summer season was off limits for Patience – she was pregnant again, and had developed a serious leg ulcer: 'Patience, if you move, you die,' the doctor told her. That Christmas, Patience found herself willing the baby not to arrive in an air raid. They named the baby – with his 'finest little monkey face' – Joseph after the embattled Stalin: 'We owed it to Stalin,' Patience would later recall. 'With his second front, he stopped the war for us.' The baby's middle name was 'Gavin' in tribute to Patience's former lover who had introduced them.[5]

Patience was back on stage again a few months after giving birth, playing varied parts at both the Garrick and Warrington Royal Court theatres in their summer season of 1942: a 'burlesque study of a gullible spinster' in Ivor Novello's *I Lived With You*, an 'embittered matron' in A. J. Cronin's hit play *Jupiter Laughs*, and Nanny Patching in Dodie Smith's *Dear Octopus*.[6] But their Manchester life was coming to a close. Harry was now engaged in war work. His contract with the University at an end, he had been recruited by ICI as a parasitologist, then seconded to the Liverpool School of Tropical Medicine. He had become a major part the programme to develop anti-malarial drugs and penicillin for the troops, and commuting was proving impractical. The family made the move to Liverpool at night by train in the blackout: it was pitch dark, 'the discomfort … unbelievable', Patience would later recall.[7]

Programme cover from the Garrick Playhouse, Altrincham, where performances continued despite the air raids.

Patience with Susan and Joe, Liverpool.

The Colliers settled into the Cressington Park area of Liverpool, and Patience resumed the household routines with the children. Susan was now at kindergarten, and once the worst of the bombing was over, they could go on 'escapades' into the city. Wartime habits had become commonplace, and war prospects now seemed much better. In 1943 and 1944, there was sporadic news of friends and relations in the forces: of Diana, who had become an officer in the Women's Royal Naval Service, of Geoff, who had now become an instructor in the RAF, and of Gavin Ewart in the Royal Artillery in North Africa and Italy. There was more regular news of another friend, John Burton, who was in the Royal Army Medical Corps.

Patience and Harry had known John Burton in Manchester. A young doctor, interested in public health issues, left-wing despite his wealthy upbringing and family connections with newspaper magnates Lords Rothermere, Harmsworth and Northcliffe, this friend of Harry's had become their mutual friend and godfather to Susan. Now, from the spring of 1943, he was corresponding very pointedly with Patience, referring with longing to a brief affair they had had when he was on leave at the start of the year.

Their letters must have been mutually enticing to write and receive. The *après-affaire* was conducted openly, yet with discretion and a certain mutual sensitivity to a Harry who was assumed to know, yet not say. Burton's letters expressed his feelings more openly than hers, but focussed most on the 'moment' of his military experience – the waiting for action in England: 'I feel a worm when the best we can do is to hold demonstrations to celebrate the victories of the Red Army.' In the summer, he was running 'a sort of music hall' for the troops, the jokes so blue, the Padré just did not get them. As his battalion moved in to military action in North Africa, his letters brought news of savage battles, the taking of German prisoners who passed through their lines 'with hands held up and smiles all over their faces'. He evoked images of the desert as he wrote by the 'soft yellow' of a hurricane lamp, his trousers 'stiff like clay pipes'. But by April, 1944, he was a prisoner of war himself: 'the worst thing in war – spiritually it hurts a lot'. His letters from Stalag XI-A in Altengrabow in Germany spoke of the 'fine mix' of 'Serbs, Poles, French, Albanians, Americans, Indians and ourselves [which] in many ways gives me the strongest impression yet of the unity of our cause'.[8]

Her letters in contrast, were chatty, full of practical stories, tales particularly of Susan, through whom they could legitimately nourish their intimacy. Patience was unwell with flu; Harry was settling into work at the 'Tropical School'; she thought of John nearly every day, she wrote in February, 1944. Yet Burton must have glimpsed the fact that with no acting or political work to stimulate her, she was becoming, in her mid-thirties, quite matronly, indeed *bourgeoise* in her outlook. Though she did all the main housework, she told him, there was a 'marvellous old girl to do the scrubbing' once a week, and they had help from a family who lived rent-free on the top floor of the house. Their child of nine months old was 'sweet, good and presentable, and perfectly fit to join with Susan and Joe'.

When she wrote to John Burton at Christmas, 1944, the world seemed altogether brighter. She made few concessions in her letter to his continued POW status. She was wrapping presents with coloured paper and string, and laughing at Harry who looked as though he was thinking of 'the expression on his bank manager's face' at all this extravagance. She was enjoying the neighbourhood – they had some 'amusing and attractive friends'; things had cheered up a great deal and people were even beginning 'to give proper dinner parties again'. Harry was running a pioneering WEA class in human physiology, his work on penicillin going splendidly.

Patience had heard nothing from her aunt and uncle in France until some months after the liberation of Paris, when Tante Irene wrote to her in January, 1945. Uncle Marcel, Paul's brother, was dead – not from the war as such, but of old age and despair at 'the future of the world in a cruel place', wrote Irene Ritscher. They had managed to leave Paris for Cannes, before the Nazis closed in on the Jews: only in early 1944 had she felt compelled to seek a hiding place in the country. How were *they* all faring? She had been so afraid for them all in the bombings. Each letter spoke of Irene's worry about her two sisters, apparently arrested and deported to Poland: 'I have no hope of their return... At their age and [state of] health, death is certain.' Confirmation of their capture came only after the war had ended. Back in Paris to wind up her affairs, Irene Ritscher found their old neighbourhood devastated, their flat looted; she would return to Cannes for good.

Patience heard from John Burton again in June, 1945, during the slow winding down of military operations. Stalag XI-A had been liberated by the Americans in April; now he was back in England, dealing with army discharges at the Millbank Military Hospital. He had news at last – after two years – of his elder sister, Christabel Bielenberg, who had been living in Germany throughout the war. As her book *The Past is Myself* would much later describe, her husband Peter, part of the German underground opposition, had been imprisoned in Ravensbrück after the bomb plot against Hitler in July, 1944: unlike his friends, he had been spared execution. John Burton had been dealing with hundreds of departments in an effort to get the Bielenbergs and their children – all German citizens – to Britain. Finally, a 'couple of officers' had agreed to bring them home.[9]

As to *their* relationship, he wrote to Patience in July, now that he was back in England he realised that their 'brief, gay, romantic week' had been a 'painful mistake': there was a 'big difference in temperament' between them. He would hate to be cut off from her family, wanted to be friends with all of them, and get back to a job in a hospital doing some real medicine for a change instead of the current endless form-filling. To Harry, he wrote to thank him 'but [could] not adequately express what *for*: perhaps the nearest I can get is just for your sense and generosity.' He also congratulated him on news of a new job – as head of the new pharmaceuticals department at Allen and Hanbury's in Ware, near London: 'It seems to be what you both want and a job with a future.'

Patience circa 1950, reading for the BBC's *Women's Hour* programme at the height of her radio career.

PART THREE

VOICES IN THE AIR

RADIO TIME

MAY 1ST, 1950. Diana Sandys was catching a bit of peace to listen to *Woman's Hour*, the children at school, her husband at the House of Commons. She was particularly keen to hear the first episode of the new serial, *Jane Eyre:* it was being read by Patience Collier, her old friend who long ago had left behind her life as Rene Ritcher.

These days, Patience seemed to be everywhere on the wireless. Tune in to a soap – *The Robinsons, Mrs Dale's Diary,* or *PC 49* – and there she would be: Diana's son was thrilled to know the owner of one of the voices in *Dick Barton*. Patience was appearing in the *Radio Times* cast lists for the big drama slots: *Curtain Up, Saturday Matinée, Saturday Night Theatre.* She was in schools programmes and documentaries; she had even been interviewed on *Woman's Hour* about how she approached her radio work, particularly the weekly *Profiles* about women in the news – the missionary, Gladys Aylward, for example, the tennis player, 'gorgeous Gussy' Moran, the Labour MP Dr Edith Summerskill – where the imagined voices of the subject's older and younger selves would often be needed. She would sit with the *Profile* subject for that week, she told *Woman's Hour* presenter Olive Shapley, listening to them intently, emptying her mind 'of all sound' except their voice. She would be alert to the 'colour, the tone, the accent, the rhythm and emphases, [absorbing their] emotional make-up', so that when she took up the script, she could subtract maturity to play them younger, or even project them forward into old age.[1]

But it was the *Jane Eyre* serial that particularly gripped the Light Programme audience. As the serial unfurled over the next three weeks, listeners wrote in, mesmerised by the voices, the intensity, the 'quiet stillness of emotions so deep kept in check', the cool calmness of Jane, the Yorkshire abruptness of Mrs Fairfax. Naomi Lewis, the *New Statesman's* critic, singled it out for praise; one listener said she would never go out at all if all serials were as good.[2]

Everything had been up in the air when Harry's Liverpool contract had finished at the end of the war. He had been keen to get an academic post – it would have far better suited his political outlook as well as his research interests – but the private sector had proved more promising. The job at Ware was so near London that it might enable Patience to restart her career. Yet she was already pregnant with Sarah when they moved into the spacious Victorian house at Hoddesdon in Hertfordshire, in the summer of 1945. She hadn't had acting work for three years.

Housebound with a baby and growing family – 'I was three stone heavier and could be heard and not seen' – Patience had seemed positively energised by the difficulties of her position.[3] She began to tug at the connections she had from Manchester with people at the BBC, pestering for interviews, appointments, auditions, then following up, unashamedly with 'I loved your production of *X* and would so have enjoyed playing *Y*.' It was the right moment – the war had hugely expanded radio audiences and BBC ambition. Radio was growing rapidly in size and capacity, as was the pace and quantity of programme production. The success of Forces radio had led to the establishment of the broad-based Light Programme; the Home Service remained the anchor, but with more challenging arts and music programmes going to the Third Programme. The BBC's structures had become more complex; bureaucracy had grown – the documentary approach of 'Features' had made them independent of 'Drama,' while 'Variety' had become distinct from both. Such was the pace of production that it was a nightmare for programme assistants to book rehearsal space in halls, studios and theatres near Broadcasting House, let alone ensure the right studio bookings for recordings and live broadcasts. BBC radio was now dominating the mainstream cultural life of the nation, popular, middle and high-brow: its stars were celebrities, 'almost more famous than film stars' in actor Charles Kay's recollection.[4]

After securing her first radio part in December, 1946, playing the socialist

Annie Besant in a documentary for a fee of seven guineas, Patience had taken anything that came up across thirty departments. She became increasingly skilled in the art of 'peskering' as she came to call it, sending a flurry of postcards to different producers when she seemed to have been forgotten, another batch when her casting seemed too restricted. She would send out updated CVs, ask for auditions, interviews, appointments, be charming, pleading, mock-desperately desperate: 'If you have any mothers, aunts, sisters, governesses, nurses, duchesses, etc. etc. to cast, please... be very kind and remember me.'[5] She piled on the gratitude when an exceptional part came her way, was always looking to broaden her work, extend her experience, move into *Children's Hour* or *Listen with Mother*, and to get more chances with serious drama. By 1950, she had provided the voices for dozens of documentaries, worked for all three departments, as well as Forces and Overseas programmes and Schools Broadcasting, and been engaged by innumerable producers. She had had some sixty jobs since that first contract, and though never a member of the BBC Repertory Players, was definitely a BBC actress. She knew her worth and – with Harry's help on occasion – how to win battles over fees. This woman is a 'good actress', noted one producer over yet another demanding, importuning Patience letter, 'but what a *menace*!'[6]

She was inordinately busy. She read the last episode of *Jane Eyre* at Broadcasting House on Friday afternoon, 19 May, only to set off again for the BBC on Sunday morning. Now thirty-nine, a handsome woman, wearing make-up and a smart dress, she closed the front door on the family, arguments about homework, altercations with Harry and the sounds of lunch preparations and caught the 9.56 Green Line bus from Hoddesdon into town.

Today, it was the *Children's Hour* radio series *Jennifer's Journeys*, tales of American-born Jennifer's 'pilgrimage' around the south of England, the country of her mother's birth, a mix of stories, eccentric characters and magic, making boundaries of time and place melt away in the listeners' imagination. There were the morning rehearsals – a complete read-through to get the pace and timing right to fill the fifty minutes of *Children's Hour* precisely, followed by work with the special effects, atmospheric music and above all, the microphones. Producer

An actress of many parts – Patience in triplicate: the postcard she had made to assist in her campaigns to interest producers.

David Davis – 'so strict', Patience commented later, 'perfectionist and fuss potty' – would move the actors away from or towards the microphones as they spoke to enhance the impact of the story. For him, there had to be a special quality of intimacy between broadcasters and their young audience. Later, Patience would lunch in the BBC canteen with Joan Duan from the cast (all but the actress playing Jennifer were taking a number of parts) before returning to the studio for their final rehearsals. Then the atmosphere would become a little light-headed as the five o'clock live transmission approached: they were broadcasting to families gathered round the Sunday tea table – her own family among them – and the weekday audience of millions of children would double. David Davis and his sound engineer would shut themselves in the listening room. Through the loudspeaker, the actors could hear the BBC Opera Orchestra playing out their closing pieces in the programme before theirs. There were a few seconds' silence, then Davis would clear his throat – 'Hello Children, in *all* regions' – announcing today's episode in his kind, intimate but authoritative voice. Then the slow, rurally evocative oboe music of Eric Coates unwound, Davis signalled, and they were on. Patience would not get home to Hoddesdon until almost eight, and she would be off to get the bus again next day for rehearsals for a documentary.[7]

That year, 1950, would prove particularly busy. The success of *Jane Eyre* would lead to a contract for another Brontë classic for *Woman's Hour*: *Villette*. In this golden period when radio and its performers were fascinating mysteries to the vast listening public, it also led to a second invitation to give a talk on how she approached her work. Every actor had their own technique, she told her listeners. For her, the first step in preparing a serial was reading the book out loud to herself at home from beginning to end, letting the writer's portrayals of her people come alive in her mind. At preliminary run-throughs and rehearsals, she and the producer would discuss and try variations, until she got the tone, timbre and pitch right. With *Villette*, Madame Beck, the jealous wife of Lucy's tutor, had at first 'sounded too beautiful and too tall': they had had to '"uglify" her a little and make her more stumpy'. But having *got* the character, Patience would no more forget their voice than she would confuse well-known friends. Above all, she would see each personality as different colours – Lucy as *blue*, Madame

David Davis, to become Head of Children's Hour, one of Patience's favourite radio producers, "perfectionist and fuss-potty."

Beck a jealous *green*, Ginevra a frivolous *lemon-yellow* – and would mark her script accordingly.[8] Yet despite her great success with serials, and the stretch of documentary work, it was always drama that stood out in her own assessment of her work, with its challenges and opportunities to learn. In Shaw's *Candida*, for example, she had acted alongside Edith Evans and Emlyn Williams; in Ivy Compton-Burnett's difficult *Men and Wives*, she listened with fascination to Beatrix Lehmann's 'double treble stresses' in a phrase or sentence. She was acquiring the ability to 'turn off the top of her head', to learn how people listen'; 'I do love a mike,' she would later reflect.[9]

Patience's BBC world was like a parallel universe to the one at Hoddesdon, some twenty miles away. But the separation was not complete. The children would come across her practising her *Jane Eyre* voices; Harry might assist her to prepare a part. Shopping and theatre expeditions to London would often include a visit to Broadcasting House, if only to use the toilets or the canteen. Patience occasionally arranged for the children and their friends to watch a recording, or even take an audition for a speaking part: she believed the BBC practice of using the voices of adult actors to fill the roles of children just did not work. She had her own social life attached to her work – drinks with producers after hours, flirtations with radio's top brass, strong friendships with the talented women presenters, editors and producers who had won their spurs during wartime broadcasting. BBC friends, particularly Olive Shapley, Eileen Hots and Audrey Jones, would visit the Colliers at home.

BBC Broadcasting House, London.

Hoddesdon in turn reflected her professional status back to her. She had become something of a celebrity. People would follow her on the radio, marvel with her at the bus stop, ask how she did her voices. Hoddesdon became a microcosm for her of the vast, anonymous radio audience. What fascinated, enthralled or amused the townspeople would probably do the same for the nation. She was soon in demand for community events, asked to give talks to the WI, adjudicate at youth drama festivals, open summer fêtes and vicarage garden parties. She took on serious commitments in the town, rushing back from London to conduct a play-reading class at the Evening Institute, keeping meticulous notes on the class members' aims, ability, voice, age, looks and personality, selecting plays appropriate to their skills, giving them detailed advice culled from her experience: 'Must avoid slight tendency to "act" acting,' she told one student.[10] Most challenging was her directing work for the Hoddesdon Evening Townswomen's Guild, for which she had to find all-women plays and lead a volunteer team of stage managers, wardrobe mistress and house manager. Her careful plans set out stage directions, plans of the stage, prop and dress requirements in special notebooks. She was as professional about this work as her own, ruthless even, ensuring she was back from the hospital where her second child had had his tonsils removed in time for dress rehearsals of a Guild production.[11]

Life for Patience and Harry – and for Patience in particular – was wonderfully arranged between Hoddesdon and London. The Green Line bus meant they could revive much of the social life and social circles they had lost from earlier days. People they knew in Cambridge or Manchester before or during the war turned up in London: Gavin Ewart, Harry's poet friend and Patience's former lover; Harold Lever, now a Labour MP for a Manchester constituency; Harry's mentor, Sage Bernal, now at Birkbeck College; John Burton, with whom Patience had had her brief wartime affair, now married, and the scientific half of the Penrose family, Lionel and his wife Margaret. There were old school friends to be seen, science colleagues and RADA friends, lunches, teas, drinks and dinners in town, at the Kardomah, the Café Royal or Olivetti's, weekly trips to the Curzon or Academy cinemas, and theatre outings. There were new friendships with the writer Naomi Lewis, with artists Pamela and Frank Freeman, with the painter Ivon Hitchens and his family.

Her own family relationships were reviving, with Margot, with Patience's godfather Arthur Davis and his daughter Ann, and with her Uncle Martin. In time, connections were also tentatively re-established with brother Geoffrey and his family, and even with their mother, Eva. Patience and Diana Sandys had been able to pick up their friendship, meeting up regularly, lunching together, with an occasional dinner at the Sandys' grand, double-fronted house in Vincent Square, or a visit by Diana to Hoddesdon. There were children's parties to attend – like Patience, Diana had three children – and Diana was godmother to Patience's youngest child, Sarah. They had years to catch up on: they had moved in very different circles, had utterly different wars.

The Freemans' daughter Sally, the special friend of Patience's eldest, remembers the Collier home at The Chart, Rose Vale, Hoddesdon: a spacious, comfortable, three-storey house, elegant and stylish, with flowers arranged in front of a mirror at the foot of a curved staircase. Children's parties there were somehow glamorous and exciting, with a conjuror, interesting adults – actors and BBC people, bohemian in outlook but without the shabbiness of her parents' circle of artists. But the house was also colourful, modern. Pamela Freeman was commissioned to make unique curtain designs for each of the children's bedrooms, Frank to paint Patience's portrait, wearing a dress in fabric designed by Pamela.[12]

The Collier children themselves knew that theirs was a life different from others around them – London-oriented in this still rural market town, their parents' money worries somehow of a different order than those of nearby neighbours, with whose children they were not supposed to mix. Their social life was highly organised by their class-conscious mother. But their parents were also left-wing, broad-minded, intellectual, and unconventional. The Festival of Britain in 1951 was eagerly anticipated: there were several family visits to the Science Pavilion in particular, for which Harry had written material. Theirs was the only house in Hoddesdon to sport Labour posters; they attended Labour rallies as the 1950 General Election approached. They were vaguely aware of the banter between their parents and the Sandys, with the Labour government now hanging on by its fingertips.

Theirs was both a modern life, intellectually without bars, unconventional, yet also intensely ordered, invoking odd echoes of Patience's own Bayswater

The Collier family at home in Hoddesdon, left to right: Joe, Patience, Sarah, Susan, Harry.

Nanny Sheldrake with the Collier children.

childhood. Their mother could be fun, making socks jump out of drawers. She was physically affectionate, a lover of group hugs – a family 'huggermunster'. But she was also uniquely embarrassing with her demanding ways: 'We need a hot, damp cloth, and a tumbler, not a glass,' she would require loudly in cafés. When the family arrived by mistake a day early for the opening of the Festival Hall, she demanded to see the architect – 'I've brought these children all the way from Hoddesdon, I'm coming in!' – and they got in. She was an extravagant, large-voiced mother, who loved to share intimacies with her teenage daughter, Susan, about the latest fashions, and who was intensely loyal if she felt one of her offspring was being short-changed, but who could also be dangerously unpredictable and volatile.[13]

Patience could not have grown her BBC career without tight organisation, careful planning, endless weekly lists meticulously noting people to be met, children's coats to be bought, hair washed, buses caught, school events attended, but also without being able to afford a team of women helpers at home to support her. There was Mrs Pilgrim, Mrs Wilde and particularly Mrs Stratton, an Irish woman who helped in the house but was there for the children too, prepared to extend her hours, and affectionately called 'Strattie' or 'Strattio'. At the end of 1948, Patience began what was to become a lifelong arrangement of having a 'liver-in'. Her old nanny, Ada Sheldrake, now seventy-three, had been ill and wrote to ask if she could come and stay with them and help out a bit: she remained with them for four years.

Sally Freeman remembers the old ladies in the Collier household: Nanny she recalls as benign, with her hair in a bun, sweet and gentle, yet – Patience would comment – she would cook, clean, iron and wash and tell the children, 'You ought to behave!' Harry's mother now stepped up as a warm and reliable granny, coming to stay, sometimes for long periods; Aunt Irene Ritscher would also arrive from France for a holiday. And now, after the long years of estrangement, Patience's mother, Eva, would occasionally come up from London for the day: egocentric, fashionable, a presence and definitely her daughter's mother, in Sally Freeman's view.

NEW ELIZABETHANS

In June, 1952, Patience gave a third talk for *Woman's Hour*. She was an old hand on the programme now; launched just before she started with the BBC, it had become one of her most consistent stages. Filling a daily afternoon slot on the network's most popular Light Programme, *Woman's Hour* had initially aimed at a 'not too sophisticated audience... the average British housewife.' But it soon attracted large and varied audiences, creating a strong bond between programme producers, presenters and listeners, and an active critical dialogue between them. Thousands of letters, ideas and criticisms were received each week; audience responses were constantly tested through the BBC's regional listening panels. The programme was produced by confident, professional women – with Patience's old friend from Manchester days, Olive Shapley, as its presenter, and editors Janet Quigley and Joanna Scott Moncrieff. While contributing to the renewed national emphasis on women's role at home, it had another thrust, covering a wide range of political and social as well as domestic subjects. *Woman's Hour*, wrote Quigley, acted as a 'kind of club.'[1]

This time Patience Collier's talk was part of the programme's series, *My Best Holiday*. It was an account of an idyllic family summer in 1950. Since the war, Patience told her audience, seaside holidays had been something of a tradition for the Colliers. It had all started in 1948 when Harry took a map and measured the distance from Hoddesdon to the nearest seaside towns. Dovercourt in Essex was found to perfectly fit the bill: sandy beach, safe bathing, with 'stretches of flawless sand and patches of rocks,' and manageable by train. Holidays had become particularly important to her, she explained; hers was an exciting life,

The Collier family at Dovercourt Bay.

but exhausting: 'the children's schools, plants for the garden, radio scripts, bills, patching the pillow cases, seeing friends, burst pipes, Christmas presents, the dentist and above all the daily question of food; these seem to come tumbling over each other at such a rate that ... my head feels as if it's going to pop. I crave to be by the sea and there to find ... maximum relaxation.' That summer of 1950, she recalled, Nanny had come with them to Dovercourt, so she and Harry could go off on their own, or take the older children for an expedition: 'She helped me to do what I wanted to do most – NOTHING!'[2]

Even the fondest of friends listening shook their heads at this picture. The truth was that the rest of the family often had to go on holiday ahead of Patience: she would join them later after making elaborate arrangements, her head still buzzing with BBC demands, messages left with producers and their secretaries as to her whereabouts should she need to be contacted. And that summer of 1950 had in fact been a period of high drama. During 1949, Patience had had another prolonged affair, and Harry had begun the preliminaries of divorce proceedings, getting as far as sending her lover's letters to a lawyer, along with his own account of 'events'. His anger had been as cold and hard as it had been during the summer of 1936; their physical relationship had ceased. Had Harry even joined the family at Dovercourt in August, 1950?

That autumn, however, the Colliers had been reconciled and Patience became pregnant – there was pleasant expectation if surprise all round – but then disaster. She developed a series of thromboses, and her gynaecologist decided that the pregnancy must be terminated. On 17 January, 1951, at University College Hospital, she had her second abortion, the legal position now protected by the threat to her life, and was sterilised. Friends from the BBC came to visit her during her fourteen miserable days in hospital – Harry daily, the children allowed to see her only in a waiting room – with Diana Sandys visiting her the day she suffered a sudden haemorrhage. 'It's a sad story', Harry wrote to his lawyer, asking for all the potential divorce material to be returned so it could be destroyed.[3] By February, Patience was sufficiently recovered to begin her usual flurry of postcards to producers at the BBC. She organised a joint birthday party with a conjuror for Joe and Sarah, noting the guests in her diary, absent-mindedly marking

Diana down as 'Diana Bailey', the name she had relinquished back in 1936. 'My Best Holiday', broadcast the following year, seemed to seal up a painful and disturbing episode.

Eras seemed to be ending, and beginning. In red ink in her diary, Patience noted the sequence of historic events that seemed to be tumbling one after the other: the fall of the Labour government to the Conservatives in October, 1951; the death of the King in February, 1952; the death of Stalin in March, 1953. British Conservatism was once more restored, with Diana's father back in charge: Patience and Harry observed Duncan Sandys' swift moves to undo steel nationalisation with dismay, now that Churchill had appointed him Minister of Supply. The two people to whom Patience had been closest since her early childhood – her old nanny and her godfather – died. At home their marriage jogged along, but was full of dangerous tensions and difficult, shouting rows. Patience had relished the power and intensity of another affair; now Harry would do likewise.

Patience's radio work had soon picked up after her surgery, and continued unabated. She was at the peak of her radio career. She sent a recording of her role as Queen Elizabeth I to Diana's father, rather pleased with the courteous reply she received from him on Prime Minister's office notepaper. Soon she would also appear in some of the television productions that were beginning to be broadcast live from the BBC studios at Alexandra Palace, impressing her son who came to the new Lime Grove studios to watch her rehearse the Dorothea Brooking children's serial, *Joey*. She pestered the BBC for more television roles, never doubting, however, that it was with radio that her main work lay. After all, those few people the Colliers knew who had a set were peering at the picture on nine inch screens. The Coronation seemed to change all that. The family were at a friend's party all that day, viewing on and off, later attending a street party and the Hoddesdon Coronation Carnival. They were all to be New Elizabethans now.

Patience and Diana had none of their usual outings and get-togethers that Coronation year. Diana was missing from her god-daughter Sarah's seventh birthday celebrations; there were no restaurant lunches, no visits to each other's homes. When they finally met over lunch at the Sandys' house in October, 1953, it had been almost a year since they had enjoyed a relaxed tête-à-tête. Patience was extremely busy with her complicated rehearsal, broadcasting and domestic schedules – but it had been Diana who had disappeared. It was the first of several periods when she seemed suddenly to fade from Patience's social diary, reappearing months later, pale and slightly glassy-eyed, after prolonged and unpleasant electroconvulsive therapy treatment for a nervous breakdown.[4]

But Patience herself was moving with energy into her early forties. Her child-bearing years were over; all three children were at school. She was at the top of her form as a talented, admired radio actress: she had a professional and busy social life. She ruled her household, was proud of her family and the status she celebrated as the actress wife of a scientist. She was locally fêted – 'Lady Hoddesdon' the actor Esmé Percy dubbed her – and nationally known on the airwaves. What next was she to be?

It was now, quite suddenly, that Patience's career took a new direction. On Thursday, 25 March, 1954, she had a lunch date with an old RADA friend, Eric Berry, at the Arts Theatre on Great Newport Street, the small, independent club theatre of which she was a member. She stopped at the box office as usual to ask if there were any messages. Yes, there was one, from John Perry, of H. M. Tennent's, the theatrical production company: 'Miss Collier, are you by this afternoon? I'd rather like to meet you.

That afternoon Patience met the charming John Perry. Sir John Gielgud would be directing Chekhov's *The Cherry Orchard* at the Lyric Theatre, Hammersmith, he told her, and was now casting. Gwen Ffrangcon Davies and Trevor Howard were lined up for the production, and Gielgud wanted her to play the part of the German governess, Charlotta Ivanovna. What did she think?

The offer came out of the blue. Gielgud seemed to have remembered her from a Third Programme radio play, *Helena*, in which he had starred to her four fleeting parts, from nun to society hostess. At the time, she had caught him 'half-smiling as he listened to her lines', but had thought nothing of it. Tennent's had never heard of her. 'John Gielgud does make a lot of mistakes,' John Perry said drily. 'We hope this isn't one of them.'

John Perry was one of the three most powerful men in London theatre. The business partner and lover of Binkie Beaumont, who had made H. M. Tennent Limited the predominant force in theatre production since the 1940s, he was friendly, sociable, outgoing, with an air of faded yet raffish Anglo-Irish gentility. He had been an actor and playwright, was a gambler and a racing man. People tended to see him as the junior partner at Tennent's, but Perry was the practical one, overseeing the business, albeit also more relaxed than Beaumont about taking risks. He ran the company's subsidiary, Tennent Productions Limited, the not-for-profit charity set up to stage more serious plays, and avoid entertainment tax. *The Cherry Orchard* would be produced under its banner.[5]

'I can't believe it,' was Patience's initial reaction to the offer.

'Neither can I,' countered Perry.

'What will you pay me for rehearsals? There's the Green Line bus there and back – that's at least £3 a week.'

'You're impossible! You don't seem at all thrilled.'

'First things come first.'

With no agent to represent her, Patience grew bolder, suggesting her billing be in slightly larger type.

'If I have another pop out of you,' Perry retorted, 'we shall bill you as "*but*" Patience Collier.' She was engaged.[6]

John Gielgud had planned to stage *The Cherry Orchard* the previous autumn. It was a follow-up to the highly successful season he had put on at the Lyric in 1952 to 1953 for Tennent Productions Ltd. Then he had created a temporary classical company with Paul Scofield, and brought in the young Peter Brook, fresh from Stratford, to direct Otway's *Venice Preserv'd*. Gielgud's success with the run seemed, to *Observer* critic Kenneth Tynan, to make him not so much an actor, but '*the* actor', the touchstone of quality, the guarantee of success.[7] That summer, he had finally received a knighthood.

But his plans had been disrupted by the horror and shame of his arrest in a public toilet for soliciting in October, 1953, in what seems to have been a concerted drive by the police and judiciary to 'clean up' the streets of Coronation

Britain. His whole career appeared to be in jeopardy. Thanks particularly to the support of his co-star Sybil Thorndike, he had been able to storm on in the play in which he was appearing. But he was stressed to the point of breakdown, and *The Cherry Orchard* had to be put off until the spring. He was still unwell when he began to cast and rehearse the play.[8]

Gielgud had a special right to be producing the play. Twenty-five years earlier he had worked with Theodore Komisarjevsky at his Barnes theatre, playing the student Trofimov in *The Cherry Orchard* and appearing also in *The Three Sisters* before audiences still bemused by the plays. He was unafraid of Chekhov, working on subtle amendments to Constance Garnett's translation to make the dialogue more colloquial, funnier yet also more poignant. His changes from passive to active verbs made the characters' speech less abrupt, more direct, personal and immediate: little phrases were opened out.[9]

The first read-through was on 13 April, 1954, at the Haymarket Theatre, with rehearsals running for a luxurious six weeks. Patience began to work on Charlotta right away, in a schedule that continued to include radio rehearsals and broadcasts, children, schools, lunches, teas, drinks and theatre visits. The role is peculiarly challenging: there is complicated stage business to be managed – a dog, ventriloquism, conjuring tricks. But more, the governess seems somehow separate from the Ranevsky household, amusing them with her tricks, yet not part of their conversations. She is absurd, enigmatic, yet takes the play somewhere else with her soliloquy; she seems to embody the themes of the play obliquely yet have her own momentum.

Patience started by building up concrete ideas: Charlotta's dress, her appearance, the *why*. Her clothes must be 'something Charlotta could wash and iron' and afford to maintain: 'navy blue serge, white collars and cuffs,' Patience decided, ideas which Gielgud would adopt and adapt with her in his directions to Bermans, the costumiers. Yet she would panic: 'I've no idea how Charlotta should be played – three ideas all wrong,' she declared at the first rehearsal. At home she shared her thoughts with friends and family, drew on their ideas in return, and began to feel she was whirling with 'six or seven Charlottes.' She learned and practised her tricks, her lines. Eight-year-old Sarah would hear her repeating her

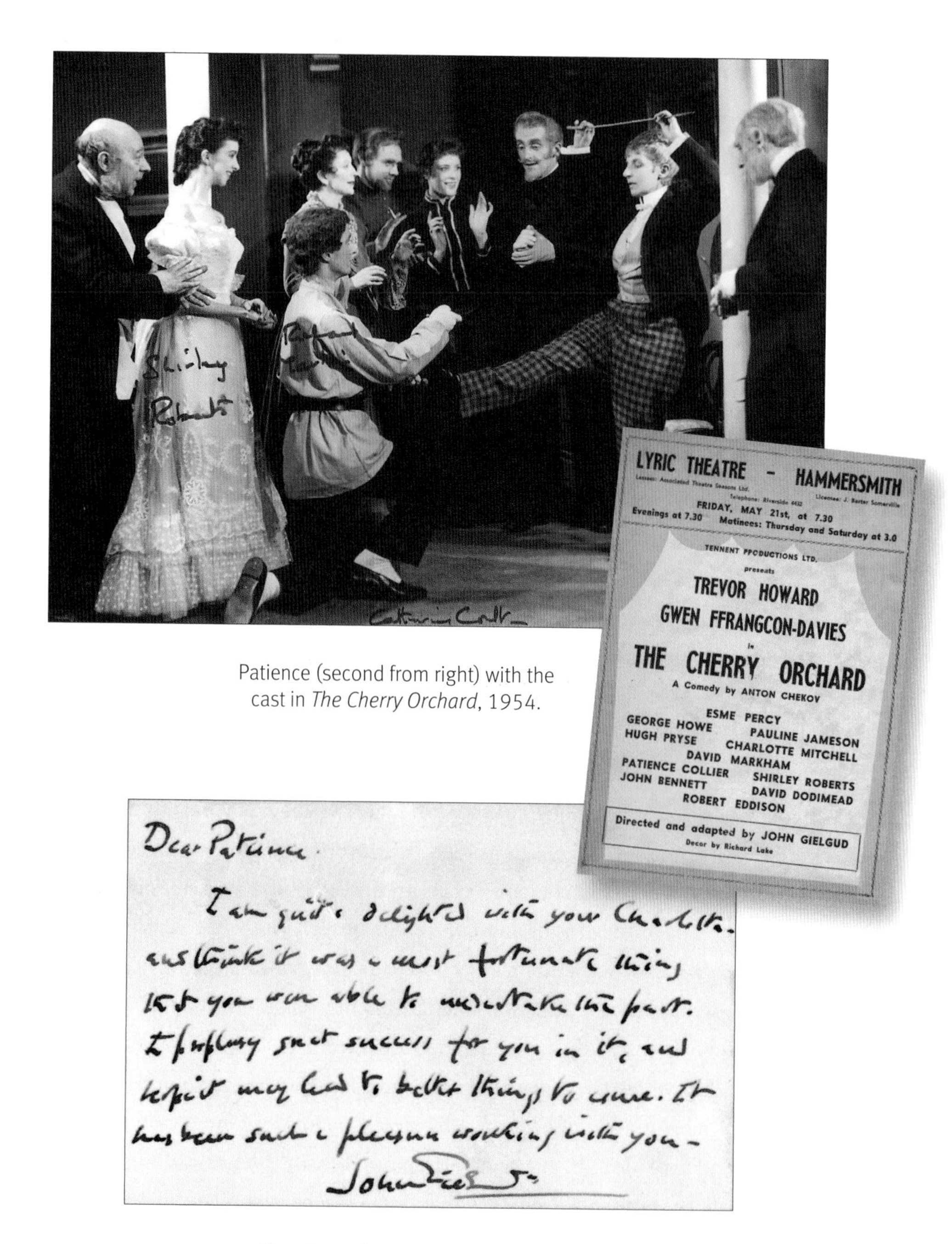

LYRIC THEATRE - HAMMERSMITH

Lessees: Associated Theatre Seasons Ltd. Telephone: Riverside 4432 Licensee: J. Baxter Somerville

FRIDAY, MAY 21st, at 7.30

Evenings at 7.30 Matinees: Thursday and Saturday at 3.0

TENNENT PRODUCTIONS LTD.

presents

TREVOR HOWARD

GWEN FFRANGCON-DAVIES

in

THE CHERRY ORCHARD

A Comedy by ANTON CHEKOV

ESME PERCY
GEORGE HOWE PAULINE JAMESON
HUGH PRYSE CHARLOTTE MITCHELL
DAVID MARKHAM
PATIENCE COLLIER SHIRLEY ROBERTS
JOHN BENNETT DAVID DODIMEAD
ROBERT EDDISON

Directed and adapted by JOHN GIELGUD

Decor by Richard Lake

Patience (second from right) with the cast in *The Cherry Orchard*, 1954.

Dear Patience.

I am quite delighted with your Charlotte and think it was a most fortunate thing that you were able to undertake the part. I prophesy great success for you in it, and hope it may lead to better things to come. It has been such a pleasure working with you –

John Gielgud

Note from *The Cherry Orchard* director, John Gielgud.

opening lines about the house – 'My little dog eats nuts' – with different emphases. Gielgud was toying with the alternative, 'My dog even eats nuts.'[10]

Artist friend Pamela Freeman sketched her idea of Charlotta. Fifteen-year-old Susan drew her own word picture, reflecting Patience's stage interpretation back to her:

> *A woman with red hair, sharp, resentful and perplexed eyes, strong features, carrying herself erect, with the balance of a circus girl. She had a good figure, but now it is disguised by the spinster-governess clothing she wears. No one will love her now, because she will not let herself be loved, perhaps she is mad, she is certainly eccentric. I think her name is as interesting and magnetic as her mysterious personality...*

Patience found Gielgud's direction made the rehearsal days 'magic.' He would arrive with 'snatches of notes'; never said good morning. He had a 'clever, light brilliance [and] changed his mind all the time. Changeable quicksilver.' He was encouraging, a 'poet director'; there was a joyousness to the work which surprised her, causing her to reflect that 'this can't be the acting that I thought I knew.'[11] Yet this project took courage. Though she knew Esmé Percy well (who would be taking the part of Gayev), and had briefly worked with Gwen Ffrangcon Davies (playing Madame Ranevsky) back in the 1930s, the starriness of the production was daunting. There was also no guarantee that the technical skills she had honed on radio would translate to the stage. But her directing at Hoddesdon, a recent substantial part in Shaw's *Candida*, her occasional work now for television, had all served to keep her performance skills whole. 'Charlotta' was a huge leap, but she was not unprepared.

The Cherry Orchard opened on 21 May. It was immediately recognised as a seminal production, scaling the 'heights of British production and acting,'[12] reviewed by every paper, from *The Observer* to *The Catholic Herald*, from *Punch* to *The Nursing Times*. It was celebrated as a fitting revival of the play some fifty years after its first performance in Moscow when Chekhov was dying. It was also thirty years after its first British production, and twenty-five since Gielgud's own performance in it. That Komisarjevsky, Gielgud's hero and mentor – and Patience's – had died in the month before the opening gave the production extra significance. Some critics saw Komisarjevsky's influence in its fluidity of tone, its 'brilliant mixture of laughter and melancholy'.[13]

The general tide of praise and celebration – with an undertone of admiration, surely, for Gielgud's rapid recovery from his personal crisis – was not without some exceptions. Eric Keown, leading the discussion for BBC radio's *The Critics,* felt the production 'notable' but a little off course, insufficiently moving. Some reviewers found Gwen Ffrangcon Davies unsatisfactory, and that Trevor Howard played the key role of Lopahin as a 'Shavian' rather than Chekhovian character. Yet even those who had criticisms felt there was something momen-

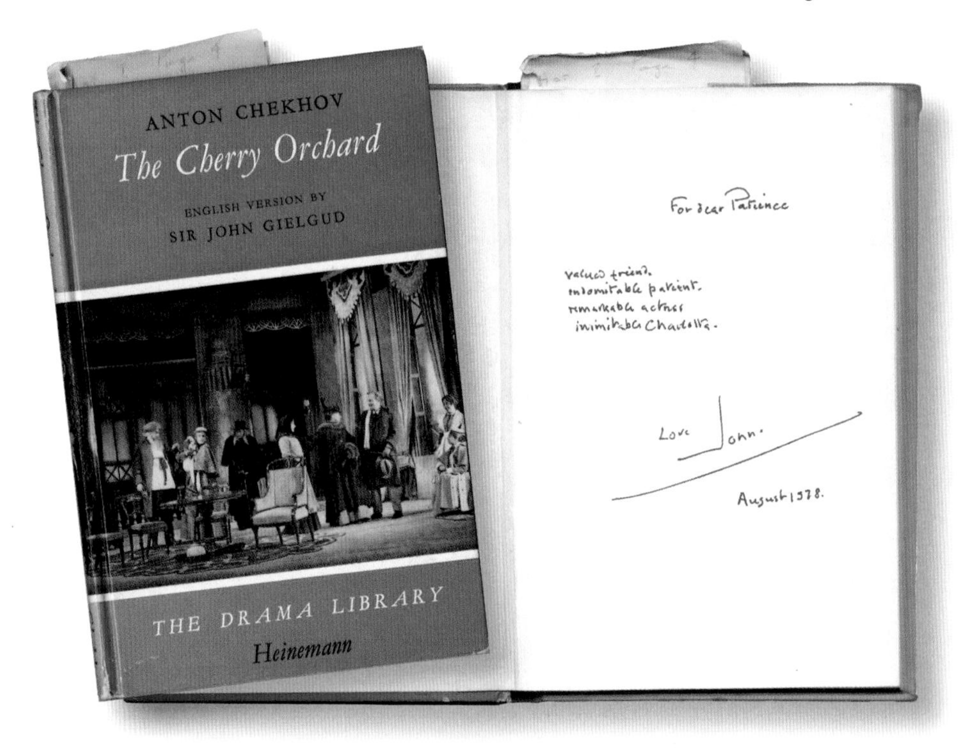

Gielgud's English version of *The Cherry Orchard*, inscribed by him 'For Dear Patience'...'Valued friend'...'Inimitable Charlotta'.

tous about the production. Revisiting the play in June, T. C. Worsley for *The New Statesman* revised his original opinion: 'Its best moments are superb, and such moments serve to remind us of the sublimities of experience which the theatre is capable of giving us.' Patience's performance was repeatedly singled out. Critics who had formerly considered the character out of step with the rest of the play now felt it made perfect sense. Those puzzling aspects which might throw the play off balance were solved by the 'straight line that Miss Patience Collier drives straight through [her]... absurd, pathetic tricks.'[14] *Punch* commented that her 'clever' performance had given 'sharp outline to that often elusive creature, the eccentric governess', *The Financial Times* that she had beautifully hit off 'the acid self-contempt' of Charlotta. *The New Statesman* called her comic performance 'extravagantly tight and monomaniac.'[15] Rose Macaulay on *The Critics* thought it the 'best part' in the production: 'very very funny and at the same time not self-conscious... admirably done.'

Backstage, Patience was getting admiring fan mail from Hoddesdon friends, the Women's Institute, the Townswomen's Guild, BBC colleagues and Wolf Mankowitz, the novelist and screenwriter. Friends, family and Hoddesdon neighbours came in parties to the show, visiting her afterwards in her dressing room. Theatre goers who worked with her later would remember it as an 'extraordinary performance': you knew you were seeing an exciting actress, yet one who contributed without ego to the ensemble.

The Cherry Orchard ran throughout the summer, with the final performance on 4 September. Harry sent her a telegram wishing her a 'happy ending to a wonderful achievement.' The children had been mesmerised by it, reflected the older Patience, but had probably found it all 'terribly hard work.' John Gielgud wrote her a thank-you note in his neat and tiny handwriting: 'I do indeed hope that the success you have made in this production will lead you on to finer opportunities and greater triumphs.' Had she been almost too successful, Patience would wonder in the aftermath. Would she top this? Could she? Or would she be destined 'to be cast as governesses'?

❧

Patience Collier, 1959 – now an established West End actress and TV star.

PART FOUR

WITH THE FIRM

THREE ANGELS

Noël Coward's *Nude with Violin* opened on 24 September, 1956, in Dublin, after three weeks' rehearsal in London. It was the epitome of a Tennent's first nighter. The audience were in full evening dress at the plush Edwardian Olympia Theatre; impresarios and critics from London and New York mixed with London celebrities and Dublin grandees. Binkie Beaumont and John Perry sat dignified but slightly anxious on either side of one of Tipperary's old Anglo-Irish elite. There was a slight delay in the start of the performance – paper darts began to whistle down from the gallery. John Gielgud, who was both directing and starring, grew nervous. But, as the London *Times* said afterwards, it was only 'Dubliners' whimsy': soon there were 'explosions of laughter ricocheting' around the theatre at this highly anticipated new comedy.[1]

Patience Collier, as a key member of the cast, was experiencing the full Tennent's treatment. A new Noël Coward play was in a league of its own: he had been a hero of hers ever since she and her father had had front stalls at the London première of *Cavalcade* in 1931. The cast were being treated like royalty, she wrote home from Dublin. Her trunk and dressing room case – including two red Turkish towels, make-up box, plate, fruit bowl, tooth mug, thermos flask – had been sent on before her. She and her fellow actors had been driven up to the steps of their plane at London Airport; at Dublin, they were met by an enormous Rolls Royce. Binkie Beaumont gave an elegant supper party at the Shelbourne Hotel after the opening performance, and she found herself given pride of place between John Gielgud and his lover, Paul Anstee, who had designed the set.

There had been no let-down, as she had feared, after the final performance

Patience Collier – then Rene – in the front row of the stalls at the first night of Noël Coward's *Cavalcade*, 1931. In the Royal Box sit King George V and Queen Mary alongside other members of the royal family.

The all-powerful Binkie Beaumont:
Angus McBean's surrealist picture of him
manipulating Angela Baddely and Emlyn
Williams on stage, 1947.

of *The Cherry Orchard* back in 1954. Instead, she had rapidly become that coveted thing in the acting world, a Tennent's fixture, an actress on whom Beaumont could rely for brilliant comic grotesques, for elegant countesses, peasant mothers, petty aunts; for serious intellectual plays, for comedies and even for musical revue. She would spend the next five years with 'the Firm', as Tennent's had become known for its controlling stakes in Theatreland.

To outsiders, the commercial power of Beaumont and Perry made them seem dangerous and unassailable: some saw Beaumont as an 'important and inevitable Mephistopheles'.[2] Their longstanding links with Noël Coward and Gielgud, their sexuality – completely known in the theatre, yet unannounced in the ordinary world – made them seem like a closed circle. But the partners brought sparkle, breadth and depth to post-war theatre, introduced new drama, revived lesser known plays at a time when the Arts Council and state subsidy were still in their infancy, and launched its stars into television. As Kenneth Tynan, the young critic at *The Evening Standard*, acknowledged in 1953, Beaumont 'has been righter...than anyone else in the Theatre of his time'.[3] It was a remarkable thing, to be a Tennent's woman at this time.

Patience had moved into rehearsals and touring for a thriller just as soon as *The Cherry Orchard* closed; a new comedy had then followed. *My Three Angels* was classic Tennent's fare, middle-brow but quality entertainment, tried and tested in Paris, a costume drama, starring popular comic actors and brought to the UK with an eye to selling film rights. Four weeks of rehearsal in December, 1954, had been followed by a pre-London tour of eleven towns and cities.

It was Patience's first experience of being on tour for over twenty years and she found touring just as stressful as she remembered it. Beaumont kept interfering with the direction, writing and acting: her role was still being reshaped as they opened in Brighton and Newcastle. But whereas in 1933 she had youthful resilience, now she was middle-aged and a mother of three. A varicose ulcer made it hard for her to walk, let alone deal with the pressures of rewrites, rehearsals and shows, and the separation from the family had proved far from easy. Whatever the ups and downs of her relationship with Harry, she depended on his support, and relished his first night telegrams:

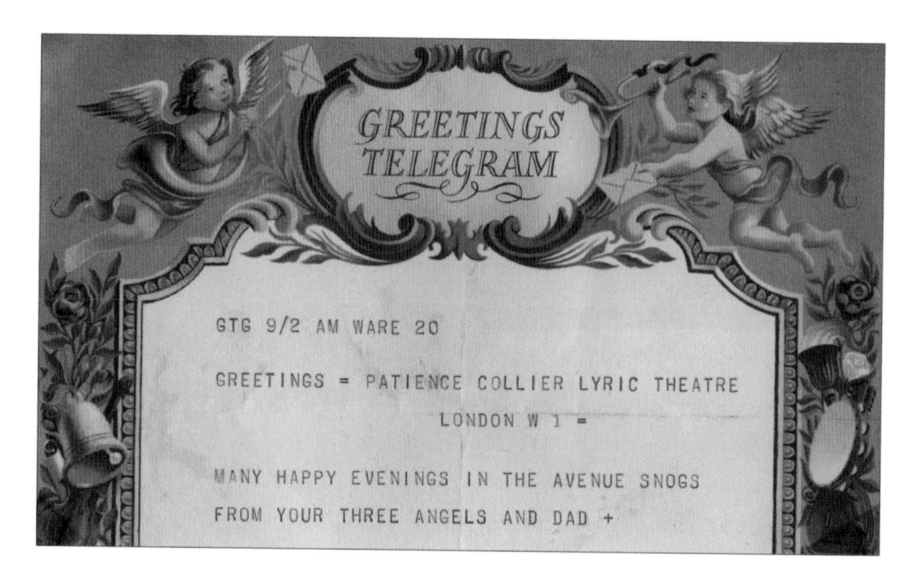

GREETINGS TELEGRAM

GTG 9/2 AM WARE 20

GREETINGS = PATIENCE COLLIER LYRIC THEATRE LONDON W 1 =

MANY HAPPY EVENINGS IN THE AVENUE SNOGS FROM YOUR THREE ANGELS AND DAD +

Support from Harry in his telegram to Patience for the first night performance of *My Three Angels* in London.

Patience as Madame Parole and Ronald Shiner as Joseph in *My Three Angels* at the Lyric Theatre, Hammersmith, 1955

MANY HAPPY EVENINGS IN THE AVENUE SNOGS FROM YOUR THREE ANGELS AND DAD

'Darling Harry' ran errands for her to get a new wig and jewels sorted during the nerve-racking early days, and liaised with doctors about her ankle. The family came to see the show, toured the set, and giggled with the cast.

It was the arrival of Greta Finch at the Hoddesdon household after the illness and death of Ada Sheldrake which made the whole thing practicable. Recently widowed, capable, friendly *and* middle-class, Greta had brought a new element to the Chart. She had had no drilling in service, and Patience could feel she was a friend. To her, Patience could confide her sense that 'Joe misses me least, and Sarah most.' But still she worried about practicalities, warning the children of a flying weekend visit and a clothes inspection: 'Darlings ...BE PREPARED!' she wrote from Aberdeen. Even as a remote mother, Patience was both funny and daunting.

Despite the stress and fatigue of the tour, Patience was determined not to take a break from the BBC, where she was now doing some television as well as radio. She slotted in rehearsals for a television play and a second set of readings of *Jane Eyre* for *Woman's Hour* around work on *Three Angels*, and once on tour, she regularly undertook radio recordings at weekends. On the last night of the Edinburgh run, her leg painful, she took the Saturday night train to London, rehearsed and broadcast on the Sunday, then caught the Flying Scotsman back to Edinburgh in the small hours, ready to catch the train to Aberdeen for the next week of the tour. She spent the next few afternoons between rehearsals and performances in bed.

From there, she listened anxiously to the broadcasts of her recordings of *Jane Eyre:* would it live up to her original performance in 1950? She thought the first episode rather dull. She liked some bits as it proceeded, but hated others: was furious at a wrong effect in one episode. In her own mind, she was a radio actress who was now also appearing in theatre. That was how she portrayed herself – that, and as a loyal mother of three children – when interviewed by the Aberdeen *Evening Express* during the tour of Scotland. For her, radio was the serious, ongoing career, the medium through which she reached millions. People in hotels recognised her name from radio; she got more publicity than other cast members due to her radio stardom. Yet she found that there was a strange snobbery about it amongst theatre people who tended 'to treat radio as a sort of amateur sideline to the acting profession,' she wrote home. 'They only take notice of high-powered Third Programme productions or an historical "World Theatre" drama.'

For all its stresses, Patience relished that tour with *My Three Angels*. She became teasing friends with the stars, with George Rose, his boyfriend Rudi, and even his mother. There were lunches and teas between the shows, outings with George, Nigel Stock, Hugh Manning and Peter Barkworth, trips to the pictures, to the new Grace Kelly and Bing Crosby film, *The Country Girl*, or the latest Hitchcock, *Rear Window*. The play improved as the tour progressed and they got good laughs. In Newcastle, the applause for her had been good; by Coventry she was basking in praise from Beaumont. When the show finally arrived at the Lyric, Hammersmith in May, 1955, it lasted until November. For the second year running, the rest of the family took their summer holiday without her.

NUDERS

Noël Coward was due to fly to Dublin on 26 September, 1956, to see *Nude with Violin* on its third night. Then, Patience wrote home, 'all the criticisms, changes and upheavals will start'.

John Gielgud had taken on the casting, direction and lead role with some trepidation: he was far from being Coward's first choice. He was new to light comedy, and not entirely confident about the play. 'It is very broad and a bit vulgar, but full of some surefire situations', he wrote to his mother. He also felt curiously challenged by the part of Sebastien, the valet who manipulates and blackmails his way into making money out of the artworks of his dead master with the confidence of a 'major domo' and the craft of a spiv and crook. It's 'a rather new kind of part for me', he wrote, 'a sort of confidential Dago valet who is the smooth arranger of everything'. And he was nervous about the maestro's reaction to his direction: 'I wish you could have been there to hold the reins, but shall look forward with some trepidation but also with great pleasure, to seeing you in Dublin', he wrote to Coward, who was basking in Bermuda.[1] Coward, the most exalted of the Tennent's grouperie, vented his own anxieties about Gielgud and the production in snide asides to Binkie Beaumont, to a leading member of the cast, and to friends: 'May the blessed Virgin have pity and keep his nibs away from the cottages and prevail upon the poor spalpeen to play divil a bit of comedy and not fuck up the whole blathering enterprise.'[2] There were tense disputes between them over casting, but Gielgud, tougher than he appeared, stuck to his guns.

Yet Patience was right. Coward's arrival brought substantial cuts and revisions: the play needed to be 'redirected from beginning to end', he later wrote

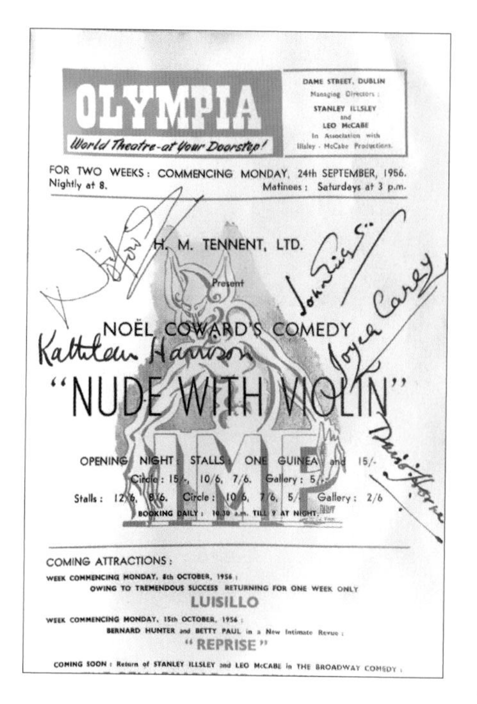

OLYMPIA
World Theatre-at Your Doorstep!
DAME STREET, DUBLIN
Managing Directors :
STANLEY ILLSLEY
and
LEO McCABE
In Association with
Illsley - McCabe Productions.
FOR TWO WEEKS : COMMENCING MONDAY, 24th SEPTEMBER, 1956.
Nightly at 8.
Matinees : Saturdays at 3 p.m.
H. M. TENNENT, LTD.
Present
NOËL COWARD'S COMEDY
"NUDE WITH VIOLIN"
OPENING NIGHT : STALLS : ONE GUINEA and 15/-
Circle : 15/-, 10/6, 7/6. Gallery : 5/-
Stalls : 12/6, 8/6. Circle : 10/6, 7/6, 5/-. Gallery : 2/6
BOOKING DAILY : 10.30 a.m. TILL 9 AT NIGHT.
COMING ATTRACTIONS :
WEEK COMMENCING MONDAY, 8th OCTOBER, 1956 :
OWING TO TREMENDOUS SUCCESS RETURNING FOR ONE WEEK ONLY
LUISILLO
WEEK COMMENCING MONDAY, 15th OCTOBER, 1956 :
BERNARD HUNTER and BETTY PAUL in a New Intimate Revue :
" REPRISE "
COMING SOON : Return of STANLEY ILLSLEY and LEO McCABE in THE BROADWAY COMEDY :

A handbill for *Nude with Violin*, signed by Noël Coward, John Gielgud, Kathleen Harrison, Joyce Carey and David Horne.

to Beaumont. He gave all the cast notes, new blockings, and terrified many of the actors, undoing much of the 'distracting comic business' of Gielgud's direction. But Patience, playing the 'doubtful Russian princess' who like the other charlatans turns up to try and outwit Sebastien, found herself admired: 'You're the best comedian that [has] turned up for years,' Coward told her. 'I want you in all my plays.' To act in a star-studded production of a new Noël Coward play *and* to be so complimented by him must have seemed the height of gloss and grandeur. But she kept her head, trying to avoid him – and more re-directions – at lunch breaks. That weekend, she escaped the hothouse of the show to go and stay with John Burton's sister and brother-in-law, Christabel and Peter Bielenberg, who after their experiences in wartime Germany had settled into life in County Carlow.[3]

As the autumn went on, *Nude with Violin* continued to be received 'uproariously' by the Dublin audiences, but, as Patience wrote home, 'the press think what *we* always thought they *would* think.' Some critics bowed to the pleasure of the audiences, and saw a Sheridan-like grotesquery in Coward's characters, a touch of the Oscar Wildes in Coward's 'best comedy since *Blithe Spirit*.'[4] Patience's elegantly extravagant, crazy Russian Anya Pavlikov – with some of the play's funniest lines and a smattering of Russian to exchange with Sebastien – was particularly and consistently admired. Yet the overwhelming critical reaction was savage. Anthony Coleman, in *The Tatler*, wrote that the great author had 'dwindled into a mere playmaker'; *Drama*'s critic that it was an 'amusing

Patience Collier as Anya Pavlikov with John Gielgud as Sebastien in *Nude with Violin*, 1956

Stage cigarette case with a real Russian Sobranie used by Anya in *Nude with Violin*, indicative of the diligence with which Patience would approach her rôles.

idea...spoiled by a paucity of wit', and Ken Tynan – now at *The Observer* – that it was 'brief and interminable'. Philip Oakes' London *Evening Standard* piece about the Dublin opening was so vicious ('described as a comedy, it emerged as a farce and ended as a corpse') that Binkie Beaumont banned the paper's regular critic – Milton Shulman – from attending the London opening.

The row followed the production as it progressed – with new revisions and innumerable changes of cast – to Liverpool, Manchester, Newcastle and Edinburgh, before opening in London at the Globe Theatre in November. But audiences continued to flock to it, despite the critics' unfavourable comparisons with a new theatre which seemed to be emerging. John Osborne's *Look Back in Anger* and Brendan Behan's *The Quare Fellow* had both opened in London in May, 1956 – raising questions in theatre circles as to what the theatre was *for*. The audience had enjoyed itself very much, noted Philip Hope-Wallace in the *Manchester Guardian*: 'The kind of audience which goes to a Noël Coward play in mild and middle-brow expectation was not let down – and why should their interests be ignored by the...sort of theatre-lover who complains...that Mr Coward is writing to formula now, that his personages are stock types, his invention effete, and many of his jokes flatly facetious?'[5] Coward for his part could predict a 'steady run', based on ticket sales in London. 'I am really thrilled about darling "Nuders" being such a wonderful success', he wrote to Joyce Carey, who played the artist's widow in the play: '...I still believe, in spite of Brecht, Peggy Ashcroft, Arthur Miller, etc. that the Theatre is primarily a place of entertainment.'[6]

The savagery with which the critics attacked *Nude* reflected not only the contrast between Coward's fluff and the new drama, but also disappointment with the apparent decline in his talents, and the British press's taunting about his tax exile status. It may also have been connected with the extraordinary roller-coaster of political events that year. The Suez Crisis was still playing itself out as the production toured, forcing the removal of some references to Egypt from the script when it opened in London.[7] For those on the left, the Colliers among them, the year had seen a series of shocks to their own past and present faiths: Soviet leader Khrushchev denouncing Stalin's purges in February, the Polish uprising in June, the Hungarian uprising – beginning the very day before

Nude opened in Dublin – followed by brutal suppression. 'Isn't the news terrible?' wrote Olive Shapley to Patience. A silly comedy of manners mocking modernism just seemed out of step with the national mood: 'Tory satire, directed at people on a moving staircase from a stationary one', as Tynan wrote.[8]

Nude was not the only commercial production to be suffering the taunts of the critics, however. To some contemporary observers, the general theatrical scene of the mid fifties was looking decidedly jaded. Britain's best actors seemed mostly occupied with playing dead authors, a series of *Times* articles observed in the spring of 1955; most interesting plays were imports, and then old ones: Londoners were not seeing the latest O'Casey, O'Neill, Tennessee Williams or Arthur Miller; and the country lacked the dynamism and experimentalism of European state-subsidised theatre.

Yet the London arts and entertainment scene enjoyed by Patience, Harry and their friends was not without its pleasures and inspirations. The musical was entering its most ebullient period, Hollywood was enjoying its golden era of genre movies, and Londoners could see foreign language films – by Fellini, De Sica, Resnais, Jacques Tati, Satyajit Ray and Bergman – at the Academy, Everyman, Curzon or National Film Theatres. And there were now alternatives to mainstream commercial theatre. Patience's old friend Joan Littlewood was attracting regular press praise for her work at Theatre Royal, Stratford East, which Theatre Workshop had occupied since 1953. The young Peter Hall had been at the Arts Theatre for a year or more, and in 1955 became its director, responsible for productions of Ionesco and Beckett which Patience saw that summer. And Peter Brook's free-wheeling directing career had been underway since the late 1940s, quite a proportion of it under the patronage of Tennent's and Binkie Beaumont.

Only months before the opening of *Nude*, indeed, Patience had performed in Peter Brook's season at the Phoenix Theatre for Tennent productions. At the age of thirty-one, Brook was already well known as a director who would always surprise and tackle the unpromising, even the apparently impossible. With his Russian Jewish inheritance, his approach to theatre was eclectic, inter-

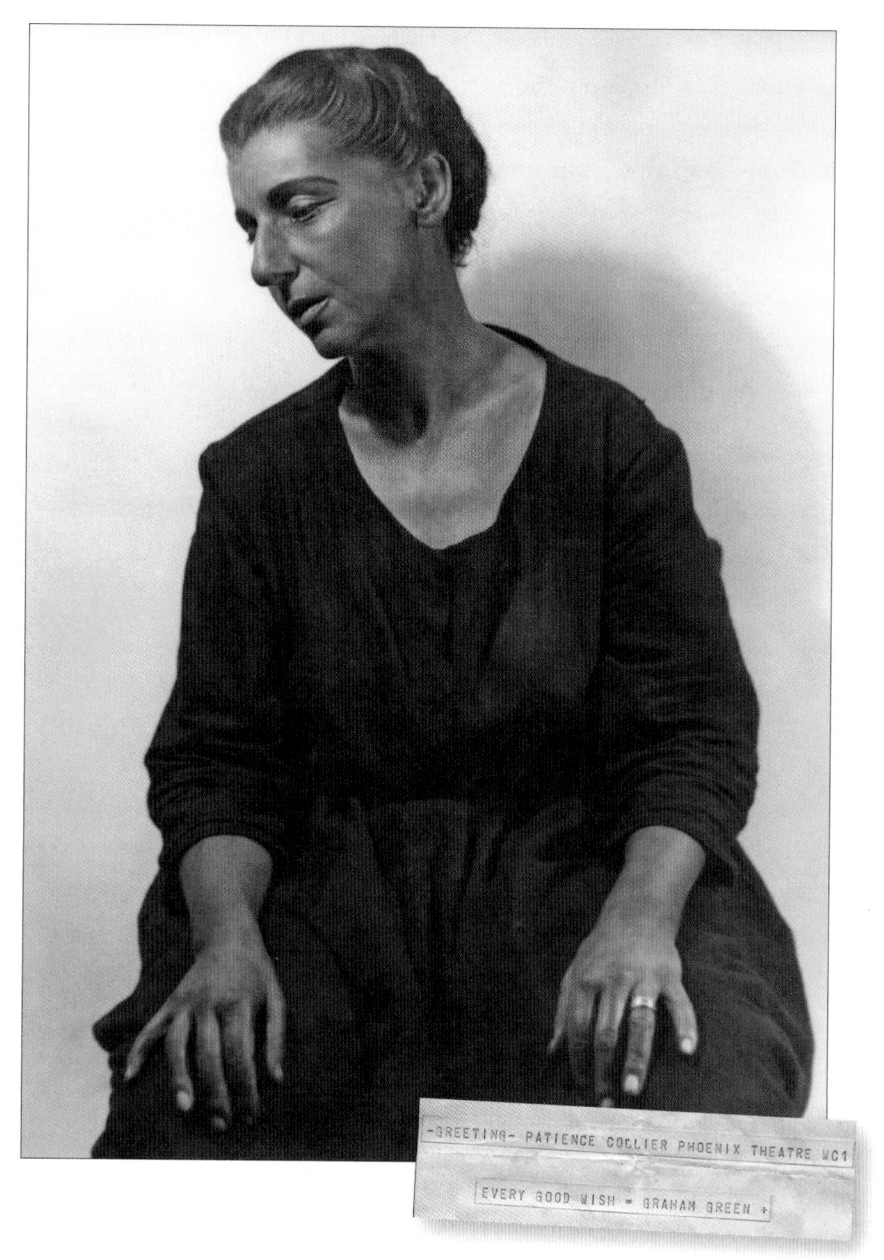

Patience Collier as Maria in Graham Greene's *The Power and the Glory* at the Phoenix Theatre, 1956, with a good wishes telegram from Greene for the first night.

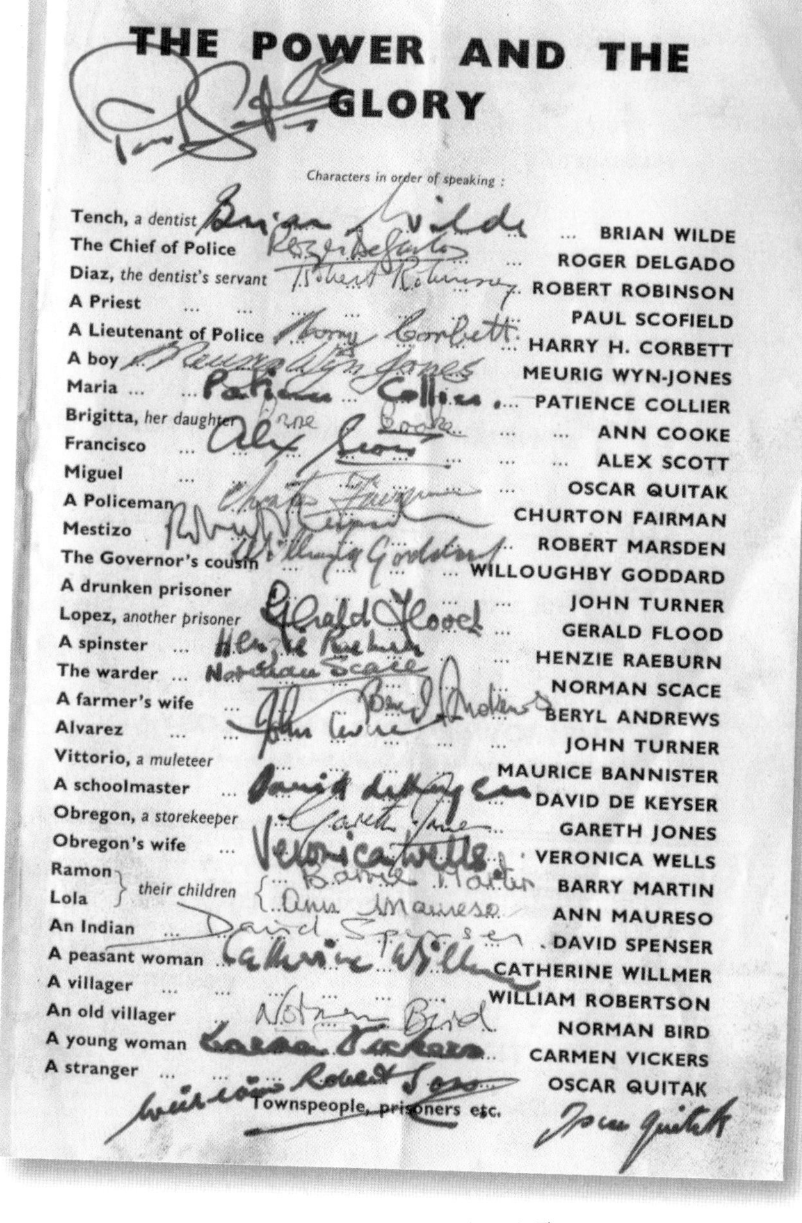

THE POWER AND THE GLORY

Characters in order of speaking:

Tench, *a dentist*	BRIAN WILDE
The Chief of Police	ROGER DELGADO
Diaz, *the dentist's servant*	ROBERT ROBINSON
A Priest	PAUL SCOFIELD
A Lieutenant of Police	HARRY H. CORBETT
A boy	MEURIG WYN-JONES
Maria	PATIENCE COLLIER
Brigitta, *her daughter*	ANN COOKE
Francisco	ALEX SCOTT
Miguel	OSCAR QUITAK
A Policeman	CHURTON FAIRMAN
Mestizo	ROBERT MARSDEN
The Governor's cousin	WILLOUGHBY GODDARD
A drunken prisoner	JOHN TURNER
Lopez, *another prisoner*	GERALD FLOOD
A spinster	HENZIE RAEBURN
The warder	NORMAN SCACE
A farmer's wife	BERYL ANDREWS
Alvarez	JOHN TURNER
Vittorio, *a muleteer*	MAURICE BANNISTER
A schoolmaster	DAVID DE KEYSER
Obregon, *a storekeeper*	GARETH JONES
Obregon's wife	VERONICA WELLS
Ramon } *their children*	BARRY MARTIN
Lola } *their children*	ANN MAURESO
An Indian	DAVID SPENSER
A peasant woman	CATHERINE WILLMER
A villager	WILLIAM ROBERTSON
An old villager	NORMAN BIRD
A young woman	CARMEN VICKERS
A stranger	OSCAR QUITAK

Townspeople, prisoners etc.

Cast of characters in the Phoenix Theatre production of *The Power and the Glory*, signed by the whole ensemble (with the exception of Maurice Bannister).

national, blurring the boundaries between the performance arts, linking back to Komisarjevsky and Gordon Craig. He had learned his trade at the Birmingham Repertory Theatre where he worked with Paul Scofield, and had directed several legendary Shakespeare productions at Stratford, opera at Covent Garden and the New York Met. Beaumont had long recognised Brook's abilities, and had used him for a Dostoyevsky and Sartre season at the Lyric in 1946, and again in 1953. He now came fresh from directing *Titus Andronicus* – the unperformable play – for Stratford, in a production of such power that it had astounded critics and audiences. This time he was directing three plays for Tennent's, all starring Paul Scofield. Patience had taken a supporting role in two, an adaptation of Graham Greene's *The Power and the Glory* and a revival of T. S. Eliot's pre-war verse play, *Family Reunion.*

The first play in this Scofield-Brook season – *Hamlet* – went well enough. But *The Power and the Glory* got a more mixed reception. The timing was unfortunate, opening on 5 April, 1956, in the same week as the London premier of *The Crucible* at the Royal Court, where George Devine and Tony Richardson launched the English Stage Company with a commitment to supporting new writing. *Plays and Players* reviewed the two side by side, under the opener, 'April was the cruellest month....' Beside the terrifying drama of Miller's play, the adaptation of Greene's novel about 1930s Mexico seemed less than satisfying: 'There was power at times, but not an ounce of glory.'

But the real test came with the eagerly anticipated third play of the season, *Family Reunion.* Eliot had achieved considerable success with *The Cocktail Party* only a few years previously, and *Murder in the Cathedral,* though now twenty years old, remained so popular that it was always being performed somewhere. Verse plays still signified 'modernism' to contemporary audiences: Christopher Fry's plays, which Brook himself had directed, were popular among intellectuals. For this production, he assembled a distinguished cast around Paul Scofield, including Sybil Thorndike, Lewis Casson and Gwen Ffrangcon-Davis, with Harry H. Corbett, Norman Scace and Patience retained from the previous play.

Patience received her usual spate of good luck telegrams and cards for her part of Violet, including a little black cat card from her youngest daughter, Sarah,

PHOENIX THEATRE
TEM. 8611

Lessees: H. M. & S. Ltd.
Licensed by the Lord Chamberlain to Prince Littler
CHARING CROSS ROAD, LONDON, W.C.2

Evenings at 7.30
Matinees: Wednesday and Saturday at 2.30
PRICES OF ADMISSION: Stalls 16/6, 10/6; Dress Circle 16/6, 12/6; Upper Circle 10/6, 7/6, 5/-; Boxes £4.

Tennent Productions Ltd. present
PAUL SCOFIELD - PETER BROOK SEASON

SYBIL THORNDIKE
PAUL SCOFIELD
GWEN FFRANGCON-DAVIES
LEWIS CASSON
DAVID HORNE

in

THE FAMILY REUNION

by T. S. ELIOT

NORA NICHOLSON
PATIENCE COLLIER
OLIVE GREGG
CYRIL LUCKHAM
CATHERINE WILLMER
NORMAN SCACE
and
HARRY H. CORBETT

Directed and Designed by PETER BROOK

FOR A LIMITED SEASON

THE FAMILY REUNION

Characters in order of speaking

Amy, Dowager Lady Monchensey ... SYBIL THORNDIKE

Agatha, *her younger sisters* ... GWEN FFRANGCON-DAVIES

Ivy, *her younger sisters* ... NORA NICHOLSON

Violet, *her younger sisters* ... PATIENCE COLLIER

The Hon. Charles Piper, *brothers of her deceased husband* ... DAVID HORNE

Col. The Hon. Gerald Piper, *brothers of her deceased husband* ... CYRIL LUCKHAM

Mary, *daughter of a deceased cousin of Lady Monchensey* OLIVE GREGG

Denman, *a parlourmaid* ... ... CATHERINE WILLMER

Harry, Lord Monchensey, *Amy's eldest son* PAUL SCOFIELD

Downing, *his servant and chauffeur* ... HARRY H. CORBETT

Dr. Warburton ... ... LEWIS CASSON

Sergeant Winchell ... ... NORMAN SCACE

NOTE

The Furies (Erinyes) of Greek mythology, the avengers of crime against kinship, who appear during Act One, were propitiated, according to the Orestes legend, by the expiation of crime, and became transformed into the Kindly Ones (Eumenides)—the "bright angels" of Act Two.

Programme from *The Family Reunion* at the Phoenix Theatre, 1956 together with good luck paper 'violets' sent to Patience on the first night.

inscribed in family joke style to 'Aunt Violet'. She played one of three sisters to Sybil Thorndike's dowager widow Amy, who awaits the return of her son in the chilly decline of Wishwood, a 'country house in the North of England'.

The play was challenging to perform, implicitly satirising drawing-room theatre, flexing itself between the absurd, the banal and the luminous, hinging on Greek myth and the arrival of the Furies but also the unravelling of mystery and scandal. Patience's character specialises in caustic remarks, but the script requires her to step aside from conventional realism at key points, and join her siblings in the stylised laments and analysis of the Chorus. Would the audience find the play absurd in the wrong places, the cast wondered, the Furies provoke giggles? Brook tried to tackle the problems with his own designs and lighting effects, encouraging the actors to develop habits and preoccupations for their characters so that even T. S. Eliot, more sceptical than any critic about his play, commented that they had made 'made these people live'.[9]

The production was generally hailed as a success. But the play itself irritated critics: an 'unsatisfactory play' (*Financial Times*), 'an artistic failure' (*Plays and Players*), a work in which the audience must 'search for the play'.[10] It had perhaps been risky reviving an earlier Eliot, which used themes and scenarios better worked through in the subsequent *Cocktail Party*. But it was something more, a feeling that Eliot was already beginning to belong to the recent past. As the Phoenix season proceeded, innumerable first nights came and went: Fry's *A Boy with a Cart*, Colette's *Gigi*, the gentle *Caucasian Chalk Circle* at the Haymarket, directed by Gielgud for Tennent's. But *Look Back in Anger* had also opened at the Royal Court to a famously mixed reception and *Waiting for Godot* acquired commercial success, transferring from the Arts Theatre to the Criterion. Beside them, some critics found works by Eliot rather absurd, lacking in truth and feeling on the one hand, failing in the manner of its symbolism on the other. Poor Paul Scofield is 'now called on to impersonate a tormented pseudo Greek', wrote Kenneth Tynan, who had acquired his scathing style in *The Observer*. He found the play 'magnificently revived' with 'fine work...by Nora Nicholson and Patience Collier', but fundamentally it was a 'has-been...glacial, a theatrical Jack Frost'. 'The whole cast inhales Mr Eliot's thin air as if it were nourishing them.'[11]

TELEVISION SETS

OLD FRIENDS OF PATIENCE came to see *Nude with Violin* as it continued its long run in London during 1956 and 1957 – Peter Brook, George Rose, even Joan Littlewood – and she was enjoying the camaraderie of the cast. She was particularly close to Kathleen Harrison, whose Cockney Cherry-May Waterton in *Nude* had charmed both audiences and critics. She knew Kathleen from radio's *Meet the Huggets*: left-wing, a national radio and film character star, eighteen years her senior. Patience caught up with the latest theatre and cinema productions, attended Ivon Hitchens's exhibitions and Count Basie concerts. She was filming, and doing occasional radio, a new *Woman's Hour* serial and a *Children's Hour* feature for David Davis. And thanks to Tennent's, she was now getting regular roles in television.

Patience's television experience had progressed slowly alongside her far more significant radio work. Her first play for BBC TV – Norman Swallow's *The Suffragette* in 1951 – had been broadcast live from Alexandra Palace, a converted dance hall, to an audience of perhaps half a million located only in London and the home counties.[1] Television managers and producers were still struggling with what factual programmes and dramas should be, and *The Radio Times* was publishing television listings as an appendix to the main sound broadcasting schedules.

Live television as it was then was something else, Patience would later say, and nothing could quite prepare the actor for its peculiar demands: the constant disasters waiting to happen, the 'sound boom...swinging over your head with its microphone swooping down on you every now and then to pick up your lightest

Patience was particularly close to Kathleen Harrison, a national radio and film character star eighteen years her senior.

murmur', enormous 'dinosaur-like cameras' trundling at you to get their close-ups. While families at home saw only the actors, they could easily feel like a 'tiny cog in an enormously mechanised wheel. The lights are very strong and flat. Just outside your acting area...carpenters wait eagerly to tear down the set as soon as you've finished it.'[2]

It took until 1954 for television to begin to rival radio seriously as a mass medium for the home. Over four million people acquired sets in the full flush of the Coronation: televisions were now cheaper and could be bought on Hire Purchase, and the Midlands, Scotland and the North were finally able to get a signal. At last the BBC recognised its potential: Alexandra Palace was largely abandoned for Lime Grove while a purpose-built television centre was constructed at White City. A new post of Head of Drama was created – and Michael Barry appointed – with the aim of reaching new audiences, building on the kind of pioneer work that producers such as Dorothea Brooking had already achieved for young viewers, with a menu to grip, amuse, move and frighten.[3]

Like the post-war radio broadcasters before them, television planners were also now developing the art of patterning the viewers' week, not only with serials and popular soaps like *The Grove Family*, but with regular drama slots which helped to promote the one-off play. Audience research showed that viewers were more likely to stay tuned even to a difficult play if it followed a popular show. On Boxing Day, 1954, fresh from her West End success in *The Cherry Orchard* and in the midst of rehearsals for *My Three Angels*, Patience appeared with veteran actor Harcourt Williams in *The Captive*, an adaptation of a Pirandello story, the live broadcast following on from *What's My Line?* and *Aladdin on Ice*.

She was gradually finding television easier as she sought to understand the perspective of each of the technicians – the cameraman, the sound man, the make-up girl, the hairdresser and the dresser. She was learning to become a partner in the enterprise and gain their support: that way she found she could focus better on achieving her performance. Television producers were now always included in Patience's BBC write-rounds, yet getting parts with BBC TV still required as much badgering and wheedling as had been needed in her early days of radio.

All this changed with the arrival of independent television. Binkie Beaumont and his circle were quickly alert to the possibilities offered by the Conservative government's breaking of the BBC's television monopoly. Beaumont was a key member of the Incorporated Television Company – one of six chosen contenders for Independent Television contracts under the 1954 Television Act – alongside other giants of the theatre-making scene. The ITC bid failed only because the Independent Television Authority feared a monopoly over the entertainment profits of the nation; but when the company instead became a supplier of programmes, Tennent protégées such as Patience were in a strong position to benefit.[4] She found herself part of the great exodus of producers, script editors, cameramen and technicians abandoning BBC Television for the opportunities of ITV.

Even before ITV's opening night – on 22 September, 1955 – Patience had a play in the bag for Channel 9, an ITC production prepared for one of the new channel's early drama slots. *The Concert* was a prototype of what would become an ITV recipe for successful drama: filmed, like many of the North American series which also became popular, and with a different feel to most television drama to date. It was a thriller, had a glamorous setting (Montreal), but dealt with a serious subject: racial prejudice. Breaking free from BBC traditions, appealing to popular audiences, it filched shamelessly from Auntie: its stars, Bernard Braden and Barbara Kelly, were household names on BBC TV and its director, Dennis Vance, had been a lead producer on BBC's *Sunday Night Theatre*. Patience cemented her success by appearing for a second time on commercial television that October, as Aunt Boffin in *The Little Round House* drama series for children produced by Associated Rediffusion.

She soon became a familiar face on ITV, in thrillers, detective series and also serious drama, while appearing in Tennent's stage productions and still undertaking regular radio broadcasting. Around this time, the Colliers grew tired of having to cadge invitations to watch TV on other people's sets, and acquired their own: a small green portable box.

During this period, Patience seemed to be growing her off-stage persona alongside her brilliant development of the roles she performed. As a Tennent's actress and a star of ITV, she needed to become again a woman who depended on a highly created appearance. She would remake herself each day before she stepped out of the house, living up to her reputation not just as a character actress, but a characterful actor, even when off-duty. There was also a need to mask some of the intrusions of middle age. She was not particularly well: early in 1957, she was experiencing the early symptoms of the menopause, had developed fibrositis and wore dentures now. *This* Patience Collier required perfect make-up, an exacting choice of clothes and scarves, and also a wig. Self-conscious about her own very fine hair, she was embracing the art of the wig-maker off stage and camera (good wigs being particularly important for television) as well as on. Regular visits to the most renowned wig-makers of the time, Wig Creations, were now a key part of her schedule, both for her private and professional selves.

Wig Creation's owners, handsome Stanley Hall and his partner, Noel Macgregor, had created a business to cater for the stars, where professionalism and attention to detail were combined with the personal care and trust necessary to deal with the intimacies of wig design and fittings. Paul Huntley, who went on to become one of New York's most famous wig-makers, remembers joining the business at about this time, and soon got to know Patience. 'We were bosom buddies; Patience used to come in almost every other week. She was a very special person [with] wonderful ideas, strong ideas…a consummate perfectionist – her ideas were always best, she knew what she wanted exactly.'[5] Wig Creations extended the camp, flirtatious, bantering and exuberant relationships of the theatre into her personal life, enabling her to be more than herself, a bigger self. Stanley and Noel's New Year parties – 'the talk of the world' – became a regular fixture in her diary.

Patience and Harry's marriage was continuing to drift. Her exhausting schedules of performances in the West End, twice-a-week matinees and broadcasting had some while ago become the perfect reason for them to have separate bedrooms, Harry setting up his in the sitting-room of the Hoddeston house. Soon, Patience would spend most nights staying over in London with friends, and in November, 1955, they secured a little pied-à-terre for her near

Alice Lytton who, during her interview for the job of housekeeper to the Colliers, responded to Patience's questioning by calling her 'Madam' throughout in what seemed like mock deference.

Swiss Cottage. Yet when Greta Finch announced her imminent engagement and departure from the Collier household, Patience – drawing up a kind of prospectus to attract a new housekeeper – painted a rosy picture of harmonious family life. It was at this point, in September, 1956, that Alice Lytton arrived, a single woman of fifty-seven who had been in service all her life. She seemed to respond to Patience's presence with measured irony, calling her 'Madam' throughout the interview. When Patience objected to her unmistakably challenging deference, Alice simply replied, 'Well, you'll have to lump it, won't you?'[6] The conversation set the tone for their extraordinary relationship for years to come.

Patience and Harry were both running serial affairs, but they were maintaining a kind of outward equilibrium. Patience assisted Harry with his public health broadcasts; he defended her interests when she seemed poorly treated professionally. Harry was often a perhaps bemused part of her theatrical circles, she of his scientific friendships. But privately they were difficult with one another and the rows were endless. Sarah, now eleven, found herself suddenly sent off to boarding school in Solihull and suspected they were planning a divorce.

Nude had a long run, over twelve months in the West End; there were celebratory drinks on stage on 7 November, 1957, the anniversary of the show's London opening. Patience played Anya throughout, but Sebastiens were switched – a short-lived Michael Wilding, Coward himself, then Robert Helpmann – each major cast change necessitating new rehearsals.

The play finally closed in February, 1958, after a brief run at various outer London theatres and Oxford. It had been a mixed bag of a show, but Patience came out of it with new acclaim for her talents as a comic actress. She earned praise even from critics bent on wiping the floor with the play. Patience Collier was 'worthy of better material', commented Philip Oakes. 'Patience Collier's rambling Russian is game, set and match, but the rest of the cast resemble a cocktail party at which the gin has run out,' said Kenneth Tynan. Charles Kay, then a young actor who saw *Nude* before he knew Patience, put it more succinctly: 'not a very good play – [but] she was wonderful in it, really wonderful.'[7]

Patience was now a firm fixture on Noël Coward's Christmas card lists; they corresponded for a while, and Coward was encouraging about casting her again.[8] When he died in 1973, hers would be among the starry collection of tributes in *Nova* magazine: "He was ruthlessly critical,' she would say, but 'the actor's greatest ally.' Once he had told her, 'My dear, always make sure that your eyebrows are properly lit. You can't play comedy without eyebrows.'

Her New York debut: Patience Collier against the backdrop of publicity for Joan Littlewood's production of *The Hostage*, 1960.

PART FIVE

THE WOMAN IN THE BLACK BERET

CAMPDEN HILL ROAD

JANUARY 6TH, 1959 and Patience was entertaining Diana Sandys to lunch. Regular evening shows in the West End were making it a little easier to have a daytime social life: for the last six months, Patience had been performing in the Tennent's revue, *Living for Pleasure*, billed just below the four stars, Dora Bryan, George Rose, Daniel Massey and Janie Marden. The physical demands were horrendous, she told Diana, the sketches and lyrics constantly changing, the backstage facilities for double quick costume switches well below her standards. She and Harry had to have a serious set-to with the management and producer, Billy Chappell, insisting that she be given better material to show off *her* talents, as well as Dora Bryan's. After all, she said, Dora 'had tits like two corks'.[1]

Tatler cartoon depicting Patience in *Living for Pleasure*, 1959

But now, though exhausting, she found the revue – her first – a huge laugh: mad, camp sketches with George Rose, the teasing pleasure of a new friendship with tall, dark and handsome Daniel Massey, the feel of glamorous skin-tight costumes created by young theatre designer Peter Rice, and, now, an affectionate relationship with Dora Bryan. Her sketches were going down a treat with West End audiences: as one of the Sloane Street ladies berating modern youth, or as fairy-godmother to Dora Bryan's Cinders, and above all her rollicking soliloquy as the 'lady who sits in the loo at the Ritz'. The critics, used now to more daring stuff from Theatre Royal Stratford East, had complained about finding the show a bit thin, the whole thing too cosy. But the critics were not everything. Patience was running a book on the show's predicted life: George Rose's original four months had already been beaten, her daughter Susan gave it ten, darling John Burton was flattering them with two to three years.

Patience and Diana were eating their lunch in the basement dining room of the Colliers' new home at 23 Campden Hill Road, Kensington. The family had moved to London from Hoddesdon only three months ago. It was Patience's first chance to show off the house to Diana, so dilapidated when they first saw it, but now boldly renovated using the proceeds from the sale of a Max Ernst painting given to Harry by Madame Ernst herself, back in the 1930s. Patience had long ago banished it to the attic – it looked like a piece of old lino, she said – but the sale had raised enough money for them to employ a designer to oversee the improvement work.

The Colliers had been looking to move into London for a couple of years at least. Harry had begun to feel restless at Allen and Hanburys and, in 1957, spotted a much bigger opportunity as Director of Pharmacological Research at the pharmaceuticals firm Parke-Davis, based in Hounslow. All the signs had been encouraging, until it became clear that his Cambridge politics had come back to haunt him: he had been blacklisted at Parke-Davis's American headquarters as a former Communist and Communist sympathiser. Strings needed to be pulled. Duncan Sandys, newly appointed Minister for Defence in Macmillan's government, agreed to vouch for Harry, and the difficulties seemed magically to melt away. On 14 October, 1957, Patience noted in her diary – using the capital letters she reserved for very special happenings – that Harry had landed the Parke-Davis job. It was yet another occasion to be grateful to Diana.

The Colliers had started to house-hunt without delay. Tall, white, stucco, No 23 Campden Hill Road made a big statement. Steep steps led up to the wide, glass-panelled front door. There was a large drawing room to the right of the hall, elegant and velvety, with bold John Piper design curtains at the windows. Downstairs at the front of the basement was the kitchen with a Belfast sink – the domain of Alice Lytton, who had moved with them to be the family's housekeeper and cook. At the back was the satin-stripe-papered dining room where

The Colliers' new home in London, 23 Campden Hill Road, drawn by Susan Collier for the family's 1958 Christmas card.

Patience entertained, overseen by a portrait of her father. On the first floor were Patience and Harry's separate bedrooms, Patience's with rose-strewn Sanderson wallpaper, her scarves hung carefully according to their colour and shade, and on the second and third floors, the children's and housekeeper's rooms. But the *pièce de résistance* was the very dramatic navy blue wall going up the stairs in a generally white-painted house.

No 23 would soon become part of the experience of knowing Patience – glamorous, a place to anticipate, a space for parties. She was shaping the house into a kind of salon, with sherry parties for discreetly matched theatre, family and scientific guests, and lunches and suppers: a place to present herself. She began to refer to their previous life as 'when we were in Hoddesdon, *Herts*', and had her photograph taken by Anthony Armstrong-Jones for her expanding gallery.[2]

Yet the house had an edge of nerves and social incongruity about it. It was often a war zone between Patience and Harry, a front for their mutual extra-marital affairs – and there was a new intensity about the relationship she was currently having, with the young film actor Jeremy Spenser: beautiful, dark, twenty-seven years younger than her and probably the love of her life. It was a place where the children led their own lives against a foreground of glamorous comings and goings. The Colliers would invite politically sympathetic friends to watch as the Aldermaston march against nuclear weapons ruffled feathers along Kensington High Street, and see if they could spot Susan, Joe or Sarah among the marchers. Meanwhile, Robyn Karney, living in a bedsit down the road, remembers knocking on the door of No 23 as part of a market research job and it being answered by an 'ill-tempered crone' like a scene from an old gothic film; Alice gave her short shrift: 'Madam's not here.'[3]

If Patience had changed in recent years since becoming a Tennent's actress, so had Diana Sandys. She had carried off the role of apparently successful society hostess as Duncan's career under her father ebbed and flowed then continued under Harold Macmillan. But that was between bouts of mental illness, savage electric shock treatment and sedation. Her marriage to Duncan had broken down. The Sandys had been separated now for a couple of years, their divorce pending as he planned to marry his mistress. Her biggest consolation lay with her

Film actor Jeremy Spenser (pictured here in *The Roman Spring of Mrs Stone*), with whom Patience – although 27 years his senior – formed an intense relationship.

children, her family and her friends. 'I am thinking of changing back to "Diana Churchill",' she confided in Patience.

Living for Pleasure was the last of Patience Collier's productions with Tennent's. She now employed an agent – Jimmy Fraser of Fraser and Dunlop – keeping him busy as her television career expanded. Contracts rolled in without let-up: it was proving to be one of her busiest times in nine years of television.

Patience had appeared in some of the most popular ITV drama shows of the mid to late fifties, the *Martin Kane, Private Eye* series (1956) and *Knight Errant Limited* (1960) among them. Television was a cut-throat business, overtaking radio; commercial television was now attracting three quarters of viewers, and the BBC appeared to be losing the battle. Theatre and cinema audiences were also under threat. Yet canny entrepreneurs like Binkie Beaumont, who had a foot in both camps, could see that theatre could be adapted and promoted for mass audiences. Patience had reprised her role of Anya Pavlikov for a Tennent's production of *Nude with Violin* for ATV's *Play of the Week.* While stars like Robert Helpmann were making their television debuts in the production, Patience – earning herself £211, around £4,600 in today's values – was already an old hand.

She had become a regular for ABC Television's *Armchair Theatre,* which occupied the prestigious Sunday night slot on the ITV network following *Sunday Night at the London Palladium.* Serious drama, melodrama, classic adaptations, and thrillers all featured in the series developed under ABC's Canadian Head of Drama, Sydney Newman; his team of ex-BBC and Canadian directors and script finders broke the mould of British television drama to date. Patience appeared in ABC's *The Lady of the Camellias* (1958), on the one hand, and *My Guess Would be Murder* (1959) on the other, both directed with years of BBC expertise by George More O'Ferrall. Bill Naughton's drama, *Honeymoon Postponed* (1960), in which Patience got top billing, was quintessential Sydney Newman Armchair Theatre, adapting 'kitchen-sink' social realism to the screen, and paving the way for *Coronation Street.* Patience, as the stuck-up mother of the bride, was all disapproval, bristling plump handsomeness and gloves even at the pub. That year she would also appear in the first of Sydney Newman's *Armchair Mystery Theatre* series (*Eyewitness* was introduced with sinister relish by Donald

Pleasance), *The Shrike*, directed by Silvio Narizzano for Granada, and *The Prodigal Parents*, for ABC. At last she was also securing parts with the BBC, thanks to her agent's intervention and her own hustling. She and actress Mary Wimbush both targeted the Controller of BBC Television at a Christmas party, stressing their keenness to be considered for BBC work. Patience Collier 'you undoubtedly know as a *character*, as well as a character actress', he wrote afterwards to the Controller of Programmes.[4] She would now appear on two BBC chat shows about books with Brian Redhead and Olive Shapley, and secure the part of Clara Hibbert in a Sunday Night Theatre production of *The Vortex*.

It was fun for a while to be free of stressful tours and late nights on stage. Though Patience was working hard, earning well, still fitting in radio contracts with her TV work, her schedule made it easier to keep up with friends and cultivate new ones, with theatre-going no longer confined to matinées. As always, she was enjoying the latest productions, including Paul Scofield in *Espresso Bongo* and Kathleen Harrison in *Watch It, Sailor!* At the new Mermaid Theatre, she saw Bernard Miles and Lionel Bart's opening of *Lock Up Your Daughters*; at the Royal Court, *Chicken Soup with Barley*, now performed as part of the Wesker Trilogy. At the Arts Theatre she attended the premier of *The Caretaker*; at Stratford East, *The Long, the Short and the Tall*. And in the West End, she enjoyed Theatre Workshop's transferred hits, *A Taste of Honey* and *Fings Ain't Wot They Used T'Be*.

Patience was biding her time in terms of her own theatre roles, consulting regularly with Jimmy Fraser. This was a crucial point in her stage career, following her successes with H. M. Tennent's. She had her eye on the West End – an interview with *Theatre World* during *Living for Pleasure* had highlighted the extraordinary development of her late-starting career, and the versatility of her acting. But George Rose drew her attention to an article by Ken Tynan, 'Summing Up', which reviewed the most significant recent developments in contemporary theatre. The Royal Court, Theatre Workshop at Stratford East and now the Mermaid in the City were mounting 'a three-pronged suburban assault on the citadel' of commercial theatre, Tynan considered, but developments at Stratford-upon-Avon were also to be watched, with Peter Hall about to assume

Patience Collier and Dora Bryan in *Living for Pleasure*, 1958

direction. Tynan shows 'the way the wind is blowing', Rose wrote to Patience from New York, and that 'one should [now] be a bit careful about doing commercial stuff in the theatre'.[5]

It was during this period of back to back television appearances, theatre and restaurant jaunts, romance, and reflection about her next step in theatre, that out of the blue, Patience had a phone call from Gerry Raffles, now Joan Littlewood's 'man' at Theatre Workshop. It was mid August, 1960, and she was due to start rehearsals for a new Armchair Theatre production. What was she doing at the moment, Raffles asked. Was she free to join the cast in the New York production of Brendan Behan's *The Hostage*, due to open on 20 September?

Patience had watched her old comrades at Theatre Workshop from her position as a rising West End actress. They had been performing innovative productions of classic and contemporary plays since 1953, when Littlewood first leased the Theatre Royal, Stratford East. With the smallest of intermittent grants from the Arts Council and local authority, Theatre Workshop began to receive international as well as initially grudging British attention, developing new plays to rival the output of the Royal Court in Sloane Square, but in a quite different mode: Littlewood remarked that the Court was 'too soft-centred and very middle-class'.[6] As with Theatre Union in the early days, their drama depended on the creative participation of the actors, and drew on musicals, circus and movies as well as European theatre. The company grew its material from a combination of talented writers, strong stories of working and offbeat lives and a company that attracted bright new actors and retained loyal company members, keen to participate in the hands-on development of shows. It was somehow hitting the right note of exuberant, brash and irreverent comedy for the times, and spawning a fistful of hits.

Only that month, East End story *Sparrers Can't Sing* had opened at Stratford East, starring the young Barbara Windsor and Roy Kinnear, as well as company stalwarts Murray Melvin, Avis Bunnage and Victor Spinetti; it was even attracting the affections of Limehouse mobsters. But in less than six months the show would transfer to the West End, following close on the heels of other

Theatre Workshop transfers: *A Taste of Honey, The Hostage and Make Me An Offer.* Alongside these, the company was still producing a stream of classics, including Brecht's *Mother Courage* in which Joan herself starred. She and her brilliant, big, Manchester Jewish, brandy-drinking partner, Gerry Raffles, Theatre Royal's owner and manager, were running a major theatrical operation. Yet they still retained a close-knit sense of a locally based company whose members worked, ate, partied and drank together.[7]

Success had now become a major logistical and artistic problem. When Raffles approached Patience, Theatre Workshop had three shows running in the West End, *Sparrers* had just been launched, and both *A Taste of Honey* and *The Hostage* were being prepared for New York. Yet the company still had to maintain its creative focus at Stratford East; indeed, some Theatre Workshop actors preferred to remain there. For New York, it was necessary to recruit a proportion of American actors to meet local union rules, but they needed the appropriate skills. There was a real yet unavoidable risk in taking on 'outsiders' who would, as Joan Littlewood would complain, 'bloody act'. But Patience was not a real outsider: Littlewood knew she would not have forgotten her past experience of Theatre Union. She had seen her recent work, even visited her backstage during *Nude*'s run, and noted her openness to new directions in *Living for Pleasure*: 'I've watched you for many years,' she told her. Patience, she felt, could help save the day.

Patience may have briefly hesitated: it would completely disrupt her busy schedule and there could be no certainty about how long the run would last. Nor did it fit with her West End ambitions. But it meant a debut appearance for her in New York – and it would be different, and fun. That she was excited by the challenge is reflected in the block capitals with which she recorded the offer and the rapid arrangements for the trip in her diary. She went to Stratford East to discuss her contract with Raffles and Littlewood.

Now forty-six, stocky, usually sporting a black beret or cap, with an extraordinary dynamism but capable of devastating put-downs to non-compliant actors, Joan was as spiky as ever to Patience's now elegant and coiffed but firmly outspoken actress of stage and screen. But when in due course Joan and Gerry Raffles

Joan Littlewood, 1963.

met her off the plane at Idlewild Airport in New York after a nineteen-hour flight, she found them warmly appreciative of her joining the production and clearly keen to flatter her – just as she would have wished. They were also amused by the incongruity of her ladylike appearance and 'queenly smile' in the midst of the mayhem of the flight arrival, with Brendan Behan striding forth amidst the rush of reporters. Only Patience Collier would insist on a New York customs officer saying 'please' before opening her bags for inspection.[8]

The play they were taking to New York was very different from Behan's original *An Giall*, about a British soldier taken hostage as the execution of an IRA man approaches. That had been a simple, poignant, almost expressionist short play written in Gaelic and first performed in Dublin in June, 1958. *The Hostage* had been rapidly created from it for its opening in Stratford East that October: Littlewood and the company working on the gaps in the author's 'translated' script, drawing on the characters, anecdotes, songs, dances and mimicry of Behan when in stage Irish playwright mode. He had been so reluctant to deliver a script that Joan Littlewood and the cast had still been revising the third act as the opening night approached. They added new characters to appeal to British humour and expectations of Irishness, camped up the play, changing the tone to make it a version of the 'knees up' style the company were finding so successful with audiences. They had arguably made it less his play, more his *show*. Patience's character, the hypocritical St Vincent de Paul social worker, Miss Gilchrist, had been one of the additional roles, developed by the young Theatre Workshop actress, Ann Beach.

Now with just five members of the cast of seventeen surviving from the West End production, no well-known stars and only a handful of actors trained in Theatre Workshop traditions, there was some uncertainty as to whether the play could retain its original vitality *and* appeal to New Yorkers. 'Joan Littlewood is very balanced about the prospects of "The Hostage", Patience wrote home from New York: '[she] gives it ... a 75% chance of being a success.'[9]

OFF PISTE

THEY HAD SEVENTEEN days to prepare the play in a sweltering New York, suddenly lashed by the high winds of Hurricane Donna. Rehearsal conditions were poor. The Cort Theatre on West 48th Street, where they were due to open on 20 September, was 'elegant, but falling to pieces', Patience wrote home, 'front of house luxurious but backstage conditions filthy, – as bad as 'second class English touring' facilities. 'I sat in the middle of an iron staircase organising the cleaning', she later remembered.[1]

Patience also felt below par for much of the time: her legs were bad with phlebitis and a bruise inflicted during too lively a dance by a fellow actor, her arm was swollen from a rushed pre-tour vaccination, and she was suffering from migraines. She learnt the part as they rehearsed: there were altogether 'too many lines, songs and dances to learn comfortably in the time'. 'Hate New York,' she told her diary, four days into rehearsals. Yet she loved Joan Littlewood's methods, her direction of such a particular kind that she would tell actors, 'Don't let yourself be produced.'

The role of Evangelina Gilchrist required fake piety combined with incongruous sexual longings, and a nauseating nostalgia in de Valera's Ireland for the old British days – 'I have nothing against the Royal Family. I think they're all lovely...' Miss Gilchrist must duet mock-religiously with the government spy masked as civil servant, Mr Mulleady. She must project *double entendre* at just the right pitch – 'Our souls. Our souls...Are souls...Arse-holes' – and sing some of the best songs in the show: *'I am a little Christ-ian, / My feet are white as snow...'* Patience told Gerry Raffles that she had never sung on stage – her songs

Brendan Behan's *The Hostage* with (left to right) Patience Collier as Miss Gilchrist, Aubrey Morris (Mr Mulleady) and Avis Bunnage (Meg) at The Cort Theatre, New York City. 1960

in *Living for Pleasure* had been at talking pitch – and she would need singing lessons. But Joan forbade it: 'Build up your top, woman, not your stomach.' She 'made me sing without a [single] lesson', Patience would later recall. 'It worked every night. I never feared it.'[2]

Patience, with an intense seven years of Tennent's grooming behind her, might have responded to Joan Littlewood's direction differently. But she took to it completely. Joan was, she felt, the 'only director who was utterly relaxed on stage'. She was a kind of 'Svengali', drawing the cast of actors of very mixed experience into a chorus of movement. Littlewood's focus on the actor's relationship with the audience was liberating. 'Have you ever thought of loving the audience or the audience loving you…stand back – put your arms out and receive them,' she would instruct. 'You've a marvellous pair of boobs. I'll teach you how to make the whole stalls like an asparagus bed.'

'She made me in love with myself, with the audience,' recalled the older Patience. 'She really understood audience reaction.'

Littlewood could be forthright, her post-rehearsal notes to actors couched in a kind of written megaphone: 'EVEN WITHOUT A VOICE YOU CAN HAVE RHYTHM IN YOUR BODY!' She would give actors notes and briefings but keep them from their colleagues, in order to disconcert and shake up routines – and do this quite late into rehearsals. *The Hostage* had its first preview with a paying audience on 14 September, less than a week before the opening. But it was at this moment that Joan chose to upset what she felt was the slightly stale playing between Alfie Lynch as the British soldier and Celia Salkeld as the young Teresa, both of them overly familiar with their parts from the long London run. Patience in Gilchrist outfit, Victor Spinetti in IRA greatcoat, were made to swap roles with them: 'I was entirely uninhibited and I've never played so well,' recalled Patience later. Suddenly, 'I was seventeen, with beautiful red hair like Celia. The applause was enormous. Now Joan could do that with people. Who else could be so daring?' Yet it was all so rushed: 'Joan's work is wonderful and she could do miracles with me,' Patience wrote home, but 'her wonderful methods shouldn't have to be assimilated [so] hurriedly.'[3]

There were ten curtain calls on the opening night. As Patience Collier and

Alfie Lynch entered Sardi's restaurant on West 44th Street after the performance, 'people stood up, came over and shook hands and hugged us.' At the first night party at Downey's, the famous actors' restaurant – 'Don't go looking like Theatre Workshop. Go looking like Balmain and Cartier,' they were instructed – the cast was 'literally smothered with congratulations' from guests who included Lauren Bacall and Jason Robards.[4] Soon people were waiting at the stage door each night, 'LOVED' the play and came back for more. Patience's song 'Don't Muck About with the Moon' got so much applause that after the first verse, she – as Miss Gilchrist – was having to put up her hand and say, furiously, 'Hush! Please let me continue!' Audiences roared at obscenities, the irreverences, the references to Khrushchev – in town, as was Castro, for a meeting of the UN General Assembly – and wanted more.

But the notices from the press were 'very anti-climactic after the people's praise,' Patience wrote home. Brendan Behan had 'no possible appreciation of play construction,' wrote John McClain in *The New York Mirror*: 'the evening is a series of soiled vignettes.' John Chapman in *The Daily News* found *The Hostage* a 'theatrical mulligatawny...madly funny...but...a ramshackle affair which wore itself and me out before the end of the first performance.' Howard Taubman, the feared chief theatre critic of *The New York Times*, thought it a 'grab bag of wonderful and dreadful prizes... If you are willing to shuttle madly between delight and distaste, you might try dancing to Mr Behan's Irish Jig.' As a result, the play felt like a success, but was 'not a smash hit': 'quite full houses but not capacity.'[5]

The company swam in Behan's wake regardless: the interviews, parties and receptions for the Behans and *Hostage* cast rolled without respite. 'Brendan is the person among us who counts,' Patience wrote. There was the party held by Tennessee Williams –'Tennessee...like a rather soft, gentle, middle-aged lady,' she noted – the receptions by the Drama League of New York, the 'do' hosted by Eli and Ann Wallach. Brendan came to every rehearsal, 'adding a little bit here, a song there.'[6]

He was orchestrating *Hostage* publicity with aplomb: he embraced New York, and its expectations of him as a 'bawdy, ballad-singing, jig-dancing, stocky, rumpled, wild-haired' playwright. He had steamed off the plane ahead of all the

Brendan Behan in New York. The copy of this photo by Sam Shaw is signed on the back "To Patience of whom I am very proud – with love Brendan".

cast to meet the press throng, meeting their every question with a pithy sally.

'What do you think of New York, Brendan?' they asked.

'The greatest city in the world,' he said. 'The place where you were least likely to get a bite from a wild goat.'[7]

Everyone loved this big, roistering character – a 'broth of a boy' – and hard-drinking was a crucial part of the legend. Yet when he arrived he was on the wagon. He had been in training for months, knowing he would have to 'marshall all his exhibitionist talents together' as his biographer Ulick O'Connor would comment.[8] His appearances at the play's performances would bring in the audiences and to their adulation, applause and laughter he would become more outrageous, more apparently drunk, yet he would drink tea for hours after the show. Some saw it purely as an act for the box office – was he even an 'Irish Uncle Tom?' barbed one commentator. He had seen Behan around town 'dressed in carefully prepared disarray,' yet as sober as a judge.[9]

Patience herself developed a real friendship with Behan and his wife Beatsie from the start: 'I like him enormously and he seems to have become surprisingly attached to me.' He seemed to see her, she thought, as 'a typically English-lady-actress, and everything I do appears to entertain him.' Her initial impression of him seemed to be about as accurate as his of her: she found him basically 'a simple, shy, good-hearted fellow...very sincere and amusing,' and Beatrice, an artist, 'a charming, quiet, simple Irish woman.'[10] But they clicked. He was the 'most delightful person you could wish,' she later recalled, and a 'wonderful host... ordering each person's meal quite separately.' Their companionship was affectionate, enjoyable, a gas: 'we fell for each other.' When Patience introduced her friends the Rices to Behan, he missed kissing Pat on the cheek and went for her bosom.[11] He sent the Collier children a postcard 'from an old Irish Republican Booser.' But he also signed a picture of himself by photographer of the stars, Sam Shaw, 'To Patience, of whom I am very proud.' When he finally fell off the wagon one memorable night on 26 October and tried to storm the stage, it fell to Patience to try to contain this 'large, wild man' in her tiny dressing room for the whole of the first act.[12] It made great headlines for the play.

Patience disliked New York at first – the 'high prices, the screaming police-car sirens, the brilliant flashing lights...the cotton-wool tasting food', the filthy public transport and the 'nightmarey' contrasts between districts. But she found herself seduced by the 'jazz oozing out of every drug-store...the iced water fountains, the real orange drinks sold everywhere, the good telephone service', and the Baked Alaska.[13] The cast were 'a lovely lot': she made particular friends with Aubrey Morris (playing Mr Mulleady), Victor Spinetti and Celia Salkeld, Beatsie Behan's sister. Patience and twenty-nine-year-old, gay Alfie Lynch developed a flirtatious, affectionate relationship. With him, she could vamp without consequence, thoughts of bad legs set aside.

This was a New York electrified with presidential election fever, as Nixon and Kennedy went head to head. Patience had a ball at the Democrats' election night party, and at the stream of after-show nights on the town: 'IT'S GOT TO STOP or I'll never see New York properly by daylight!' It did not do to be in bed before 3 a.m. She was enraptured by the celebrities they were meeting – a chat with Bette Davis at the Drama League of New York Reception, a glimpse of Marilyn Monroe at Lee Strasberg's studio where Alfie, Victor and she had an open invitation to visit and observe. Mischievous colleagues took her down a peg or two by setting her and socialite actor Roddy McDowall up for a non-existent late night party.[14]

She was feeling particularly good about her performance and reception as Miss Gilchrist: 'She has become as composite and magnetic [a] character as "Charlotta"', she wrote home. She had earned special mention from the critics: 'Some of the funniest efforts emerge from Patience Collier...Her strange screeching and songs are a delight as she tries to comfort the poor hostage.' She 'bring[s] whatever there is in the play to a dead stop any time she feels a hymn coming on' wrote John Chapman in *The Daily News*. People at the stage door, in cafés, in hotels, were 'spoilingly praising of "Gillie"'.15

But within the privacy of her letters home, Patience began to feel slightly prima-donna-ish about her situation. She felt frustrated that she could not get better billing, and was not being seen in London. This was essentially a 'team play', in which she was regarded as 'just a very good member of the Brendan Behan Joan Littlewood Repertory Company'. Would she even 'get other work from

Alfie Lynch and Patience Collier at the weekend house of Bill Frohlich in East Hampton, Long Island, October 1960.

such a WEIRDY as Gillie?' In this ambition-thwarted mood, she felt less than attracted by an offer from Peter Hall, newly in charge at Stratford, to reprise *The Cherry Orchard* and take on some Shakespearean roles. How could she want to 'do Charlotta again, ever, after John Gielgud had magicked me into it?' The other parts Hall was offering 'are absurd at this juncture...after this New York success', she wrote. She and her agent decided together to 'kill that job'.[16]

Winter came on. Alice sent Patience her winter coat, liner and boots from home; she bought a mink hat, got chilblains. She and Alfie both moved their rooms at the Hotel Bristol to the eighth floor, making themselves cosy in his 'efficiency' room, buying tablecloth and plants, sharing domestic life. The play was switched from the Cort Theatre to the Ethel Barrymore, suffered a temporary drop in takings, and moved again after four weeks to the Eugene O'Neill. There was talk of going on tour if another theatre could not be secured by their backers at the end of the four-week lease. Patience would definitely *not* tour, she wrote home: Alfie and Celia Salkeld, her two best friends in the company, had given their notice. Even if another theatre was found, the cast would be very much a replacement one. She was tired, homesick, could not cope with 'an understudy cast and a play whose critical spirit had worn down'.[17] The last night of the show was confirmed for 7 January.

Patience returned to London ready to resume her life – a read-through for ABC TV's new series, *The Avengers*, organising the wedding of her twenty-two year old daughter, Susan. Harry was on the warpath over the ostentatious way she was conducting her relationship with Jeremy Spenser; she had her sights set on developing her West End career. Nothing seemed to have changed.

But *The Hostage* had taken her off piste and somehow she found herself staying there. In the summer of 1961, she accepted a part in Bernard Miles's production of *'Tis Pity She's a Whore* at the Mermaid, the new theatre created out of a blitzed warehouse in Blackfriars through public subscription and London Corporation support. The play was completely out of her comfort zone, unknown to contemporary audiences, the production 'alternative'. It was probably Celia Salkeld, Patience's friend from *The Hostage*, who convinced Patience

Programme cover for Bernard Miles' production of *'Tis Pity She's a Whore* at the Mermaid Theatre, 1961

of the attractions of working with Bernard Miles. She had been staying with the Colliers while performing in an O'Casey play at the Mermaid.

The critical response to *'Tis Pity* was uneven. Ken Tynan found himself laughing at all the 'writhing and posturing in bad blank verse, accompanied by dying agonies reminiscent of Jonathan Miller's in *Beyond the Fringe*'. But Patience's performance as Putana was almost universally praised for its style and sensuality. A 'splendid red-haired figure straight out of a Titian' reported *Plays and Players*; the lead actors 'could take a number of lessons from Patience Collier's fine performance as Annabella's tutoress' declared *The Financial Times.* She had the necessary 'bite and style', a sheer sexiness, suiting the pattern of the play's inversion of values exactly.

And so she found herself becoming, at the age of fifty-one, part of the theatrical new wave, in a move almost as swift, but also more tentative, as the launch of her West End career in *The Cherry Orchard.* Peter Hall, the new director at Stratford, wooed her again following *The Hostage*, offering her one of the precious three-year contracts with his new Royal Shakespeare Company. She still wanted to be able to say no, particularly to reprising Charlotta in a production to be directed by Michel Saint-Denis. She was not sure she even liked or trusted Hall when he smiled his appeal over coffee at his house in Montpelier Square. But 'yes' she finally said, so that when she appeared in *'Tis Pity* it was already by 'kind permission' of the RSC. She carefully nurtured the transformation she was making, ensuring that her profile in the Mermaid programme notes carried just the right note of gravitas: *in* were references to Komisarjevsky, Gielgud, Scofield, Brook and *The Hostage*; *out* were her radio and TV work, *My Three Angels* and *Living for Pleasure.*

Peter Hall's company was making news, was 'fashionable, and hot'. At the age of twenty-nine, he had taken over what had been essentially a family-dominated private company with a prestigious but uneven past, and given it all the shine and promise of 'the new'. Stylishness and bravery of approach had been apparent on every page of the company's giant programme for Hall's first season at the Stratford Memorial Theatre the previous year: lavish black and white photographs of each production in rehearsal and performance: design sketches in full colour. Penelope Gilliatt wrote of a new era, a new regime: alterations to the austere 1930s stage and theatre, an 'organic sequence' of Shakespeare's comedies in repertoire, new members of the company more familiar to audiences at the Royal Court and Arts Theatres than at Stratford.[18] The company was also laying claim to modern and international theatre with the launch of its London branch at the Aldwych Theatre in December, 1960. What Hall was offering Patience – a fresh, young, ambitious company, the potential to expand her experience and repertoire into Shakespeare and classical as well as modern theatre, and an unprecedented three-year contract – made her feel her eventual 'yes' had a strange inevitability about it. Relenting, she had accepted even 'Charlotta'. Later, she must have wondered why she had ever turned him down. She began investigating Stratford over the early summer – the theatre, the staff, hotels and digs.

Patience, set for the 1960s.

PART SIX

O SWEET MR SHAKESPEARE!

RIVALRY

PATIENCE COLLIER MADE her presence felt at once among the ranks of the RSC that autumn, beckoning handsome young actor Paul Greenhalgh over to sit by her at the first company meeting she attended, sending nudges and giggles around: 'Ooo, there she goes, one of her young men.' She came with quite a reputation.[1] Yet her first months were not particularly comfortable.

Saint-Denis's production of *The Cherry Orchard* with John Gielgud, Peggy Ashcroft and a very young Judi Dench was hailed by some critics as one of the finest productions of the time but yawned through by others, and Patience's Charlotta – peculiarly puppet-like under Saint-Denis's direction – was less acclaimed than her 1954 role. Her second RSC part as the masked and arrogant Governor's wife in *The Caucasian Chalk Circle* was seen as a spirited and talented performance, developing her understanding of the Brechtian concepts so central to Hall's company. But it was Shakespeare that brought her up short, with the role of the Queen in *Cymbeline* – mother to Vanessa Redgrave's Imogen – which opened in July, 1962. 'I'd never spoken Shakespeare before,' she would recall, at least not since RADA, some thirty years earlier: 'I *hated* it.'[2]

The threat of failure led Patience to take coaching not only from John Barton, who was training the assorted talents of the company in a new, analytic, non-rhetorical approach to Shakespearian verse, but from the RSC's singing teacher, Denne Gilkes, who gave her the techniques to project her relatively light voice through the lines, and across the vast and difficult Stratford auditorium. But the production went down badly with the critics, and she received the first bad notices of her career, her wicked Queen described as 'lightweight,' more 'acid drop... than deadly potion'.[3] It was not until Clifford Williams's *Comedy of Errors* that she got into her stride, her send-up of the Abbess's 'sly machinations' earning her general acclaim in what was dubbed 'the funniest show in town' – although that performance was disrupted by ill health.[4] But her first major Shakespeare challenge was to come.

Patience Collier noted the first day of rehearsals for *King Lear* at Stratford in her diary: 1 October, 1962. It had all the makings of a ground-breaking production. Peter Brook, directing, wanted to set it on the barest of stages with the brightest of lights, the thunder sheets for the storm on view, a 'leather and rusted iron world'. Lear, played by Paul Scofield, would no longer be the tragic hero, nor his daughters Goneril and Regan simply villains. This was to be a play given meaning by its different stories and characters, the look of the production utterly simplified, the Fool's role heightened; this would be *Lear* as an 'arch example of the theatre of the absurd'.[5] Alec McCowen would play the Fool, Diana Rigg, Cordelia, and Patience, Regan.

There was a lot riding on this production. Peter Hall had begun his RSC project in a highly competitive and rapidly changing environment: in London, the Royal Court, Theatre Workshop and his own Arts Theatre had brought on new writers, actors, directors and designers, but the mafia around H. M. Tennent's was still powerful. Most threatening was the revival of the campaign – begun as far back as 1908 – to secure a National Theatre as a monument to Shakespeare and a repository of British drama. By the late 1950s, Laurence Olivier had become its unofficial director-designate, a South Bank site had been identified, and government support pledged. For a while there had been negotiations about a joint approach between Stratford and the National, but Hall had pulled away, not wanting his rising RSC to be submerged. The company now needed to move fast to stake a prior claim to being *the* theatre of Shakespeare and thus the natural national theatre, but set in a modern and international context.

Above all, the company needed to prove that it was worthy of substantial government subsidy: this was crucial to Hall's ambitious programme but a principle still relatively new in Britain. The problem was that if there were to be Arts

Council grant for theatre, the National Theatre project was the unquestioned favourite. In 1962, not only had Hall received no grant for his grand schemes for remodelling the Stratford Theatre, but the RSC was beginning to lose money and the lease on the Aldwych Theatre was at risk. Peter Hall and his joint Artistic Directors Michel Saint-Denis and Peter Brook urgently needed a big heavyweight Shakespeare production to beef up their campaign, and to counteract the somewhat uneven critical response to the RSC's first seasons.

The *Lear* cast began rehearsals that autumn, as was Brook's way, with lengthy reading and discussion. For Brook, the first day was always a bit of 'the blind leading the blind', his main purpose being simply to get to the second, another all-day affair, when a 'process' would begin to be at work.[6] But though the project was one which Patience Collier had longed for – working again with Brook and Scofield – she felt stressed and had difficulty sleeping. She was still not very well, nor particularly confident about the challenging role of Regan. As rehearsals got going, they seemed relentlessly long. The pace and timing of the drama was protracted, the more gruelling scenes – Gloucester's blinding not least – repeated again and again. Brook could be a bully, Kenneth Lintott would later reflect, working people into the night and still wanting more.[7] Though she always deeply admired Brook – 'he taught me what I should never do' – and he drew on her ideas for the opening scene of the play, he could be difficult, inexact, even nebulous in his directions. '*Lear* was a nightmare,' she would later say.[8]

Patience's difficulties were multiplied by the problems she had with the actress who played Goneril to her Regan, Irene Worth. Irene was forty-six to Patience's fifty-two, an American screen and stage actor who had had a considerable Shakespearian career before joining the RSC that year. Patience may have seen in her the kind of achievements to which she might have aspired, had she not married: the breadth and depth of Irene's classical experience was far greater. Yet in their own particular manner they were rather alike: mature, strong-minded, intelligent, authoritative, charismatic, and, it may be said, rather pompous and at times eccentric. 'It was inevitable that an actress of Irene Worth's calibre wouldn't take an actress of Patience Collier's – Irene was as strong as Patience,' reflects Susan Engel, then a young actress with the RSC.[9]

Irene Worth as Goneril, Patience as Regan, in Peter Brook's production of *King Lear*.

Irene Worth became Patience's *enemy*. Their rivalry and antagonism became legendary: 'If Patience could upstage Irene she would do it!' recalled Alec McCowen. Irene Worth was a 'very obedient actress, especially to Peter Brook, and did everything she was told'. Patience, on the other hand, was 'never an obedient actress: she would argue, and often get her own way'. But in Patience's mind, the fault lay on Irene's side: 'If we had a scene together she would throw me',[10] she would later recall.

Irene never acted the grande dame as Patience did, according to Paul Greenhalgh, then a very young member of the *Lear* cast. But she could certainly play to colleagues at Patience's expense, joshing with the younger actors in the wings before the play's opening scene. 'Had they made up the back of their necks?' she would ask, peering round behind them. 'Only *amateurs* don't make up the back of their necks! As for *Patience...*' Here Irene took an exaggerated look at the back of her rival's neck as Patience stood aloof, self-absorbed, eyes closed, getting in to her part. Irene shrugged meaningfully, making no comment but bringing helpless giggles all round.[11]

The tension between the two women was palpable. 'It wasn't easy, these two actresses playing sisters', reflected McCowen. Irene Worth would be driven to an exasperated: 'Oh, Patience, come *on*!' But for Peter Brook, playing up the differences between the 'two wicked ladies' was essential to the production; even the contrast between their voices, Irene's strong and powerful, Patience's higher and thinner. In most versions, he told Peter Roberts in an interview in *Plays and Players*, Goneril and Regan are made to seem almost identical. But on his reading, Goneril is 'consistently dominant'; where Goneril 'wears the boots... Regan wears the skirt. Goneril's masculinity fires Regan, whose squelchy softness of core is very opposed to the steely hardness of her sister'. It is Goneril as the older sister who makes the first declaration of love and loyalty to Lear; Goneril who has the furious speeches about Lear's 'insolent retinue', and who assumes her sister's mind is one with hers in seeking to tame him. They are rivals for attractive arch-villain Edmund, but at the last Regan is poisoned by Goneril and creeps 'ignominiously off the stage... like a squashed spider, whereas Goneril takes her leave defiantly'.[12]

The antagonism between the two actresses was hardly helped by the reviews. The initial notices were not particularly kind to either of them, nor to the production, which some critics felt had made 'this mountain of a play… a molehill'. But following the London opening, when the relationship was at its most acidic, Irene Worth's Goneril began to be singled out as particularly powerful, 'a deeply frightening tragic character', oozing sexual power even towards her servants.[13] Patience, in contrast, received some devastating reviews amongst the praise, particularly from Harold Hobson in *The Sunday Times*: 'Whilst Miss Worth's Goneril almost bursts with sexual magnetism, Miss Collier's Regan discussed the private parts with the no-nonsense air of an emancipated Suffragette debating a matter of public importance.' Friends rallied to assure her that her performance was an 'undiluted pleasure', and that London would be falling at her feet. Anna Pollak – Erica Marx's lover and a leading opera singer – sent her a consolatory postcard: 'As for your bleak Press – take comfort! Erica's book hasn't been reviewed and *I* haven't any work!!'[14]

For the cast, the production required immense stamina. The exhaustion of Saturday double-headers – a four-hour matinee followed by a four-hour evening performance, with only one interval apiece – was added to by extra rehearsals summoned by Brook before or even in between shows. Most of the actors, including Patience, were also engaged on other productions already in repertory, or in rehearsal: on *Comedy of Errors*, or Dürenmatt's *The Physicists*, again directed by Brook, which opened on 9 January, 1963.

As the production settled, it began to be recognised as a 'runaway success' for Brook, the cast and the RSC. More critics now 'got it' than not, Tynan on a second visit to the play giving it particular status as a *Lear* for the time, directed from 'the perspective of moral neutrality', a production which 'burns itself into your mind'.[15]

There was quite a delegation to meet the cast of *Lear* at the Sarah Bernhardt Theatre when the production team arrived in Paris on the morning of 30 April, 1963, just ten days after the play closed in London. It had been chosen as Britain's entry for the tenth year of the prestigious Théatre des Nations festival.

Patience berating a bemused Jean-Louis Barrault, director of the Odéon Theatre, Paris, while Paul Scofield listens in.

Paul Greenhalgh recalls the whole company assembling that morning for a photograph with their hosts. But there was a slight delay in the formalities, a moment of panic. A huge bouquet had been prepared for presentation to Irene Worth, who was deemed to be the production's leading lady. But, the RSC's manager saw with dismay, there was no bouquet for Patience Collier. Someone spotted flowers in a vase – they were hurriedly grabbed and wrapped, dripping wet, so that the presentations could proceed. Patience held hers for the formal photographs, smiling, elegant, poised, water dripping down the front of her, as if nothing had happened.[16]

The production was a huge hit in Paris; tickets could only be obtained on the *boeuf et fromage* black market. The cast was entertained by Jean-Louis Barrault, Director of the Odéon, and his wife and co-director, Madeline Renaud. The formal invitations flowed, from the British Cultural Attaché, Le Syndicat Français des Acteurs, and the Conseil International du Cinéma et de la Télévision, which sent their invitation beguilingly to 'Mrs *Passion Colliers*'. Marlene Dietrich was among the celebrities in the audience on their first night, visiting Patience in her dressing room (it was not Irene who got such honours, observed Paul Greenhalgh). On the last night – a 'NIGHTMARE EVENING,' Patience noted in her diary, with Alan Webb [Gloucester] definitely 'OFF' – the cast had a private showing of Peter Brook's new film, *Lord of the Flies*, followed by supper with the Brooks.

DEATH AND SCANDAL

At home that summer of 1963, the Collier household came and went around Patience's engagements. The intensity of her relationship with Jeremy Spenser had gradually faded the previous year, superseded by an altogether lighter affair with another young actor, Barry Justice. She was touring with *The Physicists,* rehearsing for *The Beggar's Opera,* snatching weekends with Barry. There was another tussle with Harry over possible divorce. Friendships were having to take second place: she and Diana Churchill had scarcely had time for more than phone calls since the New Year, though at Easter, Patience was touched to learn, Diana had installed herself by the window at the Normandie Hotel in Knightsbridge to watch the Aldermaston marchers come by, her god-daughter, Sarah, among them.

The Colliers were observing Labour's exposure of the 'death throes of the establishment' with amusement as the drama of the Profumo scandal unrolled: on 5 June, John Profumo, Secretary of State for War in the Macmillan government, had resigned for lying to the House of Commons. But the affair seemed to be washing up in strange places, the establishment taking revenge. Stephen Ward, the alleged Communist sympathiser at the heart of the Profumo–Keeler affair, was put on trial; the Security Services revived their investigations into the identity of the 'third man' involved in the Burgess and Maclean defections back in 1951 and questioned even a frightened Harry about his knowledge of the Cambridge spy ring.[1] There were rumours that Diana's former husband Duncan Sandys might somehow be caught up in the atmosphere of sexual scandal and paranoia. Threatened with blackmail over sexually explicit photographs with the

Actor Barry Justice, who superseded Jeremy Spenser as the main subject of Patience's affections.

Duchess of Argyll taken at a time when he was Secretary of State for Defence, he even offered the Prime Minister his resignation. Patience wondered about the impact on Diana.

By the autumn, Duncan Sandys seemed to be off the hook: Lord Denning's prurient report into the Profumo scandal had cleared the 'anonymous minister' in the Argyll affair.[2] Patience was playing the 'raddled Mrs Traipes' in *The Beggar's Opera* at the Aldwych with a 'shameless gusto' which, the critics said, the production otherwise lacked;[3] she was filming, recording a radio play, and organising improvements for a flat to be let at the top of No 23, now that her eldest children had left home.

On Wednesday, 16 October there was a sudden crisis. Peter Brook came to see her: it seemed *King Lear* was to go on international tour without her. Furious, Patience gave him short shrift – and he called again later that day. Another phone call from him on the seventeenth was hardly enough to appease her; even tea with Peter Hall, over which he tried to explain how she was needed for the forthcoming RSC season, soothed her only a little. Afterwards she attended rehearsals at the Aldwych, gave her evening performance, and got sympathy from Barry.

It was three days later that Patience received the news of Diana Churchill's sudden death. On the night of Saturday, 19 October, there had been a party on stage at the Aldwych to celebrate the end of *The Beggar's Opera* run: Patience rose late on the Sunday and was just settling down for a day at home, tackling income tax forms, when the call came: Diana had been found dead in her home in Belgravia early that morning. It was almost impossible to believe. Next day, Patience rang the Sandys family to share the shock.

Had Diana meant to kill herself? Patience reflected on her own dramatic suicidal gesture all those years ago on the banks of the River Cam, and wondered. It seemed that only hours before she took the overdose, Diana had lunched cheerfully with her daughter Edwina, who was expecting her second child; she had planned to visit her mother in hospital on the Sunday, and to dine with her father at Chartwell in the evening. The family had thought her so much better that year – a stronger person altogether. She seemed to have found a life, immersed in voluntary work for the Samaritans as a friend of the Reverend Chad Varah. The

Patience as Mrs Traipes with Ronald Radd as Peachum and Tony Church as Lockit in Peter Wood's *The Beggar's Opera*, RSC, 1963

tragedy seemed to have come quite out of the blue. Witnesses at the Inquest on 24 October – Diana's son, and Chad Varah himself – suggested it was quite out of character, that the death was either an accident or a cry for help. But then there was the pathologist's evidence that Mrs Churchill had taken such a large amount of sleeping tablets and a third of a bottle of spirits that it was quite 'impossible to see how a lady of her intellect could have made a mistake about dosage'. He was forced to conclude it a deliberate act: the Coroner agreed.[4]

Later that afternoon, Patience and their old mutual RADA friend Gwyneth Lloyd drove to Golders Green to attend Diana Churchill's brief cremation service. The number of mourners was small, Winston and Clementine Churchill being both too ill to attend. Patience and Gwyneth stood behind Diana's children, her former husband and her siblings Randolph, Sarah and Mary, together with a few other close family friends, to sing Psalm 23 and 'Abide with Me'. They listened to the verses from the Book of Revelation promising salvation to those who 'come out of great tribulation'.

But life had to go on, as they always said. The following day, Patience met Arnold Wesker about a new television play; there was an RSC company meeting at the Aldwych, and a splendid offer of the role of Mistress Quickly in the Shakespeare history cycle from Peter Hall. Some months later, Patience heard from Diana's son Julian that she had been left a small legacy in memory of their friendship; for Sarah Collier, Diana's god-daughter, there was a little gold crucifix, set with fourteen pearls.

When, just over a year later, Winston Churchill himself was buried in an orgy of patriotic fervour and pomp, the Colliers – like many on the left – did not join in: Patience, usually keen to record events of state importance, made no mention of it in her diary. But she carefully filed away Diana's RADA portrait, and the cuttings and invitations she had kept from her weddings. Into an envelope, she tucked the thank-you note she had received from Winston Churchill in 1952 for her gift of a recording, together with the order of Diana's cremation service, and Julian Sandys' legacy letter.

15

A COMPANY IT IS

THE YEAR 1964 was her happiest period with the RSC, Patience Collier would later reflect. It was the time when the whole of Shakespeare's history cycle was in production, and she and the company took root in Stratford.

Up until now, she had been dividing her time between Stratford and London, identifying colleagues with cars who would give her lifts, Eric Porter and Patrick Wymark among them. Alec McCowen was one of those she spotted early on, during the *Comedy* and *Lear* seasons. She was not a difficult passenger, he recalled, as one might imagine, but a wonderful one during long journeys: sometimes he would play Noël Coward to her Gertrude Lawrence. Charles Kay, another of her reluctant drivers, also found her great company: she was incapable of telling a joke, he recalls, or of seeing the point of one, yet she was a wicked raconteur, getting everything in exactly the right order: the 'most *un*boring person'.[1]

At Stratford, she had established herself as a presence, as a larger than life character, who linked arms with her latest boyfriend round the town and cultivated an adoring circle of gay actors, teasing the younger, better-looking men in the company with her come-ons. 'Are you terribly queer?' she asked nineteen-year-old Paul Greenhalgh while they sat in the wings during rehearsals of *Cymbeline*. 'Are you hopelessly queer? I mean, is it possible for you not to be?' trying him out with a passionate kiss.[2] She infuriated, provoked ridicule, of course, dislike, as well as exuberant enjoyment. Even among actors, her behaviour was regarded as scandalous – 'scandal with a sort of envy', McCowen would reflect: 'envy that anybody had that much courage to conduct their life in that extraordinary way'.[3]

In London, RSC colleagues were added to the expanding map of her social circles. Parties at Campden Hill Road were now a rich blend of past and present friends. Old friends from Stratford East, more rough and ready than the RSC crowd, would sometimes come along and startle them a little; members of Harry's scientific circles would mix with family, actors and directors. Ruth Schachter, whose husband, Mel, was a talented research colleague of Harry's, recalls how she would approach these parties with a kind of dread. 'We found a lot of the behaviour reprehensible,' she says, remembering her shock at being invited by Harry to lie down on the sofa. 'We didn't approve of Patience.' Television script editor Robyn Karney remembers the grandness of some of the gatherings: 'John Gielgud, Paul Scofield – really the aristocracy.' Yet whatever the elegance of the company, when she had had enough, Patience would clap her hands and tell people it was time to leave.[4]

Friends were always being invited to dine at No 23 – Joan Littlewood would come with a rose in her beret if it was evening. Patience would present herself to her favourite guests for their approval through the glass of the front door before opening it, as though it were she who was making an entrance. But the first question she would ask visitors when they arrived, actor Vernon Dobtcheff remembers, was: '"What time are you leaving?" She would say, "Now let me see, 7.15 now, I think 9.20 would be good." And so at 9.17, I would stand up and she would say, "Oh, you're such a good boy, I wish they were all like that."'[5]

To be invited to an Alice-made lunch was something – Alice was an excellent cook. But the meal would be marked by the tension between her and her employer: Alice's backchat addressed to the cat: Patience's loud comments on the cooking: the slam of the hatch door. 'She loathes my guts, of course,' Patience would later say, adding strangely, 'Psychologically terribly good, of course, if you allow yourself to be loathed.'[6]

Theatrical friends would feel they were getting only a glimpse of Patience's other world: of Harry, the scientist, working on allergic reactions and the treatment of asthma, and perhaps Sarah, still at school. Paul Greenhalgh remembers Patience being quite different when she introduced him to Harry – not giggly as usual, but quite formal, more subdued: 'not the grand actress she played with everybody else but… the nice wife, and he was very kind.' Robyn Karney got to know Harry quite well: 'quite a shy man, I think, unless it was just the shadow of Patience [made him] appear so. It was a very odd marriage.' But despite the parties Patience seemed increasingly to be keeping her lives separate. 'Harry was around,' Alec McCowen remembered, 'but like an early chapter.'[7]

The year 1964 had to be a make or break year for the RSC. The structures Hall had developed for the company were expensive to run and arduous to manage, and debts were continuing to mount. Though the Arts Council had eventually granted £47,000 for the 1963/4 year, it was far less than what was needed: the National Theatre had begun its first season at the Old Vic in October, 1963, under Laurence Olivier, with a subsidy five times that of the RSC. Peter Hall's response to the pressures was to go for the bold, take risks. For this historic year, the 400th anniversary of Shakespeare's birth, the Aldwych would host a World Theatre Season; *Lear* and *Comedy of Errors* would go on international tour, while the remaining 'armies' of the RSC – some eighty actors in all – would move in on Stratford to play all seven of Shakespeare's histories, amid brilliantly orchestrated advance publicity.

The staging of the complete history cycle was highly ambitious. Building on the success of the previous year's 'Wars of the Roses' season, the project was planned to display a range and integrity of style and interpretation not previously attempted. Performances would be scheduled to enable audiences to see the plays in sequence; Peter Hall, John Barton and Clifford Williams would work together as the directing team throughout, with John Bury designing all the sets and costumes. They were supported by the company's highly skilled in-house teams: make-up and wigs led by Kenneth Lintott (who had trained under Stanley Hall); Reg Samuel, with his experience from opera, ballet and theatre, supervising the costumes team; Rosemary Beattie with television as well as theatre experience as the Stage Manager. Continuity of actors in key roles was part of the strategy – Eric Porter as Bolingbroke and Henry IV, Ian Holm as Hal and Henry V – but there was also a democracy about the sharing out of roles. The audience could see David Warner playing *Richard II* one night, and then taking the small part of Falstaff's companion Mouldy in *Henry IV Part II* the next. Hall had Patience marked down for the Duchess of York in *Richard II*, and Mistress Quickly in *Henry IV Parts I* and *II* and *Henry V*, offers which helped to mollify her after the mortification of the Regan business.

Rehearsals began in London at the end of January, but first there were verse-speaking classes with John Barton at the Donmar Warehouse. With Hall and Barton directing, there was strong insistence on the cast honing their skills in speaking Shakespeare's lines. Both had very specific views on how blank verse should be spoken – the importance of line structures, the understanding of iambic pentameter 'contradicted' with irregularities and cross rhythms – but also regarding Shakespeare's prose. It should not be seen with relief as 'more natural', Hall would say, but always as a 'formality, avowedly artificial'.[8]

Patience secured regular coaching from her friend Peter Barkworth to give her additional focus, and – as was her practice – seized on friends to hear her lines as rehearsals began in earnest. They had an apparently luxurious eleven weeks before performance, but, with plans to enable the public to see the plays in rapid sequence, the cast were soon rehearsing *Richard II* and *Henry IV Parts I* and *II* in parallel.

Patience took advantage of this period to see shows, catching legendary American star Ethel Merman at the Talk of the Town nightclub, supporting Vivian Matalon's production of *The Diary of Anne Frank* at the LAMDA Theatre, and enjoying *Who's Afraid of Virginia Woolf.* The play had scandalised the Lord Chamberlain, getting his office in such a twist that it imposed sanctions against 'screw you', while retaining the word 'hump'. She snuck a look at the National Theatre opposition with *The Recruiting Officer* at the Old Vic, and, with Paul Anstee, John Gielgud's former lover for support, saw the first night of *Lear* now being played without her at the Aldwych. She socialised with the young actor John Hurt, with whom she had recently starred in Wesker's first television drama, *Menace*, and still saw Jeremy occasionally, and Barry. The weeks at home also enabled her to perform at the World Campaign for Release of South African Political Prisoners event at Central Hall, Westminster, on 29 February, for which Marlon Brando had been persuaded to speak.

The move to Stratford came in mid March. Previously Patience had relied on digs in Stratford: for the 1962 season, she had taken a room at the Arden hotel, making her room cosy with a transistor radio and extra furniture. Now with months of Stratford in view, she rented rooms in the Old Ferry House by the river, close to the theatre, and was shown round personally by the agents who were, she noted in her diary, called Mr and Mrs Shakespeare.

With the Old Ferry House came James, who lodged in the house, but who also looked after her. He was right up her street – a lover of the theatrical, a fan of the bard, a man to both tease and cosset her. He would leave her intimate domestic notes in round copperplate, often in verse:

> *Oh! Madam dear, you looked not for ME*
> *At the hour of about, I think, Six Thirtee,*
> *I did wonder if you wanted a cup of Tea*
> *But decided you didn't, well, not from ME!*

Schedules for the cycle were tight and complicated, with *Richard II* and *Henry IV Parts 1* and *2* due to open in rapid succession in mid April. There was now an intense month, with scenes rehearsed across the three plays. As the opening approached, there was a sequence of dress rehearsals boxed and coxed with replays of sections still causing concern: two scenes in *Richard II* had to be completely re-staged after the dress rehearsal and club performance. Meanwhile, Hugh Griffith, brilliant at his best as Falstaff, was also often drunk and rude, causing huge tensions among the cast as to whether he should be allowed to continue. Peter Hall collapsed under the strain only a few days before the opening. There were any number of panicked meetings.

Patience had been building the look and feel of her characters since January. She saw the costume people about her Duchess of York dress even before it had been designed, and was soon in deep discussion with Peter Hall and John Bury about the look of Mistress Quickly. She was an actress who had a clear 'eye to how a character would look or sound', Alec McCowen recalled, demanding her props right at the start of rehearsals, and early wig-fittings. When she started a new character – 'making a new person' was her description – she drove designers and directors 'screaming'. 'She was relentless like a steamroller,' says Ken Lintott, in charge of make-up. 'She could be very difficult – absolutely particular – fairly intimidating I must admit,' Reg Samuel recalls, even commandeering a key member of the costume staff to attend to her. 'You tore your hair out. But she always turned in a super performance so one always forgave her.' She was as demanding as if she were a star actress in a starry company. Trevor Nunn would later say, exasperated, 'Have you ever thought of being a star?'[9]

For her, it was essential to pin down the exact details of her dress at an early stage, believing that 'until you know what you're wearing, what the shoes look like, whether the colours suit you, how you do your hair, then you can't move as the character would move and therefore you can't possibly know how you're going to say the lines.' For Patience, it was about building a 'totally accurate view of the character'. 'She was always after the essence of a character, says Lintott: 'She would get in the midst of that character – always referred to them by name... not as an extension of herself but as another person altogether.'[10]

The care for quality and detail was one of the things she loved about the RSC. She would later reminisce about the 'luxury and spoil of Stratford', the 'weight' of the Duchess of York's dress, the design of Mistress Quickly's bag. 'All I want is for it to be right,' she would comment. The demanding days of rehearsals were interspersed with endless costume try-ons and headdress fittings. Only after a long evening rehearsal and dress parade for *Henry IV* on 20 March, would she declare in her diary: 'MISTRESS QUICKLY CREATED.'

Richard II opened on Wednesday, 15 April, 1964, followed the next day, in a gruelling schedule, by *Henry IV Part 1* at 2 p.m., and *Henry IV Part 2*, at 7 p.m. There was an intense camaraderie amongst the cast as presents, good luck telegrams and cards were exchanged. 'Dear, fond, mad, frantic, unruly and much loved wife,' wrote Paul Hardwick, Patience's stage husband in *Richard II*, sending love and good wishes. 'Now Mistress, Get on and do it girl. You will be lovely. But Stop worrying,' wrote John Normington (playing Bardolph in *Henry IV Part 2*). Hugh Griffith, bringing off his Falstaff at high risk to the rest of the cast (actress

Paola Dionisotti remembers the fascination with which she and other school friends watched his hand going further and further up Doll Tearsheet's leg) was in apologetic mode: 'In spite of my impatience and ruderies, I love, and bless you with every good wish for today and always, with the really grand performance you are giving of M. Quickly.' Peter Hall sought forgiveness for it all having 'been such hell.' From outside the company came similar support: from Celia Salkeld, an embroidered heart, from Sarah a deliciously naughty painting; from Barry, 'HOLD YOUR BREATH MY DEAR DIVE IN AND MAKE THE BIGGEST SPLASH OF ALL TIME.'[11]

The RSC management had stoked anticipation of the opening of the history cycle, making grand claims as to its significance. The programmes, larger and shinier than ever, underlined the ambition of the enterprise and featured academic articles and genealogy charts with 'conversations' between the directors about the plays. But how would critics react, deal with the inter-relatedness of the plays, or cope with the practical problems of deadlines? The press did indeed seem a little caught out, some responding to the first night of the series, others holding off to write up all three plays. The launch of the histories was, moreover, now competing for press attention with Olivier's *Othello* at the National.

Opinion was mixed among those critics who had delayed their write-ups to see the whole cycle. Some suggested that 'three first performances in a row' appeared to be taking their toll on cast and critics alike. John Davenport in *The Queen* felt Peter Hall was overrated, and needed to put more pace in his productions. He hated the pretentiousness of the project: 'I, for one, am not prepared to be lectured into insensibility by the comparatively illiterate.' But from others came the kind of recognition that Hall and his directors had been waiting for. See the plays consecutively on a spring day in Stratford, wrote Pat Wallace in *The Tatler*, and watch the company 'giving their best. For a company it is, in the most exact and rewarding sense of the word…' Harold Matthews in *Theatre World* felt the RSC is 'now yielding a dividend on performance… Only a company well used to working as a team could survive four directors.'[12]

For Patience, the stress of the three first nights yielded enviable reviews. In *Richard II*, she and Paul Hardwick as the Duke of York played for laughs the

Sarah Collier's good luck card for the 1964 season of Shakespeare's histories.

rather strange scenes in which they fight over the fate of their disloyal son, to the delight of audiences and critics. Hall could feel the response 'absolutely proves the point of those neglected scenes'. With *Henry IV*, there was universal praise for the fooling at Mistress Quickly's. Her portrayal 'is a wonderfully funny low-life performance... rounded, real and human as well as funny', wrote Bernard Levin in *The Daily Mail*, while Harold Hobson found her narration of the death of Falstaff in *Henry V*, 'extremely moving'.[13]

It was only as rehearsals for *Henry V* began at the end of April that Patience was advised that she was to play a second part, in addition to Mistress Quickly. This was the role of Alice, the lady-in-waiting at the French court, whose coy and suggestive English lessons to the French princess had been made famous by Ivy St Helier's performance in the Olivier film of 1944, still very familiar to audiences. The decision proved a masterstroke. Alan Brien, in *The Sunday Telegraph*, called her skills in both roles those of 'an actress who blossoms in disguise and wears a false face more convincingly than her own'. Erica Marx and Anna Pollak, who had commiserated with her over *Cymbeline* and *Lear*, now wrote of their delight at 'your universal splendid notices'.

But Patience kept – and was kept – on her toes throughout the histories, chumming with Ian Holm and Eric Porter in next door dressing rooms, doing 'spy work' for each other: 'If ever I started resting on a laurel, using a trick, being pleased with something, they would know', she later recalled.[14]

The prolonged time in Stratford brought people particularly close. It was quite different from performing at the Aldwych, where everyone dispersed to their homes after the performance. Here, there was close socialising, lunches at the theatre or the Dirty Duck, picnics, suppers, banter, teasing, flirting, gossip. Patience would remember this time at the RSC as one of 'real democracy', where you 'breathed in a marvellous atmosphere'. There would be great meetings of all those involved in a production – with 'wig people, dress people, all departments working... a huge theatre workshop' – to raise issues. Not all actors shared this benign view of Stratford at this time: to some it was all a cover for Peter Hall 'to do whatever he wanted'. But it was, in Patience's view, a 'real Peter democracy –

he listened to everything we said.'[15]

Patience chaired a small Catering Committee over the summer, with Susan Engel (Doll Tearsheet in *Henry IV*) and Paul Hardwick. There was a great restlessness in the company, Patience recorded in the minutes she took, particularly over the opening times of the Green Room and the quality of refreshments. In tones well-rehearsed in her role as embarrassing mother, she drew up a list of essential requirements and standards. 'All cups should be chipless… Table tops should be regularly wiped over with freshly wrung-out cloths', and there should be 'serious research' into the making of good coffee. Patience was delegated to speak to Gladys about the canteen, while Peter Hall himself was invited to meet with the Committee. At his request, she wrote a 'very hard-hitting report' for him to take to the Governors.[16]

Paul Greenhalgh remembers one member of the canteen staff mouthing off: 'There's that bloody Constance Collier, she's always coming in here and wanting this, wanting that… Who does she think she is?'[17] Confusing her with the long dead Constance Collier was always bound to rile Patience. Yet though she was

Best Wishes
from
Jerry
and all
the boys
in
Proproom
xxx
ALL HANDS ON DECK
TONIGHT
FOR OUR
REGAN

One of Jerry's pro-Regan cartoons

often provoking, she was also often liked by the backstage staff – the dressers, dress-makers, make-up artists and stage hands. She was naughty, open about her feelings, adventurous. Jerry and colleagues in the props department would send her up affectionately with 'pro Regan' cartoons and good luck cards after the *Lear* affair.

That special summer seemed non-stop. Patience performed in the company cabaret, despite her painful legs, with Johnnie Normington in drag as 'Norah' and Charlie Kay as 'Charlena'. She attended the Mayor's reception for the company with her landlords, the Shakespeares, flaunting her New York mink hat, and went to glamorous parties thrown by Peter Hall and Leslie Caron. She was at the honorary degree ceremony for Peter Brook at Birmingham University and, accompanied by Harry, the celebratory garden party at Buckingham Palace on 7 July. She gave snug little dinner parties at which James would fulfil the Alice Lytton role, and had friends to stay throughout the season: Barry, but also Kathleen Harrison, the Rices, John Hurt, Audrey Postgate, and Erica and Anna who sent special thanks and love to 'pretty James'.

On 6 September, as the 400th centenary celebrations drew to a close, she and Tony Church performed William Walton's *Façade* with the RSC Wind Band. They rehearsed the atmospheric and witty Edith Sitwell poems in the open air, then in the Town Hall (where the acoustics were 'miserable'), getting their emphases, their phrasing, their timing, their sound exact against the music:

> *In the early spring-time, after their tea,*
> *Through the young fields of the springing Bohea,*
> *Jemima, Jocasta, Dinah and Deb*
> *Walked with their father Sir Joshua Jebb*
> *An admiral red...*

'LABOUR GOVERNMENT. Majority of 4', noted Patience in her diary on 16 October of Harold Wilson's narrow General Election victory. The clocks went back, the company parties accelerated as the close of season approached: at the one she hosted, Charles Kay spoofed her performance as Alice in *Henry V* wearing a hat 'five times the size' of her wimple, completely blotting out the princess, and making Patience roar.[18] In mid November, the last performances of the Histories were given. 'FINIS', she wrote. 'My acting school was Peter Hall's RSC', she would later say.

WHAT'S IT ALL ABOUT, SLAWOMIR?

It was Sunday, 4 July, 1965, a day snatched between rehearsals and performances. Patience had been to see *The Killing of Sister George* at the Duke of York Theatre the night before, dining out afterwards at Chez Solange; that morning she and the producer Patrick Garland discussed a new television project before she ate brunch with Harry and her friend Naomi Lewis. Afterwards Joe Collier called to take her and Naomi down to Crowthorne in Berkshire. They were going to 'BROADMOOR', as Patience noted in her diary, to visit a Mrs Erna Hannan. Intrigued by the notoriety of the place, they drove up to the imposing Victorian gatehouse, registering the high walls and the security apparatus nervously administered after another scandalous escape.

Something had attracted Naomi, her sister Edina and Patience to befriend Erna Hannan, under the more enlightened regime at Broadmoor Hospital brought in by the superintendent, Dr Pat McGrath. The hospital was now encouraging volunteers to visit 'lifers' like Erna, who seemed to have no other friends or family, prior to their discharge to more conventional psychiatric hospitals. Perhaps it was Erna's Central European origins, her eagerness for friendship and attention, her evident – and apparently self-taught – writing skills that drew these women to her.

Erna Hannan greeted them in her own room with her cat, Ginger. She was in her seventies, still with a trace of her Austrian accent: a woman who loved their visits, the presents of clothes, the chats, the family photographs, the postcards and the letters. But almost forty years earlier, in 1928, she had been arrested for cutting her former lover about the face when he had tried to blackmail her.

Unable to follow the court proceedings in her traumatised state and with her uncertain English, Erna had been remanded in custody for medical observation and subsequently detained at Broadmoor Criminal Lunatic Asylum.

There, as she would later write, she had been initially placed in solitary confinement: trussed, as was then the 'Rule', in a 'heavy canvas straight Jacket Gown fastened at the back with heavy locked Brassbuttons, so stiff that Gown was it could stand up by itself'. Salt, pepper, vinegar and mustard were all strictly forbidden and even 'good' patients were allowed only paper plates and wooden spoons, 'bad' ones eating off newspapers with their hands. She had been surrounded by 'crying shrieking singing screaming and swearing women'. She had seen nothing of the war, nothing of all the changes in everyday life – traffic, modern conveniences, greater prosperity. Her marriage had melted away. She had been like Rip Van Winkle, removed from history. Yet she had seen extraordinary changes in this other world of which Patience and Naomi knew nothing. Now the Criminal Lunatic Asylum was 'Broadmoor Hospital', attendants were called nurses, and the screaming patients were quietened with drugs. Erna had become a kind of trusty, moved to a nicer block; she had her own 'Best Boy Friend', and contributed to the monthly newsletter, *The Broadmoor Chronicle*. The families of staff and doctors came for the hospital bowls matches; trusted patients could sit in the garden when it was fine. 'I wanted so much to show you around', Erna wrote following that visit of 4 July, bitterly disappointed that the weather had been too poor for them to go outside.[1]

These visits to Broadmoor must have seemed strangely apposite. This was the period when the RSC was focussing on the Theatre of the Absurd at its Aldwych flagship – on plays which explored the boundaries between sanity and madness, between dark fantasies and political realities, between farce, metaphysical truth and tragedy. It had begun with Dürrenmatt's *The Physicists*. The play is set in a private asylum – soon littered with the corpses of nurses – where a physicist pretends madness in order to preserve his dangerous nuclear secrets, and is pursued by two other scientists also feigning insanity.

In Peter Brook's 1963 British première of the Swiss dramatist's play – starring Cyril Cusack, Michael Horden and Alan Webb as the physicists – Patience's rival, Irene Worth, had staged another theatrical coup as the psychiatrist who becomes madder than any of the inmates. But Patience, playing the wife of one of the patients, quietly staged another, getting Harry to advise designer John Bury about the scientific context of the play. With the Cuban missile crisis only just recently avoided, the play's political themes were highly topical. At the first night party on the Aldwych stage, to Patience's great satisfaction, Harry had secured the presence of some of the most eminent scientists of the day: Doctors Linus Pauling, J. D. Bernal, P. M. S. Blackett and Jacob Bronowski.[2]

Patience was not involved in the RSC's 'Theatre of Cruelty' plays, the most notable of which was Peter Brook's highly-charged production of Peter Weiss's *The Persecution and Assassination of Jean-Paul Marat as Performed by the Inmates of the Asylum of Charenton Under the Direction of the Marquis de Sade* in 1964. But later that year, she was invited by David Jones, the new Artistic Controller of the company and in charge of productions at the Aldwych, to participate in a special project to encourage young playwrights and attract new audiences, linking short plays under a general theme: *Expeditions.*

The *Expeditions Two* series, which ran for only five performances in February and March, 1965, consisted of four short plays under the theme of 'Home and Colonial'. Patience had been immediately attracted by the part that David Jones brought her: that of Lady Harriet Broscoe in David Mercer's *The Governor's Lady.* Lady Harriet is the deluded widow of a colonial governor, and her racist fantasies and sexual nightmares in a newly independent African country bring her husband back to life – as a rapacious gorilla.

There were comfortable discussions between Patience, Jones, and Mercer about the project at 23 Campden Hill Road, and, as rehearsals began in January, 1965, they focussed separately on the narrations – Lady Harriet's demented, soliloquising reflections on what is happening – and the interactive scenes between Patience, Timothy West as the emergent Sir Gilbert gorilla and Elizabeth Spriggs, playing the concerned family friend. Ken Lintott recalls devising the make-up for Timothy West: 'The key thing was the bananas', he says; they even went to London Zoo to have a look at the prize gorilla. They rehearsed in the cold of the Dean Street synagogue – the stage manager required to arrange two electric heaters to be placed near Patience, and moved around as she moved – before going back to meals at No 23, then lines and more rehearsing: heater switches were pushed to 'off' there, Timothy West recalls.[3]

There was almost universal critical dislike for the *Expeditions Two* project, when it opened on 4 February. The press were already weary of imitation Ionesco, Brecht and Beckett, and vied with each other to insult the trend. 'We seem to be moving swiftly from the Theatre of Bloody-Mindedness into the era of the Theatre of Boneheadedness. Or from the Theatre of the Absurd into the Theatre of the Obscured Obvious' claimed John Gardner in *The Stratford-upon-Avon Herald*. But the fourth play, *The Governor's Lady*, emerged, as *The Financial Times* had it, as the 'bull' against 'three outers'. What a pity it came at the end of 'all this mock pseudo... at least the lines did 'not sound as if they had been written by Beckett in his sleep', wrote Iain Shaw in *Tribune*. It was written with 'beautiful formality', thought *The Times*, and provided excellent material for the 'splendidly developing performances by Patience Collier and Timothy West'.[4]

Praise for those performances was almost overwhelming: 'Miss Collier's performance is not acting: it is the total assumption of a personality... And is Timothy West given a cage rather than a dressing room?' Critics admired the fineness and exactitude of Patience's performance: 'the most brilliant piece of controlled observation since she joined the RSC'. One friend had been 'irritated almost to the point of no return' by the plays which preceded *The Governor's Lady*, staying only for her performance, but they had been more than amply rewarded: 'To have portrayed that lady without ANY sense of caricature, with that observation and poignancy is a great great achievement'.[5]

Patience's relationship with Barry Justice was now occasional; with Jeremy Spenser, one of affection and friendship. This was a period of short flings with young actors, of socialising and companionable outings with straight and gay friends. After *The Governor's Lady*, Patience took a little holiday to Greece with perhaps her closest friend at the RSC, Alec McCowen, whose flat she would occasionally borrow for her liaisons. There was little time for serious preparation – a trip to see *Zorba the Greek* with Barry, a basic Greek lesson with a friend of

Good luck messages for *The Governor's Lady* – Jerry's of the RSC, *left*, and Timothy West's, *right*. West, her co-star, wrote 'With love and great admiration.'

Sarah's. 'Rather you than me,' mouthed Alice in Alec's ear as Harry saw them into the car to take them to the airport. They saw the Acropolis of a million shades of white, joined Greek families who were roasting lamb on a spit, singing and dancing, saw dawn at Delphi, declaimed in an amphitheatre, bathed naked. Alec watched one performance after another; Patience screaming at the hotel manager when her bungalow was more than the promised fifteen yards from the beach, weeping when a young pick-up failed to turn up, and flirting with the airline clerk in order to get an extension of their stay: 'I've fallen in love with your country!' Afterwards, they entertained their friends Jeremy Brett and Gary Bond with a home movie of the trip.[6]

Patience Collier was resuming her television career again. Time between RSC productions was short, but there were opportunities in abundance. Drama of every kind had become the staple of TV scheduling: the BBC was hitting back at ITV competition by securing ABC's Sydney Newman to be Head of Drama as its second channel was launched. Coverage of television, particularly plays, soaps and serials had become the bread and butter of every newspaper: puffs of programmes and personalities to come, reviews of last night's programmes, discussions about their quality. Was there too much drama? critics asked. Was there sufficient quality material? Such was the power of television drama that the schedules could become a matter of political sensitivity: a play broadcast on the eve of a by-election must be tame enough not to cause political ructions.

With this quantity of material, Patience found herself in demand for a varied palette of roles. She could easily have acquired a reputation as a good jobbing television actress in the stream of so-so dramas that critics were these days bemoaning. But her solo role as Regency courtesan Harriette Wilson in August, 1965, was something else, not least because she had to perform a 25-minute monologue entirely in bed. Patrick Garland's series for BBC 1 was featuring a slightly odd mix of historical and fictional figures, from John Aubrey to Oscar Wilde, from Parson Yorick to Squire Mytton, and starred a range of brilliant character actors, all male: Roy Dotrice, Max Adrian, Nigel Stock, Alan Bennett and Alan Badel. 'Angelic Harry,' who had bedded a string of famous lovers including the Prince of Wales and the Duke of Wellington and then, down on her luck, threatened to include them in her memoirs, was the only woman featured. 'Many women have been mistresses and many women have been writers but few women writers have been mistresses', went Garland's arch proposal for the programme; there is no equivalent to Harriette Wilson today, he added, 'unless it is Christine Keeler...'[7]

The role required Patience as Harriette to recall her lovers and escapades in sole flirtation with the camera: the mood had to be suggestive ('with the pungency of heavy perfume', one critic wrote), but also conveying her strength of character, one to be both 'admired and feared'. Garland's treatment was challenging – critics and viewers alike were not entirely easy with the static screenplay – but the general consensus was that this was one of the most successful of the series, and particularly suitable to *her*. 'Dear Patience, What a strumpet!' one friend wrote to her.

Patience studied her part and organised her birthday lunch from her own bed at No 23 that August: she was still performing in *Henry V*, and *Puntila* was now underway. Patrick Garland was one of the guests at her birthday buffet, but behind the scenes he had found her immensely difficult. She had decided the tape equipment for her voice-over recording as Harriette's younger self was not up to scratch and insisted on better, so that a recording engineer had to hire taxis to bring equipment over for rehearsals at her home. From Patience's own perspective it was not a matter of being difficult for its own sake, though that she could do: she simply had to ensure that she could achieve the excellence to which she always aspired. As RSC stage manager Rosemary Beattie would comment, having endured innumerable Patience strops, you would eventually know that if she was being difficult that she was right.[8]

Peter Hall's production of Gogol's *The Government Inspector* opened in January, 1966, to a warm and relieved reception after the perceived tedium of yet more Brecht the previous year. Michel Saint-Denis's *Squire Puntila and his Servant Matti* – the British première of Brecht's only comedy – opening in July, had been universally slated by the press: 'a bore, whatever the label, remains a bore'.[9]

Patience had also a gloomy time over *Puntila*, in which she played Emma, and after the success of a revived *Henry V* she relapsed into physical exhaustion and 'DEEP DEPRESSION'. She was interleaving too many stage performances and exacting television roles, and the disliked *Puntila* seemed to drag on and on. In September, she had required painful surgery on her foot; her youngest child was now planning to leave home. Friends and family attended on her daily in hospital.

With *The Government Inspector*, Hall seemed to be fighting back against the competition – Feydeau and Arden at the National, Edward Bond and Ann Jellicoe at the Royal Court. It could even be seen as a 'propagandist gesture by Peter Hall to show that the RSC is not just the home of sick plays about insanity, nymphomania, incest, concentration camps and other such unpleasant themes'.[10] Patience could now feel the potent reviving qualities of a true ensemble piece. The cast was enormous, everyone was in it. Paul Scofield starred, and she played the part of the pretentious, ageing flirt and bossy mother, Anna Andreyevna, the mayor's wife.

Rehearsals were fun: Paul Scofield, 'very naughty', would deliberately try to put people off. She would tease Charles Kay, who was playing Dobchinsky, one half of the Tweedledum–Tweedledee pairing of two town squires, and give him marks out of ten for his performances. They vied with one another as to which of their characters should have a lisp. Her make-up and costumes (three changes) with their green, pink, gold and blue sheens, the spark between the leading characters, the sure-footed direction of Peter Hall attempting to strike a balance between the actors' exuberance for the comedy and the 'logical, pseudo-realistic humour' of Nikolai Gogol, made it all challenging and exhilarating. This was the RSC, and 'theatre of the absurd' at its finest. Though there was unease among some critics at the overly extravagant indulgence in farce, Patience's was among those performances singled out for special praise for its subtle detail, comedy and pathos.

The play was already proving a hit when Peter Hall announced the forthcoming RSC season to the press that month, January, 1966. 'Happy Mr Hall!' *The Stage* headlined its coverage: the new programme would include a David Warner *Hamlet*, and the première of Harold Pinter's *The Homecoming*. Despite the bitter

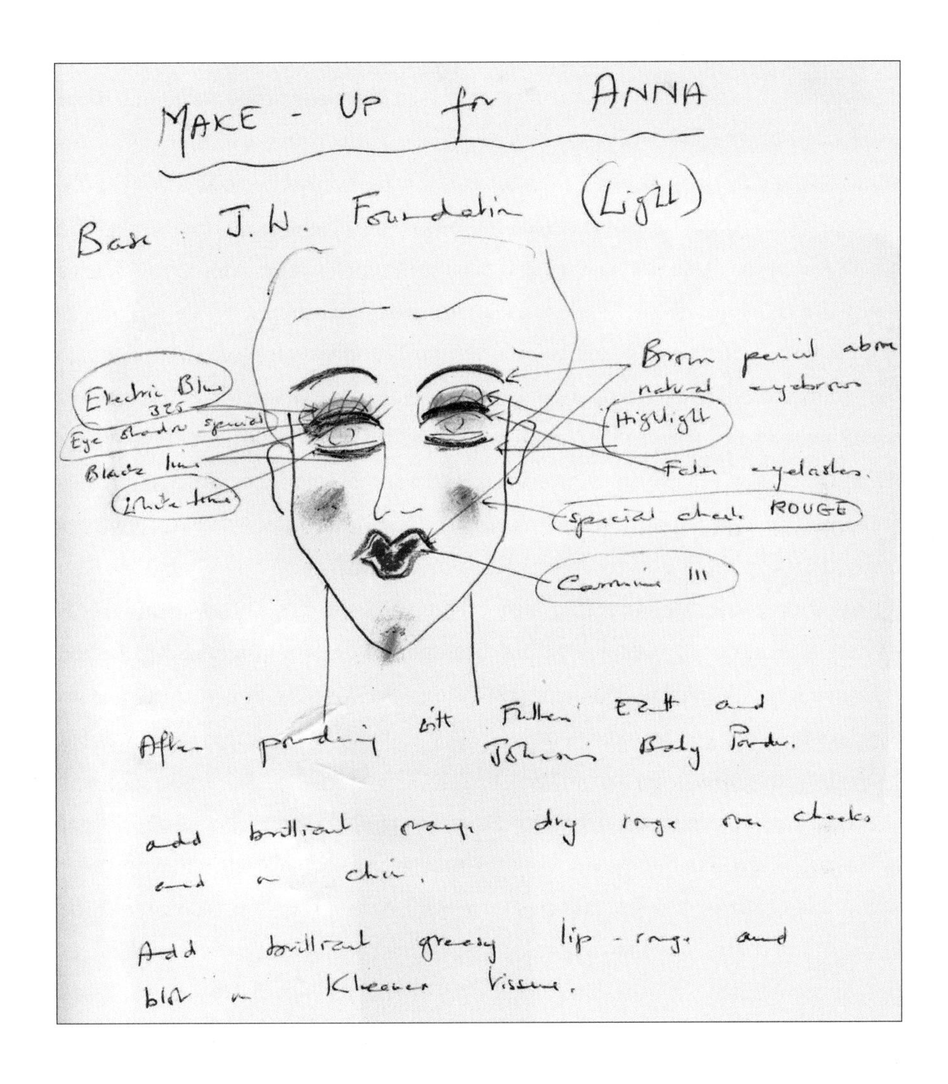

Make-up diagram for the role of Anna Andreyevna in *The Government Inspector*, directed by Peter Hall.

rows around it, *Marat Sade* was proving to be an enormous success in the States. But behind the scenes, things were difficult: financial crises around operations at the Aldwych continued to grow, while the Arts Council and Harold Wilson's Arts Minister, Jennie Lee, seemed forever biased in favour of the National. There were continuing rows with the censor, the RSC governors and the press over some of the company's more political work, in particular Peter Brook's *US*. To some critics, work at Stratford seemed to become duller – more revivals – while at the Aldwych, the insistence on producing modern European comedies with one-word titles seemed hell-bent on alienating supporters.

Patience Collier continued to be often profoundly depressed that spring as they rehearsed satiric writer Slawomir Mrozek's *Tango*. As with *Puntila*, the play itself seemed to be the problem: her own role as the grandmother involved playing the part as an elderly butch woman in a suit and tennis shoes, with a large key and pipe as props. Dudley Sutton, playing the lead, attempted suicide a few days before the first night and the part had to be hurriedly and courageously taken for the moment by the director, Trevor Nunn. As the bad notices came out – 'What's it all about, Slawomir?' Milton Shulman of *The Evening Standard* asked – Patience and Peter Hall concurred that they were 'faced with failure'. She spent the days between performances with Dudley Sutton where he was recovering at a health farm.[11]

Things were not much better for Dürrenmatt's *Meteor*, directed by Clifford Williams, despite its send-up comedy about a Nobel Prize winner who, after numerous death scenes and tributes, just will not die. The critics seemed to be in the mood to dislike what they saw as plays of a certain kind – evenings 'knee-deep in symbolism with LIFE in capital letters being discussed in abstruse, [and] portentous terms'. For Patience, playing a bawdy lavatory attendant who faces up to the protagonist in the closing scenes, it was a personal triumph. But even her 'stupendously bedizened and authoritative troll' did not quite save the evening, nor raise the play 'out of its doughy mediocrity of humour, its apparent purposelessness of undirected satire'.[12] She was feeling rather emotionally vulnerable, not very well, and gloomy. She and Harry had their thirtieth wedding anniversary, but thoughts of reviving some fun in their marriage, following the end of her affair with Barry Justice, seem to have long died. Joe and Sarah moved out: 'Very sad for me', she wrote in her diary.

It was while Patience was appearing in Edward Albee's *A Delicate Balance* in March, 1969, that her close friend Erica Marx became critically ill.

It was proving a packed year, playing Mrs Heagan in *The Silver Tassie*, Dame Purecraft in *Bartholomew Fair*, and the Duchess in *The Revenger's Tragedy*. This was Trevor Nunn's first season as artistic director, cartooned slightly after his first press conference for his 'ever-increasing side-boards and downswept moustache', endlessly clearing his throat. The regime was changing with Peter Hall's departure, the Berliner Ensemble naturalism being replaced by a more flamboyant style. Trevor Nunn had courted Patience to remain part of the company that now included Sheila Hancock, Norman Rodway, Ben Kingsley and Helen Mirren, drawing back stars like Peggy Ashcroft for *A Delicate Balance*. The new associate status, to which Patience signed up in February, 1969, was less costly to the company, enabling it to bring in big names but also give the regular members greater career flexibility.

Erica Marx had been Patience's oldest friend, a warm, lively and generous person. They had been at school together, and had a similar background: Central European, Jewish, with prosperous stockbrokers for fathers. But Erica had been a risk-taker, escaping Paris and the Nazi invasion with her lover, the artist Mariette Lydis. A poet, she had used her inherited wealth to promote other writers, particularly through her Hand and Flower Press, and her Poems in Pamphlet. She was an unashamed eccentric, 'always elegant, but [with] something of the "*gamin*" about her', living briefly on a barge on the Thames despite her rambling house in Kent, and eventually selling up the Press to help fund research into 'paraphysics and sonic therapy'.[13] 'She was very much part of the language of the [Collier] household, the language of Patience', Sarah Collier remembers, reflecting that Harry had also liked her. 'Erica seemed to know how to live. She had money and she made things beautiful.'[14] Though guarded, some friends thought, by her partner the opera singer Anna Pollak, Erica – and 'EricAnna' – had always sent loving messages to Patience on first nights, together

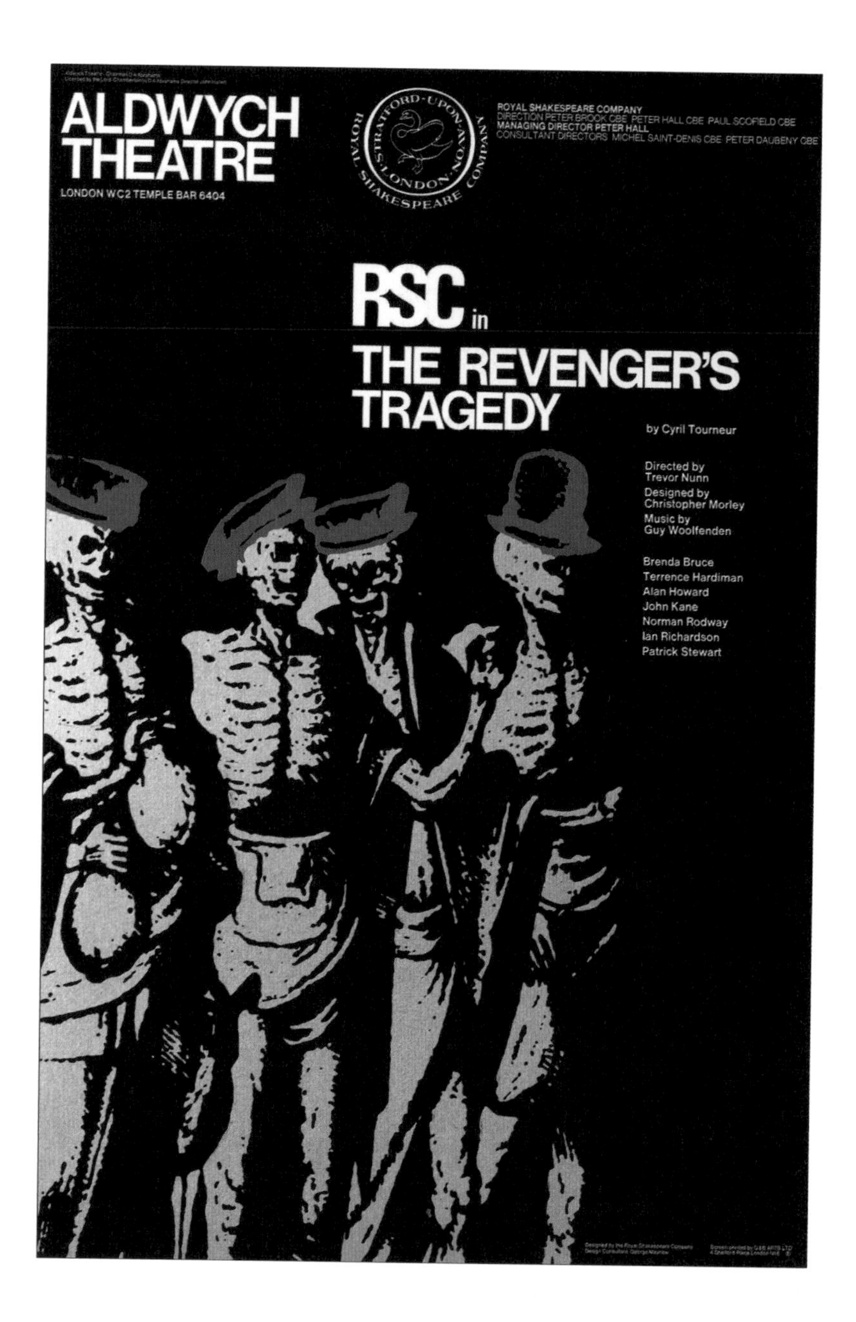

Poster for the RSC's *The Revenger's Tragedy*,
directed by Trevor Nunn.

with wicked limericks. They had commiserated with her when things felt less good, and celebrated when they were fine, staying with her at Stratford.

Now surgery for cancer had failed, it seemed, and early in the new year Erica was admitted to the Royal Homeopathic Hospital on Great Ormond Street. Yet though falling to pieces, she would tell Patience to 'do Mrs Dale's Diary', and laugh through all the pain. Visiting her on 7 March, Patience found her emaciated and desperate-looking: 'Belsen above, Biafra below,' Erica had quipped, horribly. Within a month she was dead. It was the third, premature death of a close friend and peer: Diana from suicide in 1963, Vivien Leigh, from tuberculosis in 1967, and now Erica, one month short of her sixtieth birthday.

Patience gave the eulogy at Erica's memorial service at St Martin in the Fields on 8 May. She took three weeks to write and develop it, seeking Naomi Lewis's advice, rehearsing it with her old BBC radio producer, David Davis, dress-rehearsing it at St Martin's, determined to make it reflect accurately and vividly Erica's 'intense intellectual spirit' and energy. She felt under intense pressure to do it well, knowing the church would be packed with artists and literati, and she tried to respond to Anna Pollak's intense grief. 'You must regard Anna as a widow… utterly heartbroken,' she told her children. She felt they had taken a dislike to Anna, noticing the frequency with which she seemed now to be around.

Patience took Anna in to her home in the days and weeks following Erica's death. They spent whole afternoons talking about Erica, sharing memories and grief, dealing first with the cremation, then the memorial service. Erica memories and the seeming unreality of her death drew them together, close affection developing somehow on the shoulders of the Erica-Anna relationship: 'Because of the death of my greatest school friend, I inherited Anna,' Patience would later say. Erica had entrusted her to 'look after Anna if you can. She was completely lost and unable to do anything.' Gradually the closeness grew: it was 'Anna for tea', 'Anna for coffee' and 'Anna stays the night'. They would mark 27 June as the real start of their relationship, Patience highlighting the date in her diary with a red star: 'MUSIC and chats.'

Reclaiming her heritage? Patience Collier as Grandma Tzeitel with Topol as Tevye in Norman Jewison's *Fiddler on the Roof*, 1971.

PART SEVEN

JUST WAITING TO PLAY BARBRA STREISAND'S MOTHER

IT'S *RITCHER*, NOT RITSCHER

HER GRANDDAUGHTERS CHARLOTTE, eight (born during Patience's second appearance in *The Cherry Orchard*) and Sophie, six, hid behind the fibre-glass trees on the eerie set, watching the endless re-takes, the dry ice, the men with clapper boards, the atmosphere cold and drafty beyond the heat of the lights. Patience had taken them to Pinewood to watch the filming of 'Tevye's Dream' sequence in *Fiddler on the Roof.* They seemed entirely unfazed by the tipped-up graves and Ruth Madoc's vampire-like Fruma Sarah arising out of the mists, or by her own role as Grandmother Tzeitel when she appeared, diminutive, waddling, clad in bride-veiled shroud: *'A blessing on your head – Mazel Tov, Mazel Tov.'*[1]

Patience Collier had first seen *Fiddler on the Roof* on stage in London in 1967, with Chaim Topol as Tevye and her friend Miriam Karlin as his wife Golde. 'GLORIOUS', she had noted in her diary of the musical, the longest-running show on Broadway and now set for similar success in the West End. When Canadian film director Norman Jewison began to cast for the film version early in 1970, Patience had at first been considered for the part of Yente, the matchmaker: she had had a wintry interview on the second floor of the West End synagogue on Dean Street, Soho. But Jewison's choice for that part became Molly Picon, the American actress who had made her career in Yiddish theatre, and Patience began instead to be considered for Grandma Tzeitel. Her contract was confirmed after 'a talk with piano' with John Williams, the film's musical director.

Patience joined the production for filming at Pinewood just before Christmas. It was nerve-wracking work – trying to concentrate on the part with the whirl of music, people and dancing around her at the studio rehearsals; she did her own obsessive rehearsing at home in her room. Recording the song half-spoken, against a 72-piece orchestra in separate studios, then lip-syncing against 'PLAYBACK' was a completely new experience: she had to borrow a tape-recording to practise. As always, she was minutely critical of her costume: 'dress and veil fitting – PERFECT!' she wrote in her diary on 1 January, but 'wig completely wrong'. They filmed the scene over two days, with its wild mixture of the dead and living, as if from an animated Chagall painting. Cinema audiences on the general release the following year would forever remember the exuberant schmaltz, the extravagant, funny and heart-wringing songs and dances, and the forced exodus of the little Jewish community from their Russian village.

These days, Patience was playing quite a clutch of Jewish roles – the outrageous Mrs Monty Levin in the Marty Feldman film, *Every Home Should Have One*, earlier in 1970, and the matriarch Lady Bland in the BBC's production of *Alien Corn* in the same year. These were followed by two significant stage roles. Yet she had not played specifically Jewish characters for some thirty-five years, when she had secured both crowd and understudy roles in the play *Magnolia Street* in 1934. That production, based on Louis Golding's hit novel of the same name, had employed Jewish actors for Jewish parts – Rebecca Goldstein, David Spiegel, Charles Levy among them – and black actor Ernest Trimmingham.

Patience – Rene then – had positively leapt when her impresario friend Maurice Browne had told her about the Charles Cochran production, to be directed by Komisarjevsky. Its timing had felt right: her father's death had been a reminder of her immigrant inheritance, and the papers were full of what was happening in Germany. Only a couple of years earlier, her brother had had to be fetched home from a visit to German cousins when the news was rife with Nazi thuggery. She had become one of ninety players playing Jewish or Gentile roles in the story of a working-class Manchester street. The essence of *Magnolia Street* was its 'crowd-vitality', *The Times* had said in its review, giving the impression of a 'mob seething and steaming, in its urban swarming and violence': 'Learn to disappear,' Komis had exhorted the cast. Each of them had had to learn every inch of the stage floor as the revolving sets changed the scenes from street to ballroom, to grocer's shop.[2]

Embarking on the first tour of her career, back in 1933, the then Rene had described herself in her diary as a 'Jewish girl with vitality...' But since then her Jewish origins had not figured strongly in Patience's sense of herself. She would summon them on occasion: in Belfast, she had appreciated the links made through a friend with the Jewish community; in Manchester, she had felt empathy with the strong political and artistic life of the city with its Jewish influences and refugee families. She would laughingly call her wig her *sheitel*, stand up to anti-Semitism, spread the word about the vital significance of the Anne Frank story as it was performed on stage. But in post-war Britain, Jewishness often seemed something to sublimate. She and others in the performance business would spot each other's Jewishness but often not acknowledge it. 'Never deny it, but never talk about it,' was the motto.[3]

But now in the late sixties, the cultural atmosphere on the London stage had shifted with the arrival of Bernard Kops, Harold Pinter and Arnold Wesker, writers whose immigrant Jewish background was part of what they were, how they wrote. All her life Patience had had to put up with snide comments about her looks, making her own outrageous jokes about them. She would tell stories of how when young men had taken her out to play golf, she used to sit swivelled round in the car, so they didn't get her profile. Now those same features were giving her interesting roles. She would laugh with *Guardian* journalist Auriol Stevens in a profile interview, 'I'm just waiting to be asked to play Barbra Streisand's mother...'[4]

Lately, indeed, she had become quite ebullient about her Jewishness. Filming in Rome in 1967, she took notes on the history of the Roman Ghetto and the building of the Coliseum by Jews brought from Jerusalem after the destruction of the Temple. 'I don't feel I could be a goy,' she pronounced. 'I just feel like somebody coloured would feel about being coloured. Somebody who comes from the ghettoes of Europe.'[5] She was becoming prone to large, sweeping remarks about 'good Jewish genes'. Though she would still mock her Jewish looks with the classic Jewish joke – 'You know, I turn to the left and whole scenes, people, everything, whole racecourses are obliterated' – she would also boast of how she had turned down the offer of a nose job in her teens, and calmly rejected the idea repeatedly during her career, even when suggested by Noël Coward. Now she *wanted* to be Jewish, to claim the diaspora story for herself.

It was not until some years later, however, that Patience really began to reflect and recall her own past. The sessions with Audrey Postgate, who had a book about her life in mind, would bring out her memories of her childhood as Rene at 63 Porchester Place, Bayswater in the early twentieth century: the chaotic household rent by arguments between her parents, the family paralysed by dread of her father's tempers. There, her life had been dominated by her nanny, Ipswich-born Ada Sheldrake – 'broad feet, broad-mouthed...she looked a Joan Littlewood kind of person' – with whom she fought constantly, her world largely confined with her brother to the top floor.

Sensations from that period would always remain with her: the curious smell of Nanny, the appetising smell of her mother. She would remember being allowed to sit on the *chaise-longue* in her mother's room before a dinner party and watch the women guests at their toilette, tidying their hair, making themselves up, the contortions on their faces, and imitating them 'uncomfortably well'. As a tiny child of not more than two years old she had already had her first intimation of getting an effect, of cultivating an audience, sitting on the floor before her mother's friends in a little white dress on a sheet sprinkled with raisins and currants for her to arrange. She heard the whispers around her ears: 'Eva, what a clever child!'

The Ritscher children's environment was the sheltered enclosure of the prosperous middle-class English household. But not quite. The voices of Krakow, Vienna and Berlin were central to Rene's childhood, her father never losing his Austrian accent. Her mother's family, the Spitzels, would visit, 'like gypsies or circus people'; her grandmother Tony like 'a little five-foot Tartar, half Polish, half Russian...with a square, Georgian kind of face', Patience would recall. 'Ach this place,' she would say, and stand on a ladder scrubbing out a cornice. There were always aunts, cousins and uncles around, together with her father's

Rene and Geoff as children by the front door
of 63 Porchester Terrace, c.1918

greatest friend, Arthur Davis, the Jewish architect who was Rene's godfather. For Rene and her brother, Geoffrey, the neighbourhood mapped not only their daily routines, but exotic legends of a mysterious family past, and lost fortunes. Two streets away from Porchester Terrace was Inverness Terrace, where numbers 1 to 3 had been converted in 1905 into the magnificent Inverness House by their grandfather, Louis Spitzel, five years before Rene's birth. Towering above its stuccoed neighbours, elaborately pinnacled, it was a familiar milestone on the way to the park. Their mother would show them the embossed album compiled to show off the French, *Beaux Arts* style of the house, designed for the Spitzels by Arthur Davis, who had made his name with the Carlton Hotel's Palm Court and the new Ritz Hotel in Piccadilly. But the children saw only the outside of the house: it had been lost to the family.

Their mother and grandmother would tell Rene and Geoffrey of the dark, panelled reception rooms of Inverness House, its Louis Seize drawing room with huge portraits and tapestries, its sweeping staircase decorated with delicately carved balustrades, the ceilings on the magnificent landing painted and embossed with cheeky gold cherubs. Its reception rooms had been an exquisite combination of turquoise and gold, their door handles made of lapis lazuli. It even had a tiny theatre – built, Eva said, just for her – with six bow-fronted and gilded boxes.[6] Yet the house had been wonderfully modern and convenient too: a lift, telephones installed on each floor, and no less than five fitted bathrooms for its seventeen bedrooms.

The children had never known their grandfather, Louis Spitzel, and found it difficult to connect these stories of grandeur with their uneducated grandmother, Tony, who would swoop down on them full of angst and criticism. But Eva would tell them of driving with her father to her wedding from the newly completed house in April, 1906, to the packed and lavishly garlanded, extravagantly decorated New West End Synagogue on St Petersburgh Place, where Paul Ritscher awaited her, immaculate in morning dress, his hair slicked down. The choir had been augmented for the occasion, and the ceremony was conducted by the Chief Rabbi himself, assisted by the New West End's own minister.

Interior of Inverness House – now the Grand Royale Hotel – in Inverness Terrace, Bayswater, showing the little theatre – built for Eva Ritscher – salon and kitchen.

The reception had been magnificent; German, Russian, French, Dutch, Australian and American-accented family and friends had mingled with the great and good, among them members of the Jewish aristocracy, who had endowed Bayswater and since moved to country estates: Sir Samuel Montagu, the former Liberal MP and now a baron, and Lady Montagu; as well as Leopold and Marie Rothschild, members of Edward VII's 'Jewish court'. Eva and Paul had received over one hundred gifts and left for their honeymoon in the south of France and Italy with the celebrations in full swing, the guests entertained to dinner and a performance in the little jewel-box theatre.[7]

Interior of the New West End Synagogue, St Petersburgh Place, London.

Louis Spitzel had died only five months after the wedding, his life, great deeds and funeral celebrated in yet another album, which the children would leaf through on a rainy day. For his funeral, the procession had stretched almost from Inverness House to St Petersburgh Place; and at the graveside at the Willesden Jewish cemetery, a hundred boys from the Commercial Road Talmud Torah in the East End had chanted prayers in recognition of his benevolence.

His had been a rags to riches story, a tale of romance, the innumerable lengthy obituaries said. Louis and Tony Spitzel had arrived in London in the 1870s from Krakow in their teens and married soon after; Louis had become an expert diamond cutter in the burgeoning Hatton Garden trade. They had then spent years scraping, peddling and living on their wits in gold and diamond-rush South Africa and Australia as their family grew – Eva had been born in gold-rich Gympie, Queensland – before returning to London. There, in the early 1890s, her father had turned himself into a colonial trader, identifying China as a potential source of wealth as it opened up to Western exploitation. Now the legend of Louis Spitzel began, of the man who introduced the Maxim gun to China – a 'pirate', Patience would call him – who became the friend and confidante to no less than Li Hung-Chang, the Qing dynasty's pro-Western viceroy. Inverness House had been filled with Chinese treasures, the children were told, the fruits of their grandfather's fourteen-year career. He had two Chinese valets.[8]

Their mother, Eva, had been brought up in more modest circumstances in London as the Spitzels made their fortune, until her parents commissioned Inverness House and moved into their life of – to her – suffocating splendour. For them, the choice of Bayswater and the proximity to the magnificent New West End Synagogue, whose oriental exoticism lay hidden behind a grand but austere street front, was a key element in the family's 'arrival'. They were becoming part of what has been described as the 'Anglican Church, Jewish division',[9] celebrating their Judaism – Louis was the son of a learned Hebrew scholar – but distinct from the waves of mid-European Jews arriving in the East End: refugees, Yiddish-speaking, foreign and poor.

Rene and Geoff grew up with the legends of Spitzel grandeur, but also with the furious family resentments about Louis Spitzel's lost wealth. Rumoured to be worth £2 million when he died, his fortune seemed rapidly to have dwindled to a mere £164,000 when Probate was granted: there were trails of debts, claimants and disputes. Eva and her two sisters' share of investment income was worth far less than that of their four brothers, and there was an irritating stipulation in the will that any Spitzel child or grandchild who left the Jewish faith or married out should forfeit their inheritance.[10]

For Paul Ritscher, walking behind his father-in-law's coffin for the *kvura* and *kaddish* while Eva and her mother remained at home, his thoughts about their prospects must have been mixed. Worse, as time went on, were the rumours of diamond-fraud scams run between Louis and his brothers Adolph and Julius, of High Court disputes about gun trading, and accusations even of shady arms deals. Against such stories the Spitzels would bridle: cunning rivals were always ready to accuse a Krakow Jew.[11] Any doubtful dealings had in any case, they felt, been more than compensated for by Louis's magnificent benevolence. Like

Paul and Eva Ritscher, 1920s.

other wealthy New West Enders, Louis's philanthropy had supported both non-Jewish and Jewish charities: colonial educational projects, hospital schemes but also many Jewish charitable and educational projects in the East End; and he had recently been elected a member of the Board of Deputies. For Louis Spitzel, an intrinsic part of becoming a Bayswater gentleman was demonstrating that he was not only pious but generous to his less fortunate fellow Jews.[12]

Rene's upbringing was rather different from her mother's. Paul and Eva Ritscher, like most of their friends, were secular Jews. Paul rented a pew at the New West End Synagogue nearby but religion was largely a hatches, matches and dispatches affair: Eva would refer to Rene's naming ceremony at the synagogue as her 'christening': the family celebrated Christmas, did not observe kosher food requirements, and hardly attended *shul,* if at all. But theirs was also largely a Jewish world, though one cemented by social, cultural and family ties rather than by religion. Paul's colleagues and partners at the stock exchange, Eva's friends, and the legendary Spitzel and Ritcher parties and outings were for the most part with family and members of the same Jewish circles. Erica Marx's home was the only one of her school friends' that Rene was allowed to visit, the older Patience would recall: 'Because the Marxes were Jewish and came from abroad, my parents could be sure I would get good nourishing food and no draughts.'[13]

Rene and Geoffrey's chafingly structured nursery childhoods were constantly marked by their parents' quarrels. Their handsome father, Paul, always exquisitely turned out and oozing confidence, was a man's man who exercised daily on dumb-bells with a visiting trainer, retired with friends to smoke in the billiard room or go out to his club, and kept a little black book of willing women. Their mother was ostentatious, dramatic, sentimental, flirtatious and easily accusing. He adored women, but 'regarded them as dolls'; she was 'totally unfair to him.' It was, reflected the older Patience, 'an intolerable marriage.'

The Ritschers were, in Patience's critical memory, highly extravagant: 'when I was a little girl everything was connected with treats. Everything was cushioned with comfort. It was nothing to be ashamed of to have the best of everything.' And they were horribly snobbish. The working classes were regarded as dirty and unhealthy, she would recall. If she wanted to give money to the organ-grinder in the park, it was, 'Have you got our gloves on?' But theirs was a household of confusion, inconsistency, drama and crises. Eva – '*sensible* Eva' she was called within the Spitzel family – surrounded herself with people about whom she made up stories. The servants starred: the 'marvellous parlour maid' was said to be sleeping with the butler, or drinking, or worse: 'She hates me... she's poisoning me – I've had the most awful stomach pains.' The children formed a passive audience to their parents' quarrels and scenes, but were also the tools of their rivalry, and subject to their ill-concealed preferences. Rene was her father's 'darling angel', but then her mother's 'own darling girlie'. Both parents acquired lovers during her teens: her father's mistress she recalled as 'Auntie Violet'; Eva flaunted her lover 'Uncle Harry' at Rene's school speech day.[14]

It was Arthur Davis, Rene's godfather and her father's best friend, who provided a stabilising presence for them all. Very successful (his Ritz Hotel commission had been followed by the Morning Post and RAC buildings), he lived just round the corner from the Ritschers at 107 Inverness Terrace. To Paul, he was joshing, a club companion, the keeper of that little black book. But he was also a 'quiet architect carefully thinking fellow', an intellectual, welcomed to the house by Eva, and beloved by the children. The young Rene felt that her godfather Arthur Davis – variously called 'Aareela', 'Gogfather Joseph' and 'Uncle Arthur', as she grew – was on her side, a real friend, a mediator with the adult world, providing the parental security she lacked, but also comfort, freedom and delight. He sent her letters illustrated with cartoons, and drew a special birthday picture of her winding the clock, as well as peeking over a doll's house model of one of his building designs. Reflecting on her childhood, the older Patience considered herself a lonely girl in the midst of the emotional chaos around her. 'I was all to myself, by myself, except my Uncle Arthur Davis,' she would say.[15]

All through Rene's childhood, her father travelled daily to work on the underground train to the Stock Exchange and Stand Fourteen, where the partnership of Gutmann, Stein and Co traded. This was a macho, larky and bullying world, a place where foreign-born members were needed to sustain the London Exchange's pre-eminence in the new global capital markets but were

Arthur Davis's birthday card to Rene, 1921, using Mewès and Davis's design for the RAC Club, Pall Mall, completed 1911.

also resented and suspected. Newcomers needed to trade on their wits, and adapt and assimilate fast. Paul Ritscher, arriving in London from Vienna with his mixed Hungarian and Austrian heritage, had applied for British citizenship in 1900, as soon as his length of residence permitted. By the age of twenty-seven, he had risen from stockbroker's clerk to full stockbroker status.[16]

But when war was declared on 4 August, 1914, many of the certainties of family life seemed rapidly to be taken from under them. The newspapers became full of calls to arms and, soon, tales of German atrocities. British citizens, the Ritschers and Spitzels had relatives in Berlin and Vienna, spoke German as easily as English, and in Paul's case, better. In the West End, not far from Bayswater, there were riots attacking shops and businesses with German-sounding – often Jewish – names, regardless of their owners' nationality.[17]

The Exchange had always been jingoistic, and easy to rally to fearsome demonstrations of loyalty in times of national crisis and triumph: now there was a huge drive to recruit young stockbrokers and clerks to the forces, and to raise a Stock Exchange Battalion of the Royal Fusiliers. The contingent of around 200 German and Austrian-born stock exchange members and clerks – no longer vital to daily trade – became sitting ducks for anti-foreign feeling, particularly after the sinking of RMS *Lusitania* in May, 1915. The atmosphere became ugly; in the country at large, the government was now rounding up enemy aliens for internment. At the Exchange, motions were put forward to deny even naturalised German and Austrian-born members re-election – fellows were jostled, roughed up, 'hustled out' – and the General Committee advised them to stay away. A Stock Exchange 'Anti-German Union' was formed. In 1916, Paul, now carrying the firm of Gutmann while his two partners served in the forces, quietly removed the 's' in the family name, so as to make it the more anglicised '*Ritcher*'.[18] It was a small yet significant change, but one which did not guarantee the family easy acceptance in fashionable circles: 'It's Ri*t*cher,' Rene would later have to say repeatedly at debutante dos.

The war came closer to home: the children were out with their nanny in Kensington Gardens when an air raid struck; their mother's beloved brothers Martin and Cecil were serving with the Canadian Overseas Expeditionary

Rene with Arthur Davis in uniform. Invalided out of the war, probably with shell shock, Davis got "better, got worse", Rene's parents said.

Force. Paul himself avoided conscription, but his friend Arthur Davis enlisted as a lieutenant, becoming an intelligence officer in France behind enemy lines. Something terrible happened there – there was talk of shellshock. In November, 1917, now a captain, he was invalided out of the forces and sent to Craiglockhart War Hospital for Officers near Edinburgh, to be treated with Dr William Rivers' hydropathic and talking cures. 'Your Uncle Arthur's going funny – got better – got worse,' Rene's parents said.[19]

The conflict came to an end: men came back, 'limped and had one leg.' In June, 1919, the eight-year-old Rene danced and recited the poem 'Armistice' before an admiring audience at the Michie Hospital for the Wounded where her mother had volunteered as a nurse. Eva, in her early thirties, had found a new role for herself in the war. It had given her independence, made her aware of the power of her own attractiveness and personality. Joining charitable committees, she was enjoying the glamour of upper-class circles well beyond her customary world. Paul's business managed to ride the storm, ducking and weaving the hysteria and chauvinism on the one hand, and exploiting the opportunity for war industry profits on the other; by 1920, he headed his own stockbroking firm, Ritcher and Co. He and Eva were increasingly going their separate ways. The war had confirmed and accelerated their assimilation with the wider world, albeit often uncomfortably on the edge of it. But when Paul died in 1933, his funeral ceremony was in accordance with Jewish tradition, with the women staying at home.

EVA

IT WAS PROBABLY INEVITABLE that for much of her life Patience would appear to discard even her parents' secular Jewish inheritance as well as much else. She had had uneasy personal relationships with her unreliable parents, and then, as her Communist-leaning cousin Margot told her, 'Your father is a wicked capitalist: the sooner you rid yourself of all that the better.'[1] Likewise, Harry had always been scornful of her family's milieu. It was only through their lives in Belfast and Manchester, and through the theatre, that Patience found Jewish culture of quite a different brand: political, warm, humorous but hard-edged from bitter past experience.

As the Colliers' family life developed, religion of whatever cast seemed largely alien. When Susan Collier proposed during a teenage religious phase that they should all get baptised, neither Patience nor Harry objected. It was not that either of them wanted to become Christians; it was simply irrelevant, a kind of joke. Neither Christianity nor Judaism of whatever strand seemed attractive to Patience with her liberated, leftish outlook. But then she had been brought up to be painfully ignorant of religious rituals: her first entry into a synagogue since early childhood had been at a friend's wedding in Belfast. The designer, Pat Albeck, would always remember the hurt Patience once clumsily inflicted on her orthodox mother, ignoring all the rules of the kosher kitchen.

But now, in her late fifties and early sixties, Patience would place herself in the same 'central European Jewish racial background' and performance traditions as Charlie Chaplin and Danny Kaye. Wrong she might have been about Chaplin's ethnicity, but she had a point about her own families of Spitzels and Ritchers.

Her parents Paul and Eva Ritcher shared an extraordinary talent for entertainment. Dancing was a big family skill, Patience would recall: 'We all four danced embarrassingly well.' When she was six years old, her mother arranged for her to have her first dancing lesson; at seven, she attended the Mayfair School of Dancing; at eight, her dancing and reciting at the Golder's Green Hippodrome were considered a great success. Dancing was something the Ritchers did together – 'We won every contest at every Palm Court.' They seemed to be competing against the world.

Performance, in her family's book, was a means to succeed, even against the odds. When at the age of ten, Rene attended her first school and found herself picked on by a snobbish and even anti-Semitic teacher and, worse, was the most disliked girl in the class, she won popularity by entering a competition for the best act: 'It got my Bolshevik blood up,' she would say. Dressing up in her brother's clothes as the wildly popular child star, Jackie Coogan, Chaplin's sidekick in *The Kid*, she brought the house down with her dancing, singing and mimicry: the other girls now 'swarmed her'. But at home with her mother on piano, she would perform a different kind of revenge, an improvised cabaret, imitating all the different teachers' walks with deadly comic accuracy, 'hips and feet going like mad'. Even when she moved on to a much more congenial school, St Monica's in Tadworth, she would use her talents as a performer, doing oriental-style dances in the nude in the absent Matron's room – 'strictly forbidden, of course'.[2]

By the early 1920s, her mother's name was occasionally reaching the society pages of the newspapers, as the hostess of glamorous dinner parties at Porchester Terrace, which were graced with stray White Russians and British titles, the house and garden decorated with fairy lights and banked with Madonna lilies. Eva was becoming a regular feature in *The Times* court circular – the benevolent fund evenings, the charity balls – dragging Paul with her and, soon, her daughter. Rene's launch, in the debutante season of 1929, seemed to represent the pinnacle of Eva's social ambition.

But Eva Ritcher wanted more. She would now become an entertainer, reinventing herself in her forties as glamorous singer and performer 'Eva Cavalle'.[3] Extravagant, newly ambitious, she secured an agent and bookings for shows

Eva Ritcher as performer 'Eva Cavalle', 1927,
photographed by Hugh Cecil.

at the West Ham Empire, then Portsmouth, and indulged in a smart car and a pianist. 'You couldn't hear her, that was the awful thing,' recalled the older Patience, remembering her shows with some embarrassment. 'She had loads of talents but never harnessed them.' But Eva was soon in the gossip columns – for her parties, her singing at charity events, her trips to New York and racy stories of Prohibition.

Eva Ritcher died in April, 1971, aged eighty-five. She had become frail and confused and, in Patience's view, very neglected in her residential home: it was a second stroke that killed her. 'It was an eerie business,' Patience noted of her visit with Harry to see her mother's body, and to collect her things.

Patience looked back on their often antagonistic relationship and recalled how, after the war, her mother – now in her sixties – had recreated herself yet again. Briefly flirting with the notion of opening a florist's shop, Eva went on to establish herself as a skilled hat maker to smart society, telling a romantic tale to the press of how she had learned to occupy herself during the long dark nights of the Blitz. By 1950, she had launched herself as Madame Eva Ritcher, 'Queensland-born' milliner and hat confectioner of Mayfair. She secured a studio at 1 Trebeck Street, within tottering distance of the Berkeley but also cheek by jowl with the notorious Shepherd's Market red-light district.

That year she had published the best-selling *The A.B.C. of Millinery*, a step-by-step guide on how to re-model your own hat; she gave talks on radio, as if to deliberately muscle in on Patience's broadcasting world. Her hats were for every stylish occasion, with names to match: 'Skyways,' 'Confidence' and 'Winner,' even 'I Hate Men': hats to indulge, attract and seduce. In time, the Collier family would go to the studio for Sunday lunch: her roast chicken and potatoes would become the stuff of her grandchildren's memories, as would her blonde, plaited assistant Irma, and the fold-out bed on which Eva slept. No one in the family had seemed surprised at Eva's transformation, regarding it with an odd mixture of disdain and amusement.[4]

Now, for Patience, there was the minutiae of death to be dealt with – contacting her brother, Geoffrey, for the first time in eight years; certifying the death;

calling the undertakers; organising the cremation; seeing Eva's friends and even getting in touch with the trustees of the Spitzel estate, which had continued to provide her mother with a small income.

Eva Ritcher was cremated on Saturday, 17 April, at the Golders Green Crematorium, located opposite the Jewish cemetery where her husband and father were buried. But the Crematorium was a secular institution. Eva, who years ago had upbraided her daughter for marrying a non-Jew and even seen to it that the Spitzel will was enforced against her, had wanted no religious service. Instead her daughter organised a non-religious ceremony in the chapel with music by Bach, Schubert and Tchaikovsky, and with her fellow actor and friend Dan Massey reading Tennyson.

The Author

THE
ABC OF MILLINERY

MADAME EVA RITCHER

With an Introduction by
ELIZABETH BOWEN

SKEFFINGTON AND SON LTD
FOUNDED 1858
11 Stratford Place, W.1
London New York Melbourne Sydney Cape Town

'Madame Eva Ritcher': the frontispiece to Eva Ritcher's *The A.B.C. of Millinery*, 1961 edition.

GOOD MOTHERS ARE HARD TO PLAY

IT WAS AROUND THE time of her mother's death that Patience was offered two notable roles, as two very different Jewish mothers.

The first part was as the monstrous, Medea-like Bessie, in Clifford Odets's Bronx-based play of the 1930s, *Awake and Sing.* The approach came from Vivian Matalon, the new director of the Hampstead Theatre Club. Patience knew Matalon well and had been produced by him in a television *Wednesday Play.* Mancunian and Jewish, he was keen to revive the left-wing American playwright Odets and very determined that Patience should take on the role.

She took her time considering the script, the story of a Jewish immigrant family which hinges on the character of the fierce matriarch, Bessie. Patience was doubtful: she had concentrated on television, film and radio work in the previous eighteen months and the Hampstead was fringe theatre: she had turned down parts there before. She read and reread the part all through 'with possible voice and accent' before deciding, writing in her diary in red: '*Would not like anyone else to be allowed to play her!*'

She began to work seriously on Bessie almost immediately. There were her clothes, her props, her wig, her face: 'Kenny [Lintott] and I spent an hour on Bessie's' head!' As usual, she was moving ahead of the designer, Saul Radomsky, yet finding Nathan at Berman's (the theatrical costumiers) 'VERY DIFFICULT'.

By the end of July, a friend from Philadelphia who had known Clifford Odets had arrived to work with her, and Harold Kasket, playing her stage husband, Myron, was coming to the house. She began to make up what she called her 'working book' of the part, the Bronx accent delineated with phonic signs.

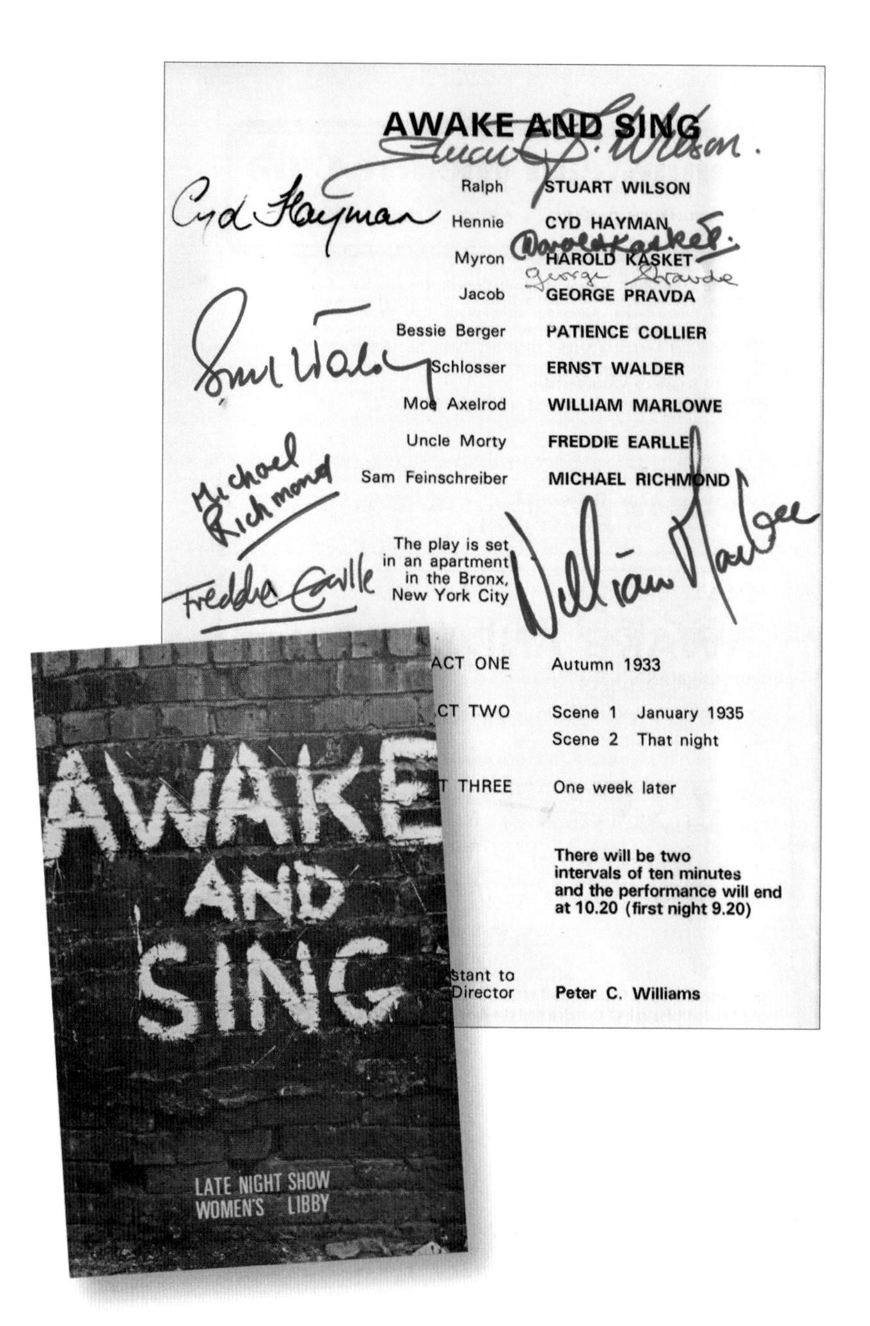

AWAKE AND SING

Ralph	STUART WILSON
Hennie	CYD HAYMAN
Myron	HAROLD KASKET
Jacob	GEORGE PRAVDA
Bessie Berger	PATIENCE COLLIER
Schlosser	ERNST WALDER
Moe Axelrod	WILLIAM MARLOWE
Uncle Morty	FREDDIE EARLLE
Sam Feinschreiber	MICHAEL RICHMOND

The play is set in an apartment in the Bronx, New York City

ACT ONE	Autumn 1933
CT TWO	Scene 1 January 1935
	Scene 2 That night
T THREE	One week later

There will be two intervals of ten minutes and the performance will end at 10.20 (first night 9.20)

stant to Director — Peter C. Williams

Programme cover and signed cast list for *Awake and Sing*, directed by Vivian Matalon at Hampstead Theatre Club.

Clifford Odets's play – his second – had originally been staged in New York in 1935, when he had become *the* playwright for the iconic Group Theatre. With Lee Strasberg, Elia Kazan and Harold Clurman, Odets had brought Stanislavsky-influenced acting techniques into his scripts. What had been so fresh and unique about him, Arthur Miller would reflect, was not only his left-wing politics – Odets, at the time, 'alone seemed pure, revolutionary, and the bearer of light' – but his 'lyricism of hopeful despair', his 'unashamed word joy'. As a very young writer, Miller had felt that 'nothing came near the work of Clifford Odets'.[1] And in Britain, he had been a favourite of left theatre groups such as Theatre Union. Since then, Odets's reputation had suffered, not only for his years of dismal service to Hollywood as a script-writer, but for his 'co-operation' with the House Un-American Activities Committee in 1952. In Edward Heath's Britain, however, in the small studio theatre at Swiss Cottage which championed new and radical writing under the direction of Matalon, *Awake and Sing* served to remind its liberal/left audiences of the fierceness and vibrancy of 1930s radical American drama. Its portrait of a Jewish family seemed, 'like a 'Jewish Chekhov', to show its members struggling for a life of their own, somehow 'in limbo before change'.[2]

When rehearsals began at the end of August, 1971, Patience struggled to find the perfection she wanted. At run-throughs, she observed of herself, 'I was very BAD' (on 16 September); 'I'm still not flowingly good. Too director-bound' (on the 17th); and on the 23rd, 'very nervous. Terrible.' At the play's second preview on 24 September, with Trevor Nunn and Janet Suzman in attendance, she found herself 'tense and not good – NOT BESSIE'. She was having bad 'tummy nerves', as well as an agonising problem with a toe, and found herself completely exhausted as performances began to roll.

The very qualities which particularly attracted Odets's contemporaries, the vigour and cut and thrust of the Berger family's aggressive/defensive exchanges, make the play particularly challenging to perform. The dialogue is caustic, the tensions within the family palpable, but their dialogue is also constantly witty. 'Second fiddle?' Bessie says of the man she has inveigled into marrying her pregnant daughter: 'By me he don't even play in the orchestra.'

The play is written for ensemble acting at its highest level, yet Bessie dominates the whole play. She is a mother who has sacrificed everything for her family but who now devours them, forcing her daughter into marriage, preventing her son from going with the girl he loves, bullying her father until he commits suicide. She is both father and mother in the Berger family, Odets explains in his script: 'She knows that when one lives in the jungle one must look out for the wild life.'

Patience was determined to make Bessie's Medea-like qualities comprehensible: 'Clifford Odets seems to have written a complete woman with her many, many facets,' she told her interviewer on BBC's Late Night Extra. The critics were impressed, saying: Bessie is a 'fearsome matriarch' and 'Patience Collier gives a stunningly impressive performance as the matriarchal mother.' *The Daily Mail* commented, 'This is a woman made ruthless by the need to survive and her implacable mask and her fury are frightening in their intensity.'[3]

Her theatre friends understood the scale of both the challenge and the achievement. 'Patience – you are very VERY VERY good,' Paul Scofield wrote to her. 'You are impossible and wonderful,' wrote Matalon, sending love and good luck for the first night: 'I have loved every minute of working with you and I mean every minute – even the rows!' But it was Jeremy Spenser who, she felt, understood the role best: 'He really appreciated BESSIE BERGER as no one else had done or could do.' It had been an extraordinary opportunity to portray the complexity of the role as written by Odets, to make what could have been an almost cartoon-like figure 'humanly understandable.'[4]

Patience came to the second of the roles, as Sarah in Arnold Wesker's *The Old Ones*, in the summer of 1972. This time it was with some relief, after a difficult reprise of Miss Gilchrist in *The Hostage* at Stratford East. Joan Littlewood – growing tired of her own battles at the Theatre Royal – had been uncomfortable to work with, unexpectedly rough-handed: 'She didn't treat me well, bloody badly actually,' Patience told *The Evening Standard*.

Yet being directed by John Dexter at the Royal Court could have been another nightmare. Dexter 'worked staggeringly hard,' Simon Callow would later say, but he was 'fuelled by booze, sex, and drugs.' 'He bruised people's egos,' said Diana

Rigg.[5] However, Patience was fortunate: she had been sought out both by him and Wesker, with whom she had worked on his first television play back in 1963.

John Dexter and Arnold Wesker were returning to the Royal Court following an absence of some twelve years, Dexter after directing opera and National Theatre productions, Wesker from the bitter demise of Centre 42. They had last worked together at the Royal Court on the Wesker trilogy, *Chicken Soup with Barley, Roots* and *I'm Talking about Jerusalem*. Dexter had mentally cast some parts while waiting for Wesker to finish the script of *The Old Ones*. Certain people had been 'inevitable', he told *Plays and Players*: the almost legendary comedian Max Wall as 'the skeletal, life-loving tailor', Manny, and Patience Collier as Sarah, his 'enclosed in domesticity' sister. John Dexter had first approached Patience back in November, when he had hoped the play would be staged at the National.

Sarah arguably is at the centre of the play: it opens in her flat. Dexter, a master of complex stage arrangements, had amended Wesker's original directions to create a one stage revolve, with each scene and domestic location overlapping with the next. The role required exacting detail – laying of tables, cooking, serving – and as with Odets, ensemble working. In complete contrast to the monstrous Bessie in *Awake and Sing*, Sarah's role is strong in her peaceability, negotiating the permanent conflict between her two quote-shouting brothers, celebrating Jewish tradition through the secular habits of cooking and eating: 'There is nothing like the solid security of a white tablecloth to solve all questions.' But she is also endowed with a kind of longing as, aided by her daughter, she seeks to clutch at religious tradition long lost and no longer understood. During the time-span of the play, the characters recreate the Jewish festival of *Sukkot* in her living room, to somehow celebrate life lived and to be lived, and to 'remember the dead'.

As usual, Patience began working on the part long before rehearsals started on 3 July, and while the script was as yet incomplete. Back in April, Wesker and his wife, Tanya, had taken Patience to visit his mother in Stoke Newington, and she had reread the part of Sarah 'with Mrs Wesker's voice in her ears'. She had discussions with him about the role throughout rehearsals: he remained closely involved in the development of the production, alternately elated and

8.VIII.72

My dear Patience,
This print of the Sabbath dinner just must be yours for your tender part in The Old Ones.
Thank you –
love
Arnold Wesker
and I thought you'd also like this old drawing of Gladys Cooper.

Arnold Wesker's gift to Patience of a print of the Sabbath dinner, with a note thanking her for her part in *The Old Ones*.

infuriated by Dexter's directing, observing the 'electrifying mixture of inspiration and malice' with which he dealt with some actors. As with 'Bessie', Patience found the part slow to build: now it was the very generosity and goodness of 'Sarah' that made it difficult to portray her with sufficient complexity and vigour. Good mothers were difficult.

Patience was full of angst and self-criticism. 'Dreadful run-through', she wrote on 27 July, ten days before the opening: 'I lost Sarah.' At dress rehearsals, she was still feeling thoroughly dissatisfied with herself: 'much too quiet and dull for "Sarah"', and 'far from reaching "Sarah"'. Her focus on the part could make her completely unmindful of other actors. Susan Engel, playing Rosa, Sarah's daughter in the play, recalls a moment in rehearsal when she had an important speech: 'There was a bit of noise behind me and I turned round and found that upstage Patience had suddenly decided business of her own, a bit of very ostentatious glass cleaning and wiping… I think John Dexter put a stop to it.' Patience was always brilliant at 'stage business' but was not always a team player.[6]

Patience found a 'NEW SARAH' halfway through the previews, but still got annoyed with her performance as the run proceeded. Yet the critics – divided as to whether they liked the play – thought that her character had exactly the blend of qualities she had been working for: 'a bundle of trimly contained energy', *Tribune* called it; 'unaffected simplicity, beautifully interpreted', said *The Jewish Chronicle*. Charlie Kay and Sybil Thorndike found her interpretation particularly admirable. But an invitation to the 'old Herxheimers' – Susan's German Jewish parents-in-law – backfired. Not particularly comfortable with the play, nor probably with Patience's study of their accents for her role, their attendance at the show followed by supper at Pizza Express turned out to be an embarrassing 'flop'.

There was another such uneasy occasion, some four years later. In June, 1976, Patience was invited to a lunch at 10 Downing Street in honour of the President of Israel. She and her son, Joe, sat down with a glittering array of Jewish artists, politicians, sportspeople and other representatives of the Anglo-Jewish community, assembled by Prime Minister Callaghan. Unaccountably, she found herself horribly bored: she seemed to have surprisingly little in common with the mix of Jewish establishment and celebrities. What meaning really had it for her? She noted the event in her diary: 'BORING for me as I wasn't Jewish enough.' Her love affair with being Jewish seemed to be waning.

But in 1982, her joke to the *Guardian* journalist almost came true. She was approached for a small part in Barbra Streisand's film *Yentl*, based on a story by Isaac Bashevis Singer: 'BEAUTIFUL! Mrs Jacobs a tiny part, but I'd really like to do it', she wrote in her diary. She was interviewed by Streisand herself: 'MOST WONDERFUL INTERVIEW OF MY LIFE!... We kissed goodbye after 1 hour together. She's warm, jewish [sic] and wonderful.' But in the event, Barbra Streisand did not think her right for the part. It was a difficult time – Patience, now seventy-two, was quite unwell: good parts, Jewish or not, seemed rare. 'Very depressing', she recorded in her diary.

Patience in typical morning pose, ready to
tackle the world.

PART EIGHT

A PERSON WITHOUT LIMITS

MOVING ON

PATIENCE COLLIER'S RELATIONSHIP with Erica Marx's former lover, Anna Pollak, ran smoothly for a few months. They had much in common, over and above Erica: their central European background, their drive, ambition and emotional volatility, and the world of performance. Their relationship 'was an enormously lucky event,' Patience would later tell her friend Audrey Postgate, 'a woman of the same age who's been in the profession...'

Anna was an extraordinary woman, two years younger than Patience. With no formal training, after a wartime performing in ENSA shows, she had made her debut at the age of thirty at Sadler's Wells in 1945 and had swiftly become the company's principal mezzo-soprano. She had sung at Glyndebourne, Covent Garden and Aldeburgh, in operas by Mozart, Strauss and Lennox Berkeley. She worked with Benjamin Britten and Peter Pears, creating the role of Bianca in the first performance of *The Rape of Lucretia*, and, in 1962, had been made an OBE for her services to music. 'She was one of those rare things, an opera singer who was a very good actress,' Charles Kay comments. It seemed a significant coincidence that one of her last key roles was as Polly Peachum in Britten's adaptation of *The Beggar's Opera*, in 1963, the same year as Patience played Mrs Traipes in the RSC production.[1]

That Patience, with her love and enjoyment of men, should have embarked in late middle age on the new adventure of an emotional and physical relationship with a woman, made it easy to disguise what it was. Patience always talked about Anna as 'her friend.' Even when Patience joined Anna at Danehurst, the large, comfortable country house in Kent which she had shared with Erica,

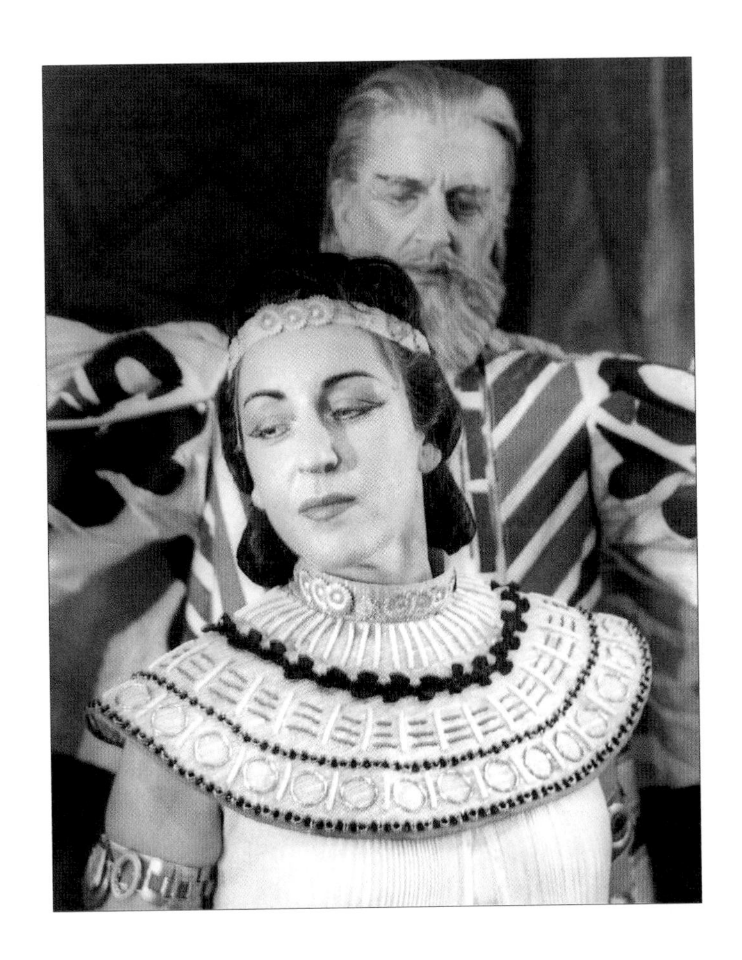

Anna Pollak in the title role in Lennox Berkeley's *Ruth*, with Peter Pears, Scala Theatre, London, 1956.

Danehurst, Erica Marx's house at Lympne in Kent, bequeathed to Anna Pollak.

they had separate bedrooms (at least at first). But there were also what Patience would call 'Anna breakfasts' in her room. Anna would be desperate with physical longing and would teasingly demand at least two hours of Patience, free from lists and Alice. Patience was discovering the unboundaried need she had for love and sexual attraction: 'I am a person without any limits,' she would say: 'I don't really feel any barrier about sex.' Gay friends, particularly, assumed what Anna meant to Patience and were glad for her, if surprised; others turned away from quite knowing.

But their relationship was soon marked with turbulent crises. 'Anna and I had another dreadful fight', Patience wrote in a typical diary entry in June, 1970. They carried the quarrel into the next day, sunbathing in silence in the heat, eating lunch still in silence and going back into the garden still determinedly not speaking: 'HORRIBLE.' Anna has been 'the worst of herself', Patience confided furiously in her diary. She reflected that Anna was still in mourning for Erica, but she herself felt unsupported, misunderstood, and got at. She 'CANNOT understand what she does to confuse and damage me. I see no hope if she can't understand.' Friends of Patience saw a different Anna, a shyer personality in the face of Patience's strength. It was not easy for Anna to play second fiddle to Patience and her work when her long-term lover was dead, and her own brilliant career appeared to be over.

Inevitably, Anna's presence in Patience's life made her relationship with Harry still more difficult. In January, 1970, Patience and Anna went on holiday together; by the spring, Harry was engaging Patience in tense, 'split-up' discussions. In May, he announced a kind of trial separation: he would rent the flat which their son, Joe, and his wife, Rohan, had vacated. In June, Anna left her own London flat and began, decorously, to rent a room at No 23; she and Patience celebrated their first anniversary. Anna was now a firm fixture in Patience's circles and increasingly Patience was in Anna's. She began to go to the opera with Anna, became close to her elderly mother, and spent regular weekends at Danehurst.

On 1 November, 1970, she and Anna flew to Malaga, spending lazy days swimming, sunbathing on their special beach, enjoying tapas lunches and special meals at the *Gilbralfaro Parador*. But on 11 November a telegram arrived from Joe: 'HARRY SERIOUSLY ILL – HEART ATTACK.' They spent the rest of the day on the phone, re-arranging tickets, washing and drying all the wet clothes so that they could pack for an early morning flight home.

Harry had been taken to St George's Hospital, and fitted with an emergency pace-maker; 'Joe had saved his father's life, without a doubt', Patience noted. Susan and Sarah were taking turns to sit with him. The next few weeks were fraught with emotions and trips to the hospital, and a new pace-maker was fitted. 'Talked to many people about Harry', Patience wrote in her diary: 'I felt tremendously sad for and about Harry.' But the situation seemed to be provoking difficult feelings for Anna: 'Long "misery" talks – she was in a furious state about ME... Several wretched talks with Anna. [She] has been vitriolic.'

Harry was discharged home on Tuesday, 8 December, following surgery to insert a more permanent pace-maker. It was a strange day – arranging flowers and plants for his homecoming, unpacking his bags from hospital with him, putting his things back in their place, observing him moving slowly but independently. He and Patience went through Christmas cards and present lists together; he rested; Joe and Rohan arrived for supper. They spent the next day doing Christmas parcels, interrupted from time to time by the power cuts imposed by the Heath government, desperate to thwart an anticipated miners' strike by conserving coal stocks. That evening they ate as a family.

Patience's professional life began to dominate once more – two television roles before Christmas – together with social life and family organisation. On Monday, 11 January, 1971, as she drove to Pinewood to work solo on the *Fiddler* set, Harry was returning to work part-time, still looking drawn and much thinner. With him back at home for the moment, there were more suppers together, sometimes with Anna. At the end of the week, Patience went down to Kent to stay with her, resuming their routine of pleasurable relaxation, before returning to supper and TV with Harry back at No 23. 'HARRY with the PACEMAKER in his HEART is improving miraculously and is changing a lot of things in the COLLIER FAMILY LIFE,' Patience wrote in her red pen as the new year began, before adding, 'ANNA is PATIENTLY THERE.'

There was spring promise. Her eldest daughter, Susan, beginning to build a brilliant career, was appointed design and colour consultant for Liberty Prints; Sarah was working as a designer with her, their partnership developing; Joe and his wife Rohan were expecting their first child. By May, Harry's career seemed once again on track. Now Laboratory Director at Miles Laboratories, he had become an authority on the body's mechanisms of tolerance and dependence, and was jetting off to major conferences on marijuana in New York.

His relationship with his mistress Paddy Dewsbery had become more of an official fixture. Patience noted their holiday departures, with the arrangements for Paddy to meet him off his plane or train, observing it all practically but not without scorn: 'Paddy and I are quite different,' she would say. 'I gave Harry three beautiful children – she carries his bags.'[2]

But the glimpse of death and decay she had experienced with Harry's emergency would not go away. She herself was often unwell, with chronic bowel problems, sore feet and 'jumpy legs,' and was having tests and x-rays at St George's Hospital. Though only sixty-one, she was feeling rather elderly. Indeed, it all seemed to be 'old ladies.' Harry's mother had grown so frail that on a trip to Richmond Park, she could walk only a few steps. Erna Hannan, now seventy-eight, seemed to be living among 'very old IDIOTS' at her hospital in Banstead. Two close friends were facing surgery; Anna's mother, Etty, was poorly, and Anna herself had decided to leave Danehurst, the house she had inherited from Erica. People began to arrive for viewings; there was the difficult job of packing and emptying cupboards, the relationship between Patience and Anna as volatile as ever. And in April, Patience's own mother died.

COSTUME DRAMAS

PATIENCE FOUND THE process of film-making intriguing and exhilarating. She was still fairly new to it when she joined the *Fiddler* cast and she observed the composite technical work required for film-making carefully. She revelled in the sheer professionalism and lavishness of a Norman Jewison production, the employment of the very best of film and production firms, designers, choreographers, film-makers, actors and musicians: 'TRIFLES MAKE PERFECTION BUT PERFECTION IS NO TRIFLE', she wrote beneath the contact details for the production at the start of her diary for 1971, only slightly misquoting Michelangelo. She even enjoyed the order of the day: the early calls, the car to the house, an hour and a half for make-up, the endless waiting about for lighting, sound and camera angles to be adjusted, and the repeated takes. Filming could be squeezed in between theatre roles and, though as intense and exacting as any of her jobs, it was less challenging physically than stage work. And then the process pampered and cosseted one in ways the theatre did not: as filming of her role in *Fiddler* finished on 20 January, she felt as though she had had 'an exhilarating holiday'.

Not all her film experience was as satisfactory. The Hammer Horror movie *The Countess Dracula*, 1970, was made on a shoe-string, 'with economy in time and cash and behaviour evident at all levels'. She played the wicked countess's loyal servant, and was almost sabotaged by a hitch with continuity. At 8.30 a.m. she had been on set, made-up, ready to film the burning of the red shawl, the last remnant of the little peasant girl whose blood had been drained to make a rejuvenating bath for the countess. Firemen were on stand-by with extinguishers; the camera, sound men and director stood ready; but after ten minutes of uncomfortable silence there was still no red shawl for Patience to burn. There were calls of 'Where's the red shawl? Who's got the red shawl?' cut through by Patience's more ringing, 'Gentlemen, please can I know where the red shawl *is*?' Then, worse, '*Whose business was it to procure it for the shot this morning?*' There was anxious blaming of Wardrobe, Costumier, Designer, until it was discovered that no order had actually been given to Berman's, because the girl who was to wear it had not yet been cast.[1]

Patience brought her RSC expectations of organisational perfection to the studio. She would challenge production management, designers' choices, directors' decisions, wanting her own work to be signed off only when it was truly complete. 'Dreadful Rushes,' she had noted during the filming of Evelyn Waugh's *Decline and Fall* in September, 1967, in which she played Flossie Fagan, telling director John Krish she was 'depressed and dissatisfied.'

But Patience understood the peculiar technical requirements of film. She got used to the problems of continuity, the strange isolation of particular scenes, which meant she might never get to meet or work with friends and colleagues playing in the same film. She learned to accept the extraordinary social hierarchy of the film world, 'ridiculously, unbelievably Feudal,' with the prioritisation of star names. She recognised the realities of the market – 'stars are there to bring in the money'; the fact that only 10 per cent of the profits on a film made in Britain could be expected to come from the home market. She was realistic about the limitations which her strong looks, and age, were likely to impose on her casting opportunities. And long years on stage had prepared her for the fact that an apparently promising and much-puffed production could fail to please audiences and critics.

Still, it could be deflating to discover at a première that a good part had ended up mostly all over the cuttings floor, as with her role of Nannie in Peter Hall's heist comedy, *Perfect Friday*. She also found to her cost that some directors could be less than respectful of her reputation. Selected for Peter Medak's film of *The Ruling Class*, starring Peter O'Toole, she made a huge fuss when it turned out the role had been erroneously double-cast – and as a result, it was she who lost the part.[2]

Patience made the most of films which gave her good acting potential, even when the film itself was only so-so.[3] 'My experience in films is only about three years old,' she told a group of drama students in 1971, 'but I already know that I love it and want to go as far as it will take me.'

'END of VERY BAD WORK YEAR: WORST for 16 YEARS,' Patience wrote in significant green ink at the tail end of her 1973 diary, and, at the start of the new year, 'DEPRESSED to start 1974 WORKLESS!' These seemed

BLACK SORT OF TIMES –
MINERS' STRIKE
RAIL MEN'S STRIKE
ELECTRICITY ECONOMIES
NIGHTMARISH!!

But it was the scarcity of work which seemed to gnaw at her, that and the volatility of her personal life: Harry still around – and not – at No 23, and the intimacy and petty, screaming rows with Anna. 'Anna and I have a horrible row about my criticising her [for] constantly listening to the radio,' she wrote in her diary in October, 1973, during a weekend together, though there was peace again the next day. She and Anna were making their wills.

There had been the difficult task of clearing and selling Danehurst, the previous year: Patience and Anna's final weekends there had been dogged by blackouts and train diversions as bitter industrial disputes continued. 'WAR TIME CONDITIONS,' Patience wrote, entertaining the Scofields to dinner by candlelight. But there had also been the excitement of plans for a new house – 'Hawthorn' at Stamford in Kent – which they saw as a joint adventure, though purchased by Anna. The move achieved, Patience and Anna wandered round the house, admiring the building work and criticising the things that were wrong, before eating a champagne supper. They had a pool built, to which Patience contributed £2,000 – money she could afford the more easily since she and Geoffrey had come to an agreement about the remains of Eva's share of the Spitzel estate.

In August, Anna, Patience and her friends Elspeth Dipper and Gwyneth Lloyd –'four elderly ladies' – swam in the nude in the new pool.

But things were as volatile as ever between Patience and Anna. The trauma of the move had brought back special grief for Anna, and her mother had died soon afterwards. They were together in Kent when it happened, but peaceful, sympathetic togetherness in the pool and garden, or watching TV, seemed easily broken by some insensitivity of Patience's. 'Anna...vitriolically against me and hysterical. Etty's death has quite unbalanced her', she wrote in her diary. They were rowing continually in a pattern reminiscent of the relationship between her and Harry: Anna began to talk wildly of selling Hawthorn, while Patience confided her exasperations and irritations in her diary. When the critic Howard Rosenthal entitled a talk they attended at the Coliseum, 'Are Opera Singers Human?', Patience probably felt that Anna was proving only too much so. But then the reconciliations, the relenting phone calls and the 'Anna breakfasts' were sweet.

Patience's main life still lay at 23 Campden Hill Road, of which Anna would be part, or not. Anna had spent Christmas with them all at No 23 – Harry, Granny Collier, Alice, Joe and Rohan and little Daniel, Sarah and her husband Alastair, and the Herxheimers – bringing the Christmas tree and holly up from the country. Patience and Anna took Charlotte and Sophie Herxheimer to *Sleeping Beauty* on Ice at Wembley on Boxing Day: 'Excellent. Wonderful skating.'

The year 1973 began promisingly enough. Patience had changed agents again (this time, from Dodo Watts to Sara Randall at the Saraband theatrical agency), and joined the new egalitarian but starry Company Theatre based at the new Greenwich Theatre in their third production.[4] This was Tom Stoppard's adaptation of Lorca's *The House of Bernarda Alba*, about a household of women in southern Spain tyrannised over by their mother, full of repressed violence; a story so unpleasant as to provoke some restless laughter from audiences, who found it hard to take. The cast of sisters – Mia Farrow, June Jago and Penelope Keith – were so disparate-looking, Penelope Keith remembers, that, 'We hardly looked as though we had breakfast together, let alone came from the same loins.'[5]

Only Patience – very 'demanding in rehearsals'– received uniformly excellent reviews as Poncia, the 'gossipy, crude, old servant woman, half chorus figure, half provider of comic relief, [spitting out] venom at the feudal society while polishing the family oak'.[6] The production had a short run and, though still an Associate Artist of the RSC, Patience was offered no other theatre work that year.

She seemed to profess little but gloom and despondence, but Patience was in fact benefitting from the rush of costume dramas that both independent television and the BBC were producing, following the huge success of *The Forsyte Saga*. The nation was fast becoming entranced with colour, bigger television sets, and lavish productions. Patience herself was now an inveterate TV addict, watching everything from serious drama to *Coronation Street, Miss World* and the wedding of Princess Ann and Mark Phillips ('a splendid performance', she noted in her diary). *Upstairs Downstairs* had become a particular favourite.

At the start of 1973, she was beginning work on the script for the first episode of John Gorrie's production of *Edward VII*, as Baroness Lehzen, Princess Victoria's governess, advisor, companion and secretary. They filmed on location at St George's Chapel, Windsor for Bertie's christening scene, followed by weeks of rehearsal and studio recording, lifts home from Gorrie and Robert Hardy (playing Prince Albert), and a somewhat bristly relationship with Alison Leggatt (the Duchess of Kent), with whom she shared a dressing room. She was 'perfect in the part', remembers John Gorrie: 'Everyone knew she would be right from the moment she was proposed... She would speak her mind but you would think: that was right.' This was to be one of the most lavish costume dramas of the period, taking a year to film and record in sequence following that first episode: ATV 'threw money at it', Gorrie recalls.[7]

Later in the year she was again filming on location for the BBC's striking six-parter on the Suffragettes, *Shoulder to Shoulder*. The series – each episode its own story – was a perfect blend of popular drama and radicalism, infused with contemporary feminist spirit and the rediscovery of lost history: 'I did not really make any connection between my right to vote today and the fight for me to have that right', wrote producer Verity Lambert in the *Radio Times* Special for

Patience Collier as Betsey Trotwood in the BBC serial *David Copperfield*, 1974.

the series. Medium budget, commissioned by new Head of Drama, Shaun Sutton, it was the work of three powerful women – Lambert herself, Midge Mackenzie and Georgia Brown – and created substantial parts for women across the age range. Patience gave a gentle and touching performance as the mother of Lady Constance Lytton (Judy Parfitt), the aristocratic suffragette who risked her health to prove she could take forced-feeding like her humbler sisters. The work cemented her friendships with Verity Lambert on the one hand, and Waris Hussein on the other, the director of the series.

It was probably difficult for Patience to gauge the merit of the television productions she took on at the time: the work itself was usually short-lived, and there was often a substantial gap between their making and transmission. That first episode of *Edward VII* was not broadcast until April, 1975, almost two years after it had been made, and as in films, actors seldom saw the whole story: the series starred Patience's friend Timothy West, but they never met on set. The time lag was far less on *Shoulder to Shoulder* – five months – but there was always a gap between performance and critical reaction, which in this case was exuberant. This was a show that was 'unexpected, jumping with content and dripping with talent. Here, for once, we have an opportunity to see a whole bunch [of actresses of quality], working on material worthy of their talents ...the girls [come on] like gangbusters...' wrote Clive James in *The Observer.*

The timescales for *David Copperfield* in late 1974, in which Patience starred as Betsey Trotwood, were rather different. There was a ten day schedule for each of the six episodes, with Patience appearing in them all; initial filming for the donkey scenes in a freezing Dunwich was followed by a strict timetable for studio recording. Broadcasting began even as they were completing the series, so Patience had feedback – and could make her own judgement – on her performance as it was rolled out. 'I was pleased, with reservations about SHOTS! Several friends phone', she wrote after the transmission of episode one, where she makes her startling appearance at Mrs Copperfield's cottage, large nose pressed to the window. The critics were immediately admiring of the 'crisp decisiveness' of her acting: 'Patience Collier's Betsey Trotwood is a masterpiece.'[8] Friends gushed to become fans: 'I was glued to *David Copperfield*', wrote John Normington. 'She's such a clear Betsey and you have made her so... loving and warm and so amusing.'

Patience herself was completely taken by Betsey: 'I've never seen another interpretation of Betsey Trotwood', she told the *Radio Times*, and 'I'm glad I haven't... All I need is Dickens, he's so brilliantly clear... The great challenge is to see how close one can get to his definitions'.

> It's an odd sensation, playing a character you admire enormously. Someone you feel you know, like a friend. What I have to concentrate on doing is steering her away from Patience Collier and making her 100 per cent herself...[9]

'I think your interpretation of Betsey is loveable, understandable, courageous', Joan Craft, the director, wrote to her at the end of the series. Craft's production was star-studded, made with an eye to the international market, and her rather pedestrian style was soon to be overtaken by less realistic interpretations of Dickens, but her choice of Patience as Betsey did seem to have been inspired.

DRESSING ROOM RITUALS

IT WAS TELEVISION appearances that now pulled in audiences to the theatre, particularly outside London. Every poster, every preview article about the touring production of the National Theatre's *Heartbreak House* in May, 1975, tagged the 'galaxy of National Theatre stars' with their recent TV appearances, 'faces...familiar to millions on television', including Patience Collier's.[1]

The tour of John Schlesinger's acclaimed production of the Shaw play alternated with performances at the Old Vic – ostensibly in line with the National's outreach policy, but mainly because the company still had no home to accommodate its current repertoire. The ambitious new building on London's South Bank had been 'topped out' two years previously, but the work of fitting out had dragged on: the latest date for the theatre's opening – April, 1975 – had come and gone. There were endless difficulties with builders, overspends, internal strife, and rampant press criticism from left and right. 'The negativism and death wish [here] is extraordinary', commented John Schlesinger in an interview with *The Evening Standard.* He had joined the National Theatre as an associate director after a stunning run of films – most recently *Midnight Cowboy* and *Sunday Bloody Sunday* – as Laurence Olivier's appointees, John Dexter, Jonathan Miller and Ken Tynan, departed. Peter Hall, the old opponent of the National project, was now firmly in charge as artistic director.

Patience had been waiting for this opportunity. There had been earlier talks with Peter Hall about her joining the company but then nothing until Schlesinger's approach in November 1974. The offer of Nurse Guinness came while she was busy with *David Copperfield,* and already engaged for a voice-over

Good luck painting for Patience on her appearance for the first time for the National Theatre from her designer daughter Sarah and family.

part in John Antrobus's play *Mrs Grabowski's Academy* at the Royal Court. She turned it down at first, only to change her mind with the promise of a second National production. She was finding such situations unpleasantly stressful, noting in her diary: 'MIGRAINES on-off ALL DAY from DECISION PRESSURE.'

Patience set about the part at once, even as she prepared for the final episode of *David Copperfield*, marking out the part in the script, receiving coaching on her Irish voice and accent from Norman Rodway. She experimented with her look: 'get ready as mock-up "Guinness"...Kenny Lintott with many red wigs to try.' She relished the feel of being part of a National Theatre project: they knew how things should be done. 'Cast welcomed by all the top people including Peter Hall,' she wrote in red in her diary of 6 January. She cultivated lift-givers as usual, Edward de Souza particularly: 'He drives at eighty excellently.' She began a warm friendship with Balliol-accented, fast-swearing John Schlesinger, enjoying dinner at the stunning Kent home he shared with partner Geoffrey Sharpe, joined by Stanley Hall, Noel MacGregor and Charles Kay – 'too good a meal! Lovely time.' And she felt exquisitely supported by Hall himself: 'My dear Patience, It's wonderful that you are here. Please stay.'[2] She had never worked at the Old Vic before; now she was introduced to the 'famous IVAN and STEPHEN and [shown] the Wonderful WORKROOM and Fitting-Rooms.' As with the RSC, she made her strongest alliances with the technical staff and got their adoration: 'GUINESS [sic] SEEMS TO LEAVE ME WANTING MORE – MORE – MORE!! YOU ARE PERFECTION!' ran their good luck card.

Touring again for the first time for years, Patience picked up old habits, saw old friends, played the tourist, was thrilled to see Norwich Cathedral and visit the Brontës' Haworth. But the audiences could be 'dreary' and 'unsophisticated:' 'It's as though we'd left our play at the Old Vic,' she wrote in Leeds. Lighting changes were in the hands of the local technicians, and backstage conditions were often cramped and cold. 'HURTY TIRED. SWOLLEN LEGS,' she would write in her diary: 'TOURING IS TIRING.' She took to knitting a brown muffler for Anna during the long waits in hotels and dressing rooms.

Her dressing room was always a most important part of her organisation of a performance. For *Heartbreak House*, she insisted on having one to herself,

Patience Collier as Nurse Guinness in the National Theatre's 1975 production of *Heartbreak House*, with Colin Blakeley as Captain Shotover.

and got Dressing Room 4 at the Old Vic, spending three hours setting up her 'Gear', cleaning and preparing it to her satisfaction before the technical 'stagger-through'. She had dressing-room rituals, stuff to be arranged, things she would always install: a screen, a 'red and purple blanket with a fringe, which might be draped over her chair, a red brocade curtain, things Susan and Sarah had designed', her daughter-in-law Rohan recalls. 'She had an old-fashioned red tin with her make-up in,' remembers daughter Sarah: 'She covered a plastic tray with her make-up tin and she'd cover that with her red and white cloth, so everything for theatre was red and white.'[3]

Patience would make great lists of her gear for touring. For *Heartbreak House*, it was:

> Folding Chair. Labels. In Mexican Basket – Blanket. Pillows.
> Small Tray – Plates. Mug. Thermos. Cutlery. Salt. Small
> Decaf – Small Marvel –Tea Bags. Sandals. Dressing-gown.
> Red Chiffons. Red Snood. Wig Block. Kleenex. Serviettes.
> Cotton-Wool Balls – Wig Wadges. Tea Towel. Large Towel.
> Make-up Towel. Striped Dressing-Table Cover. Calendar.
> Long Hand Mirror. Scent. Lauria Lacquer. Acitone-Solvent
> – gum. 'Guinness' SPECS and SHOES – Stockings – Hankie
> TRAY with all the USUALS. TOILET BAG with Flannel. Soap.
> Scrubbing Brush. Tooth Brush. Paste – 2 Tooth Mugs. Dylan
> Quick Wash. Toilet Paper. Brush and 2 combs. Suede Brush.

– all 'very, very organised'. Her dressing room was a place to prepare, to retreat, relax and retrench, and to receive family and friends after the show – less so while on tour, of course. But still there was the opportunity to greet friends in Norwich backstage, and to shock their very proper Northern Irish aunt by flinging open the door of Captain Shotover's dressing room to reveal Colin Blakeley, peeling off his beard and make-up, and naked from the waist up.

Heartbreak House finished on 29 July, 1975. It had been a huge hit, and Peter Hall wrote to each cast member of his hope that the production would return to the National's repertoire, 'when we are on the South Bank', perhaps next spring, or the early summer. 'This all sounds very vague I know but I can't be more precise when we are in the hands of the building contractors, the Arts Council, the GLC and the Treasury. No one has given us the final assurances we are seeking...' The contract for her next National production arrived – a Ben Travers farce – and staff director, Sebastian Graham-Jones, wrote a fond note: 'It has been an excellent time for me – for you, I hope too – and I look forward to "Plunder".'

Patience fully expected to be part of the National Theatre when it moved across from the Old Vic to the South Bank, step by painful step. But reluctantly she had to withdraw from *Plunder* due to her slow recovery from major surgery, undertaken only four days after the last night of *Heartbreak House*. She looked suddenly far older: she had taken to wearing snoods at home but now had a perm and was occasionally venturing out without a wig. But feeling much stronger by the new year, she refreshed her 'peskering' skills to remind the National of her readiness, making a direct approach to the Deputy Director, Lord Michael Birkett. She attended a meeting with Peter Hall at his stylish new offices overlooking the river in the still unfinished building, and had 'scintillating talks' with Christopher Hampton and Maximilian Schell about their plans for *Tales from the Vienna Woods*. But when she was finally offered two parts, she judged neither good enough for her: 'VERY DISAPPOINTED'.

Meanwhile she found herself being courted by Trevor Nunn, who wanted her to return to the RSC. Rather enjoying the excitement of the negotiations her new agent, Joyce Edwards, was conducting between the two companies, she decided to plump for the summer season at the Aldwych. She would now watch the National's year of hell from the outside, adoring the 'wonderful clothes and spectacle' of the Olivier Theatre's long-awaited opening in the autumn when she went to see *Tamburlaine* with Audrey Postgate, but found the play 'BORING', and the theatre 'restless and uncomfortable'. They took sandwiches to eat in the interval of the four and a half hour production.

It was exhilarating to be back at the Aldwych and her familiar dressing room that summer: 'MARVELLOUS! I love that little room!' Her two parts – as Dick Dudgeon's 'appalling mother' in Shaw's *The Devil's Disciple* and as Avdotya, 'an

A dressing room photo of Patience dressed for the part of Avdotya in the RSC's production of Chekhov's *Ivanov*, 1976.

old lady of indefinite profession' in Chekhov's *Ivanov* – were ones she could excel in. She was relished by Jack Gold, the highly successful television and film director who was producing the first, and warmly welcomed back by David Jones for the second. Tom Conti, Norman Rodway and T. P. McKenna brought her fun and support: 'Have a happy and wicked time to-night dear Patience', McKenna wrote for the first night of *Ivanov*: ...you're very *funny* and *good* in it.' Gwyneth Lloyd's niece, Louise Walker, joining the wardrobe department for the production, struck the right note of endearment and respect when she wrote to say how much she was looking forward to working with her.

Others in the company were undoubtedly frightened of Patience, her reputation and her bite. But Zoë Wanamaker, joining the RSC for the first time, found her funny, and kind. Whether because 'I was Jewish, or because of my father, whom she knew', they formed a friendship in this rather inflated atmosphere where people 'stood around with their legs apart and did the *Times* crossword'.

'I kind of "got" her,' she reflects. 'There was a spirit about her – she was independent. And I was part of a generation that would argue, which Patience enjoyed. She also gave me a lot of kind attention. She taught me the importance of wigs – mine was dreadful – summoning the wig people down from the top floor [to sort it out]... She taught me the need to throw your weight around, sometimes.'[4]

The two RSC performances and productions were critical successes at a time when the National was struggling to emerge from its own chaos. Yet Patience found the experience unnerving, even frightening at times. The night of the dress rehearsal for *Devil's Disciple*, frustrated with the ill-fitting costumes from Berman's, weighed down by the heat, she was terrified at what she felt to be her

The Ivanov Household

IVANOV, Nikolai Alekseyich, *permanent member of the Zemstvo, with special responsibility for the peasantry*	**John Wood**
BORKIN, Mikhail Mikhailich, *a distant relative and manager of Ivanov's estate*	**Bob Hoskins**
ANNA Petrovna, *Ivanov's wife, formerly named Sarah Abramson*	**Estelle Kohler**
SHABELSKY, Count Matvey Semyonich, *Ivanov's maternal uncle*	**Sebastian Shaw**
PYOTR, *Ivanov's manservant*	**Joe Dunlop**

The Lebedev Household

LEBEDEV, Pavel Kirillich, *Chairman of the Zemstvo Council*	**Norman Rodway**
ZINAEEDA Savishna, *his wife*	**Carol Gillies**
SASHA Pavlovna, *their daughter*	**Mia Farrow**
OLGA Semyonova, *a family dependant*	**Valerie Colgan**
GAVRILA, *the Lebedevs' manservant*	**Larry Hoodekoff**

The District

LVOV, Yevgeny Konstantinich, *a young doctor working for the Zemstvo Council*	**Kenneth Cranham**
BABAKINA, Marfa Yegorovna, *a young widow*	**Zoë Wanamaker**
KOSYCH, Dimitri Nikitich, *an excise officer*	**Patrick Godfrey**
AVDOTYA Nazarovna, *an old woman of indefinite profession*	**Patience Collier**
FIRST GUEST	**Richard Simpson**
SECOND GUEST	**Raymond Marlowe**
THIRD GUEST	**Doyne Byrd**

PARTY GUESTS, WEDDING GUESTS, etc
Steven Beard, Joe Dunlop, Diana Rowan, Clare Shenstone, Norman Tipton

Musicians:
Jeremy Barlow, *flute*
Gordon Kember, *piano*
Henry Krein, *accordion*
Christopher Le Bon, *cello*
Peter Whittaker, *bassoon*

Directed by David Jones
Designed by William Dudley
Music by Carl Davis
Lighting by Stewart Leviton

Stage Manager: Maggie Whitlum
Deputy Stage Manager: Titus Grant
Assistant Stage Manager: Caroline Howard
Sound: Roland Morrow
First performance of this production: 2nd September 1976
Aldwych Theatre London WC2
Licensees: Theatres Consolidated Ltd
Chairman: P. D. Abrahams
Managing Director: John Hallett
This programme is 15p

Programme cover and cast list for the RSC's 1976 production of *Ivanov*, directed by David Jones.

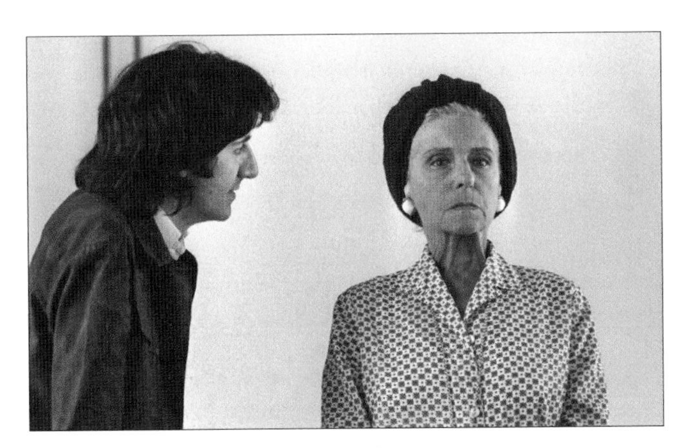

Patience Collier rehearsing with Tom Conti for the RSC's 1976 production of *The Devil's Disciple*, directed by Jack Gold.

lack of adequate preparation. She staged her own private practice in the theatre, with her props, before the dress rehearsal proper: 'I was anaesthetised with fear (like an operation).' Migraines debilitated her and her stomach troubles returned, so virulent that at one August performance she only just made it to the curtain.

'Harry has run away!' Patience telephoned her daughter, at the end of March, 1976, making it sound so melodramatic that Susan had to laugh. Harry now began what she called a 'A TRIAL RUN!' of living with his mistress, Paddy Dewsbery: two months later, he decided to make it a permanent arrangement.

Yet he was still frequently around at No 23, visiting weekly to give Alice housekeeping money and go through the accounts, staying on for dinner, occasionally fixing a curtain rail and supervising repairs; furious when a dripping tap had been ignored and an emergency plumber had to be called. Always quite matter-of-fact about these things, Patience would eventually invite Harry and Paddy to supper: 'very pleasant evening', she recorded in her diary, though they had arrived at eight o'clock and left at nine forty-five.

In many ways, arrangements at No 23 remained much the same after Harry's departure: the upstairs flat let, or not; the flow of friends and family for lunch and dinner; kitchen lunches and suppers with Alice, their roles reversed from time to time – 'ALICE VERY BAD WITH FLU. PUT HER TO BED.' RSC and television work – *Barney's Last Stand* by Ted Willis, a Dickens drama series for Paul Annett, a new version of *Bernarda Alba* for BBC TV – went alongside her picking up her GLC senior bus pass, and the usual trips to theatre, cinema and restaurants. There were glamorous occasions: at John Schlesinger's fiftieth birthday party, Patience sat in the place of honour. There were the usual late night chats with Anna, the weekends in Kent, gardening, swimming, relaxing in front of the TV or listening to opera records, before 'very lovingly to bed'.

Patience was now – almost – acknowledging part of her private life as lesbian. There were the circles of friends to whom Anna introduced her, the relaxed evenings with them, the viewing of soft porn films together, such as *Emmanuelle* and '*HOT GIRLS* and *PRISON GIRLS*,' as she noted in her diary: she tended to find these intensely boring. Their rows – so often about couple trivia – could turn on sexual jealousy. 'Tried to have open talk [with Anna] about her flirting with Gwyneth [Lloyd]', Patience noted one Friday: 'SHE WAS LIVID and left in a HUFF at 12, [said] we had FINISHED for good. I am completely wrecked.' It took the whole weekend, letters, a telegram and talks with Jeremy Spenser to bring about a reconciliation.

Their relationship drifted easily enough into Patience's wide-ranging and long-standing close friendships with gay men; she and Anna visited regularly with Stanley Hall and Noel MacGregor at Stanley's house at Soggs Parva during their Kent weekends. Yet she never seemed to embrace lesbian circles in the way that she had long loved and enjoyed the company of men, gay or straight. Within the family, still, only her daughter-in-law, Rohan, seemed to recognise the nature of her close relationship with Anna: we can only surmise about Harry or indeed Alice.

Crises and tragedies came and went. Granny Collier died after a stroke; Harry had a new pacemaker fitted; Audrey Postgate was diagnosed with breast cancer and needed surgery; Erna Hannan, whom Patience was still supporting with Anna, seemed 'much changed'. There was an IRA bomb at the bottom of Campden Hill Road. Wig Creations was collapsing – Noel was unwell, Stanley thin and growing muddled – and the business was finally sold at the end of 1975. In June, 1976, Patience's friend from RSC days, 35-year-old Mike Pratt, died of lung cancer. She saw his body before the funeral – 'like a beautiful saint with ivory skin' – and attended the star-studded memorial show at the Aldwych.

But she was also relishing others' triumphs. John Hurt was doing brilliantly; she lunched with him and his partner at the King's Head, Islington soon after his success as Quentin Crisp in *The Naked Civil Servant:* 'Quentin and I took 19 Bus home!' Anna was coming back into her own, giving highly successful talks on opera life at the London Coliseum. And Alec McCowen was winning stunning reviews for his performance of the complete text of St Mark's Gospel.

Patience could be critical, even childishly jealous of her adult children, but she was also relishing their growing success. Joe, now a member of the Royal College of Physicians, was, like Harry, popularising and explaining medical matters with an appearance on the television show *Tomorrow's World.* Susan and

Patience with grandson Louis Campbell, Summer, 1978.

Sarah had formed a highly successful textile design partnership, soon to be Collier Campbell. Patience toured the Liberty centenary exhibition at the Victoria and Albert with them, kept their newspaper cuttings in triplicate, and got a kick out of being photographed in their *Sunday Times* offer of wrap-around skirt and peasant blouse.

She now had five grandchildren. Her diaries record her irritation with the mess and noise of her younger grandchildren and she was opinionated about their upbringing. Yet she was also intrigued by the 'otherness' of small children, their unexpectedness and funniness; Daniel Collier 'jiving like John Travolta' or organising Christmas singing, and later, little Louis Campbell with his curious and probing questions. 'How long do you think you are going to last, Patience?' he would ask.

For the older ones, Patience organised special outings. Yet she was not a '*real* granny', Charlotte and Sophie Herxheimer reflect, unlike their warm Jewish German grandmother on their father's side. Though both were now at school nearby, 'you knew you couldn't [just] drop in' at No 23. A surprise visit to show off bargains from the closing-down sale at Biba's on High Street, Kensington was met with a 'Darling, you didn't *ring!*'

'She wasn't prepared to drop everything and give you a hug,' recalls Sophie. 'I don't remember her ever giving me a hug. She might have given you a kiss – more like air kissing, holding you by both shoulders and kissing you on both sides – ritualistic hello and goodbye, darling.' Patience could also be startlingly inappropriate, as Sophie wrote much later in a poem:

> *Do you smoke yet, Darling? Index finger holding open her*
> *Gauloises' in my alarmed twelve-year-old face, as she sits before*
> *The dramatic floor to ceiling fall of those John Piper curtains.*[5]

WHO PAYS?

'WHAT NEXT?' PATIENCE began her 1977 diary. It was promising to be an excellent period for television: she was filming the part of Queen Elizabeth I for ATV's *Life of Shakespeare* series, a role which required multiple discussions on her dress, face, teeth and hair, visits to galleries, poring over portraits, samples of fabrics – fur, velvet, sequins. 'This time I had to have my eyebrows shaved off and part of my hair as well,' she told the press. She researched the art that had gone into the daily making of the Virgin Queen with fascination, being someone who went through her own private version of the process each day. Two 'bladders' – 'two baldies' – had to be made to secure the right effect, with ATV's make-up designers working in close consultation with Kenny Lintott, and special dentures were required. Rehearsals for her episodes with Tim Curry as Shakespeare were particularly tiring with the '"PLASTIC" head make-up and heavy, corseted dress.'[1]

Shakespeare was closely followed by *Come Back Little Sheba*, one of Laurence Olivier's *Best Play of*... series for Granada Television, in which the seventy-year-old former director of the National, classical actor and star was astonishing popular audiences with his performances. *Little Sheba* was an intense and compelling 1940s classic by William Inge, set in a small university town in the American Midwest. Patience played the part of Mrs Coffman, the practical Central European neighbour to Joanne Woodward and Olivier's disintegrating and volatile couple: her remedy for all their ills is, 'Get busy and forget it, lady.'

It was delightful to be in Manchester again for the recording, visiting the set of her favourite soap, *Coronation Street*, meeting Hilda Ogden, Rita and Elsie

Patience Collier as Queen Elizabeth I in *The Life of Shakespeare* series for ATV, directed by Robert Knights for ATV, 1976/77.

Tanner. She dined out with director Silvio Narizzano – the Italian Canadian with whom she had worked in Armchair Theatre days – and Olivier, socialising too with Timothy West, Derek Jacobi and Alan Bates. But the experience as a whole was exhausting. Her small but significant part was constantly threatened with reductions as the recording schedules in Manchester slipped and slipped again, the electricians and cameramen at Granada working to rule. Worse, she was again seriously unwell and often in intense pain. She had to be met off the train with a wheelchair, and was in despair if the train or her helper were late, or arrangements fell through.

Yet she began preparations for her next role – as Katerina Matakis in the BBC's *Who Pays the Ferryman?* – even before *Sheba* was complete. *Who Pays* became a hit series for the BBC, with its haunting theme tune by Yannis Markopoulos, its sun-bared setting and its themes of high emotions and revenge. Patience had almost turned down the part: 'Not high-powered literature!! Heterosexual *Woman's Own*!' she noted in her diary as she slogged through the scripts, loathing Katerina, and added that she was 'really wicked and vile!!! Should I identify myself with her?'

Filming took place in Greece in May, followed by rehearsals and recording at Pebble Mill. But she found the whole process difficult, the conditions problematic, herself in 'PAIN! PAIN! PAIN!', resolving to 'USE PAIN for voice harshness.' She was slow to learn the lines, grew furious with herself, and desperate when travel arrangements failed to work properly. But she joined in with relish at the last night party on 15 August at the Pebble Mill cricket pavilion, transformed, for the occasion, into a 'TAVERNA!'

A week later, and Patience was preparing to go into hospital for the second time that year. In February, she had been diagnosed as requiring pelvic surgery that had been declared impossible; now doctors were to undertake colon surgery at the prestigious Fitzroy Nuffield Hospital, with its hefty fees. She was in such pain that the spelling of her diary entries – never very consistent – began to go to pot: 'Lunch with JOHNN GIELGED...JOHNN DIVINE...FEELING RESOLUTE ABOUT EVERYTHING', she wrote as she was admitted, before succumbing to confusion as she went through weeks of surgery, pain, mess and drugs.

Patience as Katerina Matakis in BBC TV's 1977 drama serial *Who Pays the Ferryman?*, produced by William Slater.

Her diary entries only resurfaced after two weeks of incoherence, recording the visits of family and friends – 'Janet Suzmannn [sic]...in wondrous red pants, scarf, gloves and pantaloons' – and flowers from Peter Hall and the National. There were nerve-wracking experimental outings, Patience dressed suitably with wig on; there was convalescent irritation with visitors calling at the wrong time, and setbacks which made her frightened, vulnerable and pathetically pleased with compliments. At home, Alice, too, now seventy-eight, had her own health problems, taking weeks to recover from a fractured femur: the two invalid ladies convalesced together. Joe had begun to raise the question of whether Patience could remain much longer at No 23.

She got down to Kent on 23 December for the first time since the early autumn, spending Christmas with Anna: 'Walked in the wind on the front at Hythe...How wonderful to be here, and whole again.' She watched the last episode of *Who Pays*, delighted at the telephone calls which followed. Anna organised a party. But suddenly they were back to their 'horrid FLARE-UPS', a tiff over television-watching versus music-listening: she 'CURSED me'. Anna, enduring no doubt a difficult convalescent, brought her breakfast 'with a glum face', though Patience had the grace to go down and make up.

It had now been two and a half years since Patience had performed at the National Theatre, a period in which the looming, grey bulk designed by Denys Lasdun on the South Bank had gone from crisis to crisis. The building and fitting-out work continued to be hit by poor organisation and bitter strikes: each of the three theatres had to open separately. Michael Blakemore, who was to have directed Patience in *Plunder*, left in fury, hurling accusations of autocracy and hypocrisy at Peter Hall. The National was devouring resources at a time of government stringency: plans for international seasons had to be thrown out and touring commitments cut back. Peter Hall's ideals of an ensemble culture for the company, so highly developed at the RSC, had to be diluted, the aim now being to develop a distinct style around the repertoires of each of the three theatres and their artistic directors.

Patience was still not particularly well when at last she got a satisfactory offer of a National Theatre role in the largest of the three theatres, the Olivier, at the start of 1978. The National had commissioned a new version of Ibsen's *Brand* from Michael Frayn for a production directed by Hall's deputy, Christopher Morahan. Patience was to play sarcastic and threatening mother to Michael Bryant's Brand.

It was a difficult play: written in verse, it had taken even nineteenth-century Scandinavian audiences years to like it. Patience 'plodded through' it when the offer came – 'didn't understand' – yet began work on her lines immediately. The cast met in the vast rehearsal room – it 'yawned in your face', Michael Blakemore would comment[2] – the place freezing as there was no heating oil. Patience had a cold and no voice, yet it was a marvellous feeling to walk on the raked stage of the Olivier alone, in her old rehearsal skirt and Nurse Guinness shoes.

Patience and Chris Morahan found a mutual respect: she thought him brilliant, noting his directions to be 'harder, less domestic': he found her 'sane and sensible, firm, and highly intelligent'.[3] The look she created with the wardrobe, wig and make-up team was satisfyingly exact: 'huge swaddled feet, thick grey skirt, long grey/dark brown overcoat...a headband swathed close'. She worked for hours on finding a *voice*, on developing a North country accent, tutored 'VERY STRICTLY' on getting it right by John Saunders and John Normington, only to find that they had overdone it and Morahan wanted it toned down. She broadened her usual range of line-learning helpers: visiting friends would find themselves corralled. Helen Taylor Robinson, a friend of Sarah's, remembers her regular sessions with Patience. She could be 'lying in state in her bedroom or in the double sitting-room and I would be told to monitor her lines exactly as set out, no other way, feeding her cues. It was a very serious task – I had to be engrossed too'; until suddenly 'I was put on hold with a phone call or interruption' and asked to call Alice. Or things would be simply brought to a finish with a 'that's enough, darling.'[4]

The whole process of lengthy rehearsals, technical run-throughs and make-up seemed more treacherous this time round. She noted her own dissatisfactions – 'went over my part too often…very nervous: too much rehearsing' – and clung to people's praise. Things were not helped by quite sudden crippling pain in her back and legs, so that she could only move like a 'Snail.' Rohan was teaching her to 'HANG ON DOORS' for sciatica so painful that some nights she had difficulty in straightening up, and she began to depend on the therapist Diana Dante and the Alexander technique. It became almost an obsession, actress Helen Bourne recalls: 'You must go to Diana *Dante*,' she would tell friends: '*Diana Dante* has told me that when I lift my foot…'[5] Anna, Patience noted, was becoming fed up with her constant problems.

Opening at the end of April, after a long succession of previews and press nights, there were glowing notices for Brand's 'pinch-faced old mother', a 'fine study in tight-fisted senility.'[6] But the applause for Patience's cameo part was muted by the generally critical press reaction to the hard-going coldness of the play, and there were depressingly empty houses in the vast Olivier Theatre. Plans for a minimum run of seven months soon came under scrutiny.

As the production came to an early end on 11 July, Peter Hall approached her with another proposal: would she play Charlotta in his own production of *The Cherry Orchard,* again in the Olivier Theatre? It was a surprising offer. It was now twenty-four years since she had first performed it, seventeen since she had reprised it for the RSC – and she was now sixty-eight years old. Moreover, the production had been running since February, with Helen Ryan in the part, 'bringing the house down' with the focus on her 'circus turn.' But Peter Hall had been disappointed with the way in which the Olivier Theatre seemed to have swallowed up the irony and delicacy of Chekhov, and the critical response had been poor: it had lacked the 'cohesive "company" feeling' necessary said *The*

Tatler, and was 'flabby, shabby and shapeless' (*Morning Star*). Moreover it had been horribly upstaged by the highly successful Riverside Studios production of the play only a few months earlier.[7] 'Poor production: Charlotta almost invisible! Confusing!' Patience had commented, when she saw the National's version. Introducing Patience, even temporarily, might just alter the dynamics of the thing, Hall must have felt: he sent associate director Michael Hallifax to her as an 'envoy', with plans and diaries to demonstrate how it could be arranged. 'Exhausting!' she noted. Three days later, however, and Charlotta was 'FIXED': she began negotiations about shoes, and was soon working on Michael Frayn's adaptation of the script. Patience also began practising Charlotta's tricks with conjuror Billy McComb. She found McComb, originally from Belfast, an 'excellent and unusual man' and was soon completely at home with him, particularly delighted by his getting her 'magical handkerchief' made from one of Sarah's scarves. With the help of his careful diagrams, she studied the techniques and practised her tricks at home, then at rehearsals. All her old excitements about Charlotta seemed to revive. She worked on stage with a pianist, and – though Joe had warned her against it with her medical problems – was even 'ABLE TO DANCE!!' She became ten or fifteen years younger, Peter Hall noted at rehearsals, by sheer 'willpower and by talent'. Even off-stage, she seemed to move with a new speed and agility: he had never seen 'such an exercise of mind over matter'.[8]

Patience loved the attention to detail and the support from the production staff: 'Darling Stephen. Wonderful clothes.' She felt exhilarated by Peter Hall's appreciation: 'It's been a joy to work with you again, and experience your courage, your application – and above all, your talent. It's a strange and wonderful feeling to meet Charlotta again...' he wrote in a series of postcards. But the energy mustered for the performance seemed rapidly to give out: her back and legs were causing her agony; she was walking with a stick, having to make herself straight, unable to stand for long, and seriously frightened. Two performances on 9 November were too much – carrying even the little dog had become 'frighteningly difficult'. She finished her run on the 18th: 'It's rotten luck your not being able to continue', wrote Hall, apologising for his distractions over pay disputes and strike threats on her last night.[9]

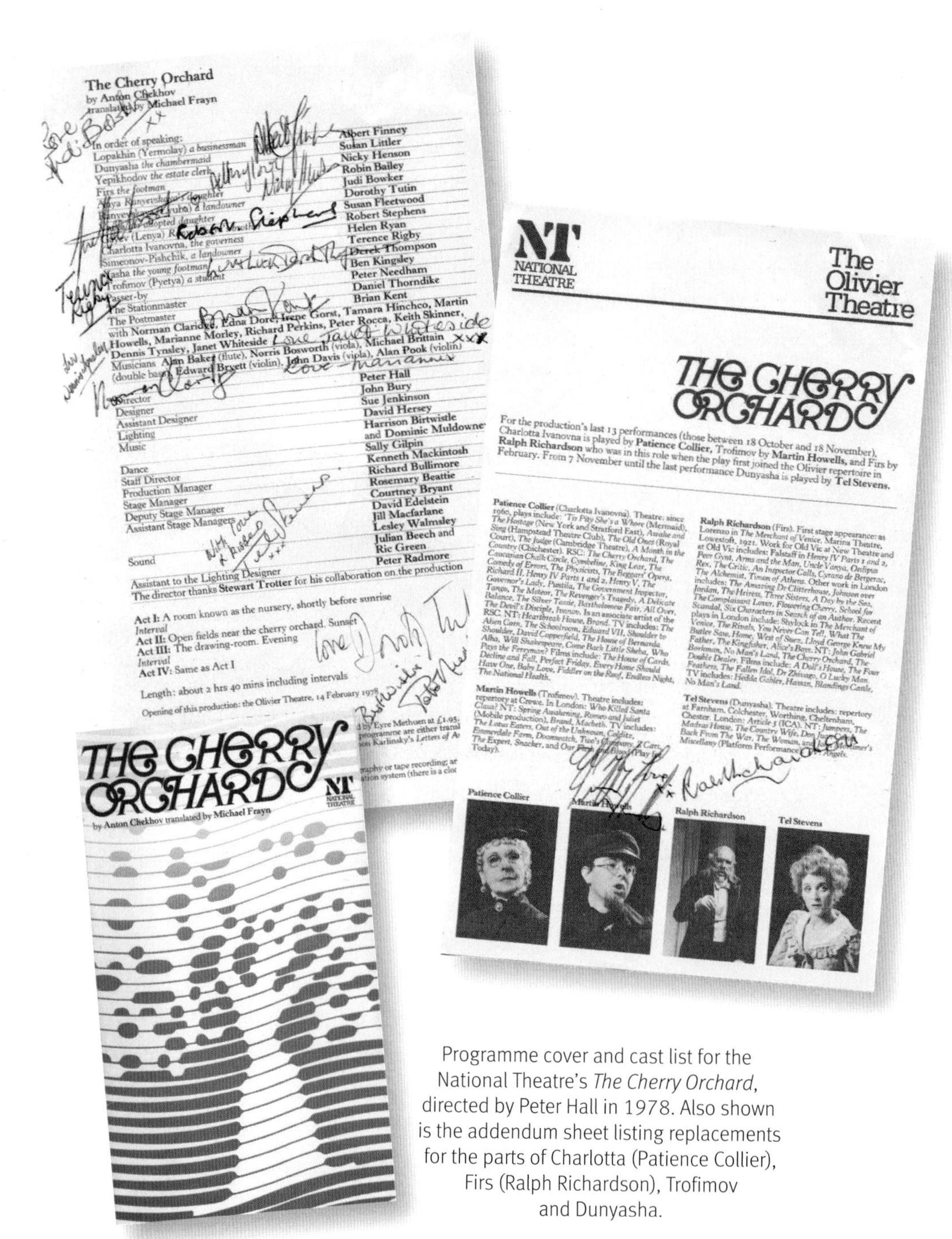

The Cherry Orchard
by Anton Chekhov
translated by Michael Frayn

In order of speaking:

Lopakhin (Yermolay) *a businessman*	Albert Finney
Dunyasha *the chambermaid*	Susan Littler
Yepikhodov *the estate clerk*	Nicky Henson
Firs *the footman*	Robin Bailey
Anya [illegible]	Judi Bowker
[illegible] (Lyuba) *a landowner*	Dorothy Tutin
[illegible] *adopted daughter*	Susan Fleetwood
Gayev (Lenya) [illegible]	Robert Stephens
Charlotta Ivanovna, *the governess*	Helen Ryan
Simeonov-Pishchik, *a landowner*	Terence Rigby
Yasha *the young footman*	Derek Thompson
Trofimov (Pyetya) *a student*	Ben Kingsley
Passer-by	Peter Needham
The Stationmaster	Daniel Thorndike
The Postmaster	Brian Kent

with **Norman Claridge, Edna Dore, Irene Gorst, Tamara Hinchco, Martin Howells, Marianne Morley, Richard Perkins, Peter Rocca, Keith Skinner, Dennis Tynsley, Janet Whiteside**

Musicians **Alan Baker** (flute), **Norris Bosworth** (viola), **Michael Brittain** (double bass), **Edward Bryett** (violin), **John Davis** (viola), **Alan Pook** (violin)

Director
Designer
Assistant Designer
Lighting
Music

Dance
Staff Director
Production Manager
Stage Manager
Deputy Stage Manager
Assistant Stage Managers

Sound

Peter Hall
John Bury
Sue Jenkinson
David Hersey
Harrison Birtwistle and Dominic Muldowney
Sally Gilpin
Kenneth Mackintosh
Richard Bullimore
Rosemary Beattie
Courtney Bryant
David Edelstein
Jill Macfarlane
Lesley Walmsley
Julian Beech and Ric Green
Peter Radmore

Assistant to the Lighting Designer
The director thanks **Stewart Trotter** for his collaboration on the production

Act I: A room known as the nursery, shortly before sunrise
Interval
Act II: Open fields near the cherry orchard. Sunset
Act III: The drawing-room. Evening
Interval
Act IV: Same as Act I

Length: about 2 hrs 40 mins including intervals

Opening of this production: the Olivier Theatre, 14 February 1978

THE CHERRY ORCHARD
by Anton Chekhov translated by Michael Frayn
NT NATIONAL THEATRE

NT NATIONAL THEATRE
The Olivier Theatre

THE CHERRY ORCHARD

For the production's last 13 performances (those between 18 October and 18 November), Charlotta Ivanovna is played by **Patience Collier,** Trofimov by **Martin Howells,** and Firs by **Ralph Richardson** who was in this role when the play first joined the Olivier repertoire in February. From 7 November until the last performance Dunyasha is played by **Tel Stevens.**

Patience Collier (Charlotta Ivanovna). Theatre: since 1960, plays include: *'Tis Pity She's a Whore* (Mermaid), *The Hostage* (New York and Stratford East), *Awake and Sing* (Hampstead Theatre Club), *The Old Ones* (Royal Court), *The Judge* (Cambridge Theatre), *A Month in the Country* (Chichester). RSC: *The Cherry Orchard, The Caucasian Chalk Circle, Cymbeline, King Lear, The Comedy of Errors, The Physicists, The Beggars' Opera, Richard II, Henry IV Parts 1 and 2, Henry V, The Governor's Lady, Puntila, The Government Inspector, Tango, The Meteor, The Revenger's Tragedy, A Delicate Balance, The Silver Tassie, Bartholomew Fair, All Over, The Devil's Disciple, Ivanov.* Is an associate artist of the RSC. NT: *Heartbreak House, Brand.* TV includes: *The Alien Corn, The Schoolroom, Edward VII, Shoulder to Shoulder, David Copperfield, The House of Bernarda Alba, Will Shakespeare, Come Back Little Sheba, Who Pays the Ferryman?* Films include: *The House of Cards, Decline and Fall, Perfect Friday, Every Home Should Have One, Baby Love, Fiddler on the Roof, Endless Night, The National Health.*

Martin Howells (Trofimov). Theatre includes: repertory at Crewe. In London: *Who Killed Santa Claus?* NT: *Spring Awakening, Romeo and Juliet* (Mobile production), *Brand, Macbeth.* TV includes: *The Lotus Eaters, Out of the Unknown, Colditz, Emmerdale Farm, Doomwatch, Two's Company, Z Cars, The Expert, Snacker,* and *Our Flesh and Blood* (Play for Today).

Ralph Richardson (Firs). First stage appearance: as Lorenzo in *The Merchant of Venice,* Marina Theatre, Lowestoft, 1921. Work for Old Vic at New Theatre and at Old Vic includes: Falstaff in *Henry IV Parts 1 and 2, Peer Gynt, Arms and the Man, Uncle Vanya, Oedipus Rex, The Critic, An Inspector Calls, Cyrano de Bergerac, The Alchemist, Timon of Athens.* Other work in London includes: *The Amazing Dr Clitterhouse, Johnson over Jordan, The Heiress, Three Sisters, A Day by the Sea, The Complaisant Lover, Flowering Cherry, School for Scandal, Six Characters in Search of an Author.* Recent plays in London include: Shylock in *The Merchant of Venice, The Rivals, You Never Can Tell, What The Butler Saw, Home, West of Suez, Lloyd George Knew My Father, The Kingfisher, Alice's Boys.* NT: *John Gabriel Borkman, No Man's Land, The Cherry Orchard, The Double Dealer.* Films include: *A Doll's House, The Four Feathers, The Fallen Idol, Dr Zhivago, O Lucky Man.* TV includes: *Hedda Gabler, Hassan, Blandings Castle, No Man's Land.*

Tel Stevens (Dunyasha). Theatre includes: repertory at Farnham, Colchester, Worthing, Cheltenham, Chester. London: *Article 5* (ICA). NT: *Jumpers, The Madras House, The Country Wife, Don Juan Comes Back From The War, The Woman,* and John Mortimer's *Miscellany* (Platform Performance) [illegible] *Angels.*

Patience Collier | Martin Howells | Ralph Richardson | Tel Stevens

Programme cover and cast list for the National Theatre's *The Cherry Orchard*, directed by Peter Hall in 1978. Also shown is the addendum sheet listing replacements for the parts of Charlotta (Patience Collier), Firs (Ralph Richardson), Trofimov and Dunyasha.

National Theatre opponents used both the *Brand* and *Cherry Orchard* productions to jibe again at Peter Hall's rule: '[He] needs to take a rest, either from running the National Theatre or from directing plays there – or, perhaps, from both.'[10] To Patience, however, he seemed ever kind and brilliant. 'You know you have a friend here', he wrote. She later reflected that even if she never worked again, it would be marvellous to end with Charlotta 'where it all began' and with 'Peter Hall – my hero'. She had got laughs where she never had them before. But this was to be her last production at the National.

Patience Collier as Mrs Poulteney in John Fowles' *The French Lieutenant's Woman* (United Artists, 1981) directed by Karel Reisz.

PART NINE

LEARN TO DISAPPEAR

FIFTY YEARS – IN CHARACTER THROUGHOUT

May 3rd, 1979, the day of the general election. Big swings were forecast against the Labour government after the so-called winter of discontent, but then only a miracle could dent the huge majority of the Colliers' local MP, the incumbent Conservative for Kensington and Chelsea. Patience Collier, who had always boasted that she used the Tories' cars to take her to the polls in order to vote Labour, now voted Liberal – perhaps as a mark of further independence from Harry; perhaps, like others, she felt frustrated by the succession of strikes and the particularly grim disputes at the National Theatre. She recorded Margaret Thatcher's victory in her diary the next day in the combination of red ink and capital letters reserved for occasions she recognised as historic: 'FIRST EUROPEAN WOMAN PRIME MINISTER!'

Harry had always said Patience was a closet Tory and as the new decade began, she seemed to be well on the way to coming out. When the Falklands War was declared in 1982, she watched the news in awe as the 'British Navy sail for BATTLE! to relieve the Falklanders'. The old Patience of her Belfast and Manchester days seemed to have long gone. Now she seemed to be shamelessly re-hashing many of the social mannerisms of her upbringing, yelling downstairs for the eighty-year-old Alice; friends always remember that prolonged screech.

But then her political and social outlook was always an enigma. She chose to play strong women, in plays with social themes, in publicly-funded and alternative theatre. She detested anti-Semitism, always identified with certain causes such as the anti-apartheid movement, and was delighted when her daughter-in-law Rohan became a Labour councillor. She was proud of Harry and Joe's work for public health. Yet she almost always chose private hospitals and clinics for herself: 'Experience of life in a TRUE POOR HOUSE atmosphere [but] with high-powered surgery, nursing and kindnesses,' she wrote of one of her few stays in an NHS hospital, the Middlesex. She was pleasantly surprised when the NHS general practice she registered with in her later years turned out to be well-set up and attentive.

She was a snob: 'Darling, he's awfully handsome, but I can't understand a word he's saying, his diction is appalling,' she would say to her teenage granddaughter Sophie about her boyfriend.[1] But then she could be bosom pals with anyone. She name-dropped even in her diary: 'ENORMOUS GLAMOROUS CROWDS,' she would note of the long-awaited opening of the Barbican by the Queen in 1982. Tony Snowden had kissed her – but then of course she knew half the guests. She had equally relished participating in the celebrations of twenty-five years of Theatre Workshop at Stratford. She was a huge fan of royal occasions and the BBC's orchestration of them, and would lap up the wedding of Charles and Diana: 'Lady Di is fairy-tale princess for all time. Brilliant clothes and colours and organisation everywhere... Alice and I had white wine and smoked salmon sandwiches in the kitchen,' she noted in her diary.

Patience had only one television role in 1979, a year of particularly poor health: a perfect cameo as the Duchesse de Sauveterre in Thames Television's *Love in a Cold Climate* with Michael Williams and Judi Dench ('delicious and very much dieted,' Patience noted). But in 1980 came the prize of Mrs Poulteney in Karel Reisz's film *The French Lieutenant's Woman*, and with it followed a succession of good television parts.

She began preparations in August for her part in the TV series *Sapphire and Steel* – as Emma Mullrine in 'Assignment 5' – while she was still working on the film. She had just finished the takes of Mrs Poulteney's grim interview of the mysterious Sarah Woodruff (Meryl Streep), when work began at Elstree on 'blocking' for *Sapphire and Steel*, and, on 22 August, she went from one studio to another. That night, she put away all her Poulteney things, feeling 'VERY SAD,' and threw herself into final preparations for the grand occasion of her seventieth birthday

Patience with Prunella Scales on Patience's 70th birthday at 23 Campden Hill Road.

party, to be held in the garden of No 23 on the 24th. Everyone from the theatre seemed to be there, noted Peter Barkworth: 'Already beginning to be frail, [Patience] sat in the centre of the lawn most of the time and people came to *her* – which was the way she liked it – to pay homage and give congratulations. She purred that day.'[2]

When rehearsals for *Sapphire and Steel* began a few days later, she found Joanna Lumley and David MacCallum – who starred as the mysterious agents of Time – 'both divine'. Director Shaun O'Riordan she also liked, but by the fourth studio day, she was feeling irritated by the 'muddle of camera and changes' and badly used, until he apologised, promising to retake two scenes. Joanna Lumley remembers Patience pointedly suggesting that she should have *her* dressing room as it was nearer to the set: she was having some difficulty walking and standing, and had a wheelchair that she used as a kind of base. Yet when the cameras rolled she seemed able to glide about with no problem in her long, black 1930s evening gown as a cool, concise Miss Emma.

So great was her focus on the detail of her character, and the need to maintain it, that she could be decidedly odd, Joanna Lumley recalls. They were rehearsing one scene which did not include Patience when there was a sudden call from off set:

Patience: 'What am *I* doing?'

O'Riordan: 'Patience, darling, you're not in this scene.'

Patience: 'I know! But what am I *doing*?

O'Riordan had to quickly invent an activity for her.[3] But when the five episodes were finally completed on 3 November, Patience had once again added to her vast layers of friends. Shaun O'Riordan came to dinner – a 'very lively evening' – and Joanna Lumley became a close friend, bringing armfuls of flowers to No 23, and invited to join the party down at Hawthorn. It was now, friends noted, '*Joanna Lumley* this, and *Joanna Lumley* that.' She would get 'obsessed with new younger actresses like Helen Mirren or Joanna Lumley', comments Robyn Karney[4]

Joanna Lumley at Hawthorn.

Sophie Herxheimer, who was in her teens, now became one of the growing team of line-hearers, as a part in Wendy Craig's TV series *Nanny f*ollowed *Sapphire and Steel,* together with the role of a sinister tailoress in *Strangled,* part of LWT's *Saturday Night Thriller* series. '[Sophie] is EXCELLENT at this job and *sympathique*!' Patience wrote in her diary. The adrenalin of work seemed to be spilling into her social life. Despite continual recurrences of her health problems, she was having fun: attending a 'gigantic GAY disco' before Christmas, enjoying New Year's Eve at John Schlesinger's. She saw Woody Allen's *Stardust Memories*, Sissy Spacek in *The Coalminer's Daughter* – 'Tommy Lee Jones the most attractive man I've come across in life after Paul Scofield' – and John Hurt in *The Elephant Man.*

The television role most to relish at this period was probably that of Mumsie in the highly successful family show *Metal Mickey* for LWT, recorded in September, 1981. The sitcom already had a raucous, resident grandma in Irene Handl, but in this episode the other, horribly bossy grandmother pays a visit, dreaded by the family and their pet robot, Mickey. The part required her to be co-ordinated in red, from copper wig to plush crimson dress; they found everything for Mumsie's outfit at John Lewis: 'Dress, slippers, pyjamas, etc.' To her own generous bosom was added a 'FALSE BUST!!' making her almost sofa-like. She arranged for her grandsons to join the studio audience: Daniel Collier remembered the extraordinary phenomenon of her continuing to play Mumsie with the robot, even off set.[5]

The French Lieutenant's Woman was now premiering in New York and London, and the reviews for the film were, on the whole, dazzling. There was some uncertainty among the critics about Harold Pinter's substitution of the modern, actors' tale for John Fowles's roaming historical and philosophical narration: 'show business within the movie', *The New York Times* called it. But much of this device, reviewers acknowledged, was fun. 'We see an actress of the stature of Patience Collier, who plays the ferociously stingy, self-righteous Mrs Poulteney... relaxing at a production-break party, chicly dressed' – this was in her Collier Campbell outfit – 'and puffing on a nicotine-packed cigarette.' The reviews of Patience's performance were almost uniformly excellent: Mrs Poulteney had come out 'HUGE', she noted when she first saw the final edits at the dubbing sessions in January. Patience Collier's Mrs Poulteney is 'magnificent', wrote *The Financial Times*.[6] But then, as Ruth Schachter says, Patience always did seem to be particularly good at horrible parts.

Patience seemed to rise on a Poulteney tide. It was a marvellous time, she later reflected. The writer Kathryn Hughes, a big fan of the film, recalls being particularly excited at catching a glimpse of her at Harvey Nicholls around this time. But Patience was in the process of furiously berating a salesgirl about something, and horrified, Kathryn beat off any idea of approaching her.[7]

For four years after the National's *The Cherry Orchard*, Patience undertook no stage work. Yet she enthusiastically embraced a rather special role as Queen Victoria at her grandson's junior school in Hammersmith to mark the school's centenary.

She took the part quite as seriously as any professional role, thoroughly alarming the teacher leading the arrangements. She summoned Kenny Lintott to supervise her Queen Victoria face and wig: 'I would dread the phone ringing – it might be several times in one day; I wasn't always in the mood,' he recalls.

Patience as Queen Victoria in a centenary enactment at her grandson Daniel's school (Brackenbury Primary, Hammersmith), 1979.

From Stephen Skatteson, cutter at the National, she borrowed the clothes; at Buckingham Palace mews, she practised getting in and out of the phaeton carriage in which she would travel, and on the day – tightly scheduled – was accompanied by a police escort and met by her well-rehearsed ladies in waiting. Everyone else at the occasion was giggly, in and out of role, remembers Daniel Collier. But she 'was in character throughout – never out of part. Teachers and pupils treated her as Queen Victoria, and everyone reacted in that way.'[8]

She took on another personal project soon afterwards. She had known Paul Alexander from when he was a child in Liverpool and acted as a kind of godmother to him. Now an experienced actor and writer, he was developing *Beau Brummel*, a one-man show, drawing on the letters of the regency dandy for a performance which required Brummel to wash, splash himself with cologne, dress 'from drawers to tailcoat' on stage in scene one, and to age twenty years in scenes two and three. He and Patience began discussing the script together in her bedroom while she was resting her legs, and before long, she was offering to direct him. She roped in Peter Rice to be their designer, got Ken Lintott to do the wigs and make-up, Anna to organise the music, and producer Tim Pitt Miller to lend them his Piccadilly flat for rehearsals.

She was an exacting and meticulous director, recording her frustrations in her diary, the work on cuts and editing, timing and clothes continuing up to the last minute: 'Paul's pronunciation not adequate. NO MUSIC HEARD.' But 'I worked very well with her,' recalls Paul. 'We had one humungous argument and I threatened to walk out, but she respected me for it.'[9] The show was a success at the 1982 Edinburgh Festival, *The Scotsman* admiring the evident 'partnership of truly professional theatrical craftsmanship,' and was well received at the Piccadilly Festival the following year, earning praise for Paul Alexander's 'easy, witty performance', Peter Rice's 'exquisite costumes', and for Patience's direction. [10]

When Peter Barkworth arrived at No 23 Campden Hill Road to interview Patience for his book, *More About Acting*, in March, 1983, he found himself squeezed in to her schedule a few hours before she readied herself for a major performance that night. She was playing the lead role in Michael Wilcox's new play, *Lent.*

Something about the success of *Beau Brummel* had lured her back into the theatre for what might now be, she knew, the last time. The play by promising writer Michael Wilcox, set in a boys' prep school in the 1950s, gave her scope and challenge as Mrs Blake, widow of the original head, who sees off the current head teacher and his wife and forges a sympathetic relationship with her lonely, adolescent grandson: much of the role would be played from a wheelchair. It was to be performed at the small, still new, Lyric Studio Theatre, and directed by Christopher Fettes, who had been building a reputation for his use of this 'lofty, stark little box of space with skill and breadth of conception.'[11]

Patience's work on the play had begun in January. She felt alternately confident and scared stiff: 'What have I taken on?' she wrote in her diary; could she cope with the learning? She had great difficulty in retaining the words, and assembled a longer list of line-hearers than usual. She stumbled through rehearsals, 'lost control' of her lines, experiencing dreadful fear, dopey sometimes from the codeine phosphate she was taking to steady her bowels, and finding the rehearsal period too short. This kind of 'scariness' she had not felt before.

Yet to all outward appearances she was tackling the role with her usual thoroughness, finding a way in to the part by talking to Wilcox about his memories of his grandmother, on whom her character was based. 'I had to get this sort of person, a mixture of softness and discipline, into me,' she told Barkworth. She summoned a navy blue and white foulard two-piece from Cosprops, finding the right shoes in her large shoe-bag 'stolen... from the RSC (but Peter Hall and Trevor Nunn knew about this)': white summer shoes, so tight she could 'wear them for hurt,' then the walk would be done.

When Rohan and her eldest son went to see the play, sitting in the front row, she seemed to speak her lines to her grandson. Reviews of the production were generally warm, for a play that would win Wilcox the 'Most Promising New Playwright' award that year. For her, the notices were particularly admiring. The play told a familiar story, Harold Hobson wrote in *The Times Literary Supplement*, but it created an amazing part for Patience Collier:

> [she] plays Mrs Blake as a charming, witty, flower-loving old lady of great charm, lethal, but with sound good sense and utter ruthlessness. It is no wonder that she is introduced to the strains of Handel's 'Arrival of the Queen of Sheba', for she is rich and mentally gorgeous.

Friends and press welcomed her back – it was her fiftieth year on the stage, *The Times* noted – and it had been at the old Lyric Theatre that she had had her first West End success. Though her dreadful nerves came and went throughout the short run, it was a very special performance from a now almost legendary actress. *Time Out*, loving the play's delicate exploration of adolescence and old age, sounded the note of prescience which her admirers might have been feeling: 'Patience Collier's clipped, strong, matronly superiority makes you rue the day when she will be "gathered in".'

LEGEND

Everyone seemed to be seeking Patience Collier's memories and reflections these days. She was interviewed about Erica Marx for the Radio 3 programme 'There was a Publisher...' and, with Anna, attended a performance of poets published by Erica's Hand and Flower Press at Kenwood in April, 1981. 'Lovely evening – ERICA THERE!' she wrote afterwards. Howard Goorney interviewed her for his book on Joan Littlewood and Theatre Workshop, and the BBC for her old friend Peter Barkworth's *This is Your Life*. She was reflecting much on the art of acting. She had found a new word to describe the essence of it, she told Barkworth when he in turn recorded her thoughts: 'pith:' 'An actor... should have inside them the pith of the part they are playing.'[1]

She and Audrey Postgate were also progressing work on the proposed book about her. Her talks with Audrey about what she now called the 'PATIENCE PAPERS' made her revisit her own early life and career, looking up old diaries: 'Strange and disturbing. Couldn't REMEMBER any of it.' With Gwyneth Lloyd, she chatted about their 'youthful times at Diana's house and when my father died'; she and Geoffrey – perhaps for the first time – talked about their father's death. It was sad and exhausting looking through old 'playbooks' and memorabilia from her times with Jeremy, with Barry (who had committed suicide in 1980) and with other lovers. But the book was beginning to take shape, she felt; she was recalling her different theatrical periods, directors she had known, her experience of the different media, in between thoughts about her sexuality, or anecdotes about Belfast. She was discussing titles with friends; would it be 'Anecdote', 'Reflections' or 'Recall?' On the whole she found the process was helping her to see things more clearly, to analyse the business of acting, and to make 'resolutions about my life.'

Patience was also renewing old friendships: with Harold Kaskett, Victor Spinetti, Kathleen Harrison ('now very old and deaf'), Strattie from Hoddesdon days, and Jeremy Spenser himself, 'very fat and burly...[but] lovely to be with.' John Gielgud would come to lunch from time to time; Paul Huntley, formerly of Wig Creations, was over on a visit from the US. When she got together with the Rices, 'we all told each other our life stories to date.' She was advising the Bielenbergs about plans for filming Christabel's book, *The Past is Myself*.[2] And she was watching the developing careers of her friends and colleagues – Alec McCowen, Timothy West, Glenda Jackson, Frances de la Tour, Paul Scofield, and also Trevor Nunn, whom she found to be 'very changed. Most strongly handsome and elegant: a personality like JET.' She was enthusiastic about the successes of the new generations – Helen Mirren, Zoë Wanamaker, John Hurt and Simon Callow, whose *Amadeus* with Scofield she found 'WONDERFUL.'

From time to time she took young actors under her wing. Helen Bourne was already an experienced actress in South Africa before she arrived in the UK in the 1970s, but as Robyn Karney's friend, she had to be introduced – no, interviewed – by Patience. 'She made me sit on a little chair opposite her,' Helen recalls. 'She would tell you where to sit... she paid me lots of compliments – [then] she said:

> Now duckie, Helen Bou-rne, that's a terrible name for an actress – I mean you don't know what it means. It could be 'Helen Burke' or 'Helen Bourke' or 'Burr'; you would be far better off being 'Helen Cigarette-end.' [By this point, Helen was smoking in total panic.] After all, ducky, you need to be remembered. The name needs to make an impression. Well, 'Helen Cigarette-end' will certainly make an impression. Nobody will forget your name. Whereas Helen Bourne – they'll say 'Bourne, Bourne? Who's that?

She followed her protégées' performances loyally. Helen recalls her coming to see *Duet for One* – a play loosely based on Jacqueline du Pré's story – at a matinée in Northampton in May, 1982:

> If Patience came to see you in a play, it was a major thing for all concerned. What only went on! She was a legend by then so anything to do with Patience arriving at a theatre – it was like the Queen Mother – everybody [would be saying] 'Oh my God!' Front of House had to be informed, the theatre manager, the director, people had to be lined up to meet her [at the station], someone to lead her to her seat…[3]

But Patience was also well-known for the frankness of her critique. 'She was very direct and had an honesty, a brutal honesty,' says Paul Alexander. '[She would say,] "Don't ask, if you don't want to know."' Joanna Lumley recalls arranging for her to come and see her in *Blithe Spirit* at the Vaudeville in January, 1986, when Patience was quite frail. Joanna organised tickets, sent her car, got someone to attend to her in the interval, arranged for her to be taken across the road to a restaurant after the show, then 'hurtled over' herself. But for about fifteen minutes, Patience didn't speak, she remembers: 'At last I asked her what she thought. After a moment she said, "I think the *maid* was all right… "'[4]

Yet equally Patience did not always convey to colleagues how highly she thought of their performances – or perhaps not till later, when she had had time to reflect and digest. At home after Blithe Spirit, she wrote in her diary, 'Joanna beautiful and very High Standard.' Her dearest friend Alec McCowen found himself similarly floored when, after his tour de force in St Mark's Gospel, she came into his dressing room and said only, 'Give me a chair. I feel battered to death.'[5] Yet the very next morning she wrote in her diary of his performance, 'Wonderful! extraordinary! mesmeric! unique!' in the green ink reserved for things of special note.

She was by now a grande dame of the theatre, enormously respected, and feared. As a member of the audience (it was always front row seats for her), she could be highly embarrassing, shifting in her seat and laughing loudly to make her presence known. 'Twelve sprouts will not be enough for six people!' she once shouted out in the midst of a kitchen scene: Alec McCowen, accompanying her, was mortified. But she was also a source of legends, adored by many. Daniel Collier, going to the theatre with her for a treat as a child, was impressed by how his grandmother was regarded: 'She would get seats straight away. We would go backstage and people would be falling over her like the parting of the Red Sea.' When they went to see the dancer Wayne Sleep, visiting him afterwards in his dressing room, Dan saw that he 'was obviously enamoured – all over her – yet it didn't show on her that he was so awestruck.'

But these theatre trips were now often gruelling for her. Robyn Karney recalls meeting her off the train after the Nottingham trip:

> It's the memory of this little figure... stocky and little and there she was, shuffling, her turban, her little sort of flat slipper shoes, little feet, getting off the train, summoning some porter who would come clattering along behind – that little figure...'[6]

RECEDING IN WAVES

PATIENCE GOT THE news about Harry on her return from a leisurely weekend with Anna in Kent, on Monday, 29 August, 1983. He had died that morning in the flat he shared with Paddy, quite suddenly in his study; after years of living with a serious cardiac condition, his heart had just given out.

It was an extraordinary situation. Patience was now a widow but so was Paddy Dewsbery, whom Harry named in correspondence with his solicitors as his common-law wife.[1] Patience and Harry had not lived in the same house for years, conducting mostly separate lives at No 23 for some time before that. But they had been married for forty-seven years, and Patience was still marking the date of their wedding anniversary – 9 September – each year in her new diary.

It had been a deeply quarrelsome marriage in which both had been serially unfaithful over decades. Behind Harry's kindly, quiet but witty manner, seen by Patience's friends, seems to have been a bitter disappointment that he had had to make compromises in his career in order to clear the way for hers.[2] He nursed, at times, a deep resentment of her. In a dark poem addressed to Gavin Ewart, he seemed to curse him for ever having introduced Patience to him, leading to his oppression under the 'tyrant's boot'. Yet even when they finally separated, there had been an underlying loyalty to each other, some mutual concern, deep enough for them never to have actually divorced, though they had often come near it. Harry had stayed around in Patience's life, not only at family dos, but seeing to things at Campden Hill Road: 'He had done everything,' Penelope Wilton reflects.[3] He and Paddy had come to see Patience's triumph in *Lent* back in March, and had 'raved' about the play.

Patience's closest friends understood the complexity of the situation and wrote sensitive, tactful but realistic condolence letters: 'Half of a practical partnership has gone, if nothing else', wrote Audrey Postgate, who had known them both from Hoddesdon days. 'You had been married a long time – however tenuous the links have become in marriage, they are, I believe, always there, invisible threads to happier years', wrote Patience's friend, the television producer, Rosemary Wilton.

There was now a strange period of 'utter misery'; 'nightmare days' of phone calls, discussions and arrangements, not helped by Anna's being 'strange, cross and critical of every Collier arrangement'. Patience and Alice travelled together to the funeral on 2 September: the splendid *Times* obituary had appeared only that morning. Harold Lever spoke, Beethoven and Schubert were played. Alec McCowen read Harry's favourite poems: from Gray's *Elegy Written in a Country Churchyard*, Shakespeare's Sonnet 116, 'Let me not to the marriage of true minds… ', a short, caustic anti-war poem by Harry himself, and the song from *Cymbeline*, 'Fear no more the heat o' the sun'. Afterwards, everyone gathered outside in the sunshine to talk and look at the flowers, and then re-assembled in Paddy's flat: 'Charming and colourful flat. Saw how Harry lived', recorded Patience afterwards. At home, she and Alice had sandwiches and decaf Nescafé and planned the weekend food for the family gatherings that would follow: 'I FELT NUMB', she wrote in her diary.

Patience was relying on friends to push her round special events in a wheelchair these days – the John Piper exhibition at the Tate, the David Hockney exhibition at the Hayward gallery. Despite this, she was still in the running for television work and, in January, 1984, her agent phoned about a job for Paul Annett in an episode of Granada TV's new *The Adventures of Sherlock Holmes.* The series starred Patience's close friend Jeremy Brett as Holmes, a part which would show off his talents brilliantly but also gradually consume him. Deep into filming the first episodes, he could be a dramatic and unexpected visitor: 'IN A CRAZY, HIGH STATE', she wrote on 14 January, when he came to dinner at No 23: 'VERY STRANGE!!!'

Patience was to play Miss Stoper, the manager of an agency for the supply of

Jeremy Brett, star of Granada TV's highly successful *The Adventures of Sherlock Holmes*, with Alice Lytton at 23 Campden Hill Road.

Patience's 'dear friend' Alec McCowen at the Mermaid Theatre, 1968.

governesses, in *The Copper Beeches,* the eighth in the series. The read-through and fittings began in February – 'am completely looked after' – with recording in Manchester a couple of weeks later. But the rail travel was now extremely challenging for her and filming was not easy, despite the delights of the set, a permanent Baker Street having been built round the corner from *Coronation Street*'s pub, the Rovers Return. She had to be sewn into her grey silk dress, and developed a migraine: even Jeremy Brett's wonderful hospitality she found over lavish. Yet the part she created, a diminutive, small-shouldered woman, made a perfect and precise contribution to the dark melodrama. 'Good!' she exclaimed when it was shown a few months later.

Patience was now working in almost reckless defiance of the deterioration in her health: she did not seem able to turn down good work, even if she had to crawl to it. Less than a week after her return from *Sherlock* taping in Manchester, she fell badly at the bottom of Campden Hill Road, and broke her hip. Yet she had barely arrived home from convalescing after surgery in late April when there was a call from BBC Scotland about a part in the television play *The House on Kirov Street.* She immediately began work on the script, assembling her line-hearers. Even when she dislocated her new hip and had to be hospitalised again, she could not resist the director's personal plea for her to continue: 'DECIDED TO WORK: AM I CRAZY?'

Tom Cotter's pursuit of her to play Chekhov's ageing sister, Maria Pavlovna, seemed worth suffering for. Set in Yalta in 1941 during the German occupation of Crimea, Maria guards the playwright's effects in his old house on Kirov Street, now full of German officers. But as Patience settled back home after convalescence at the end of May, the realities of what she had taken on were becoming clear. She was finding work on the script with Paul Alexander 'extremely tiring', and the first read-through and rehearsals were 'THE MOST UNCOMFORTABLE DAY OF MY LIFE'. Even having fittings at Cosprops was 'EXHAUSTING… I ached beyond the possibility of bearing.' But she got through it, increasingly pleased with the way she and Tom Cotter were working on her part: 'I begin to BE MARIA PAVLOVNA', she wrote in June.

That feeling of success made it easier to say yes to another television role, even as rehearsals and filming in Glasgow for *Kirov Street* were still in train: that of old Mrs Wardle, in BBC Television's *Pickwick Papers*. To be back in a classic Dickens serial felt particularly good, among a large cast, many of them old friends and colleagues – Clive Swift in particular from RSC days (playing Mr Tupman), Nigel Stock (Pickwick) and Fenella Fielding (Mrs Hunter). Her role as the selectively deaf and ear-trumpeted old lady, Mrs Wardle, was small but not unsatisfactory, her tiny frame dominated by a bustled dress, topped with an enormous mob cap; she managed even to dance. But at the end of filming, she had another fall, and a further spell in hospital. Back home, watching the serial as it began to roll in January, 1985, she was annoyed: '*Not* excellent…BAD photography.' But it was the critical eye of the professional, not a querying of whether it had been personally worthwhile.

It was Alice's health, not hers, which suddenly changed things. One moment in January, 1985, Patience and 84-year-old Alice were having supper together in front of the TV, with Alice feeling rather poorly with an infected foot, and in bed by nine. And the next, Alice's problem had become suspected gangrene and an ambulance had to be called.

There was snow on the ground as family and friends rallied to visit Alice – now confused and bewildered, with 'MORE GANGRENE' suspected – and to support Patience. Would Alice recover, and be herself again? The doctors seemed to think she might; there was talk of her managing on one level at No 23. But then came the shocking news of further gangrene, and on 27 January that she would have to have her leg amputated above the knee.

Alice Lytton became bright and cheerful remarkably quickly after the operation, but now wheelchair bound, it was clear that she would not be returning to Campden Hill Road: she needed her own looking-after. In April, she moved into a nursing home and, by May, Patience found her 'settled and happy with well-groomed hair' when she visited. She seemed to rally and enjoy a new kind of life away from No 23: 'Alice always lands on her *foot*,' Patience told friends, with a strange, black precision. She is 'well and brave and very well cared for', she wrote in her diary and when she visited, it was a pleasant, friendly, social time.

Patience at 23 Campden Hill Road.

Patience had contemplated a move from No 23 before. She and Alice had been rattling round in the large house; it was expensive to run, and with its steps up to the front door and many stairs, hardly suitable for either of them as they grew older. The family had been urging her to plan for the future and indeed, she had begun sketching her 'BASIC REQUIREMENTS for my NEXT and LAST HOME' back in 1983. She would need, she considered, a flat, bungalow or ground floor of a house, with one large and one small bedroom, and a 'flat for liver-inner'. Anna, she thought then, might live next door, in a smaller house, 'QUITE SEPARATE'. But all that had been speculative. Harry's death, financial considerations and her reduced mobility were all forcing her to review her position, and Alice's sudden retirement settled it.

At first things moved fast. Estate agents Roy Brooks – the firm whose wittily frank house advertisements and left-wing credentials had amused the London intelligentsia until Brooks's death in 1971 – valued the house at the very Kensington price of £345,000: prospective buyers started to arrive and had to be shown 'round MY HOME! All very RICH', she noted, with a Mrs S 'in Black Mink'. Susan and Sarah found a flat at No 51 The Chase in Clapham, where they both lived and worked, and 'in spite of MANY DIFFICULTIES', she was charmed by it. On 22 April, 1986, the deed seemed done – a price agreed for No 23 and for the purchase of the Chase.

But now plans and anxieties about the move began to take over her daily life. There was the emotional side of it all: 'despairing of leaving this District', she wrote on 18 May; and 'very depressed about HOUSE-FLAT situation' on 1 June. Things grew worse as the tenant of the top flat moved out: one moment the hall and stairs were filled with her belongings, then she had gone, leaving the place empty. But Patience took hold of herself, drawing in friends and family, and eventually employing a secretary to progress the vast operation. She made interminable lists, overseeing a detailed room-by-room schedule of everything in the house, and where it was to go. Family memorabilia turned up and had to be found a home, including a dozen of Paul Ritcher's stock exchange caricatures circa 1907, a picture of her and Geoffrey aged seven and five, and cousin Margot's portrait of her as a young woman. Geoffrey Ritcher carried off the portrait of their father that had hung in the Collier dining rooms at both Hoddesdon and Campden Hill Road, now 'swathed in candlewick counterpains' [sic]. There were sad and disturbing memories.

Through it all, Anna seemed often to react to her obsessions with irritation and fury: 'she wants no responsibilities towards me', Patience wrote in her diary on 21 July. 'My heart grew very heavy: my leg was VERY SORE.' When in August, she finally moved out of No 23 to begin a temporary stay in a Putney convalescent home while work on the Chase was completed, she felt 'FRIGHTENED AND DEPRESSED... ALL FUTURE PROSPECTS SEEMED HOPELESS.'

When Patience moved into the flat in January, 1986, after five months in the convalescent home and a host of horrors with the alterations – a collapsed ceiling, tiles falling off the wall, quarrels with Susan about a Habitat sofa in Collier Campbell fabric – she found it 'wonderful to be in my own home'. The Chase was bright and light in comparison with No 23, but of 'the same era', her daughter Sarah recalls: 'a bay window, high ceilings, a flat in a double-fronted house'. And the sitting room was like Campden Hill Road, running from front to back. Patience had her John Piper curtains, and her Ivon Hitchens had been hung: 'SUPERB.' Friends visited to inspect and admire: Alec 'mad about the flat', she wrote in her diary, Charlie Kay too. She settled down to organise things: 'I was the GENERAL. A GREAT DEAL WAS DONE.'

More challenging was the need to find a 'liver-inner'; the flat had a spare room for a housekeeper/helper with its own kitchenette and bathroom. It was the first time Patience had needed to recruit such help in thirty years. She began to advertise and interview, summarising applicants in quick pen portraits as though they were students in her Hoddesdon drama classes: 'Mrs B, clean, honest, capable and home loving'; 'Mr C, a fantasist... not right but longing to come to me'; 'Miss E... LAME DUCK! Needs domestic job. HOPEFUL. Has had illness... tragedie [sic]. WANTS to COME.' Some took fright before they even started, but for those that accepted the job, a pattern of events began to emerge. Patience would take them through her meticulous work plan; she would get to be interested in them; then they would start to reveal problems of their own.

For anyone becoming a 'liver-in' there would be the non-stop challenge of *her*, with her increasing physical complaints, difficult, exacting ways and unrealistic expectations of help in the 1980s. None of them stayed long, Sarah remembers, and Patience was forever phoning Universal Aunts for someone else.

Health problems and the dramas of her relationships with her current liver-in often dominated her diary, but her social life was still in good shape thanks to her small army of friends, her list of drivers who could be summoned, and the GLC's Dial-A-Ride service. The Alexanders were often around (Paul's wife, Robin, the photographer, regularly worked with Patience) and Jeremy Brett lived nearby, as did Miriam Margolyes whom Patience had got to know in recent years.

She was continuing to dine out, the stories of her latest extraordinary behaviour in inappropriate evening dress and feathers in her hair circulating among her friends the next day: she could be monstrous. She was, as always, to be seen at the latest films and theatre productions, including *Chorus Line, The Colour Purple, A Room with a View* and *A Prick Up Your Ears*. Rosemary Wilton had to 'DRAG ME UPSTAIRS' in the cinema, Patience noted, so that they could see *Mona Lisa*. Old theatre friends would call, come for a meal, greet her at previews and new productions; she would grace colleagues backstage yet relish the respect shown to her. She was needy now. Robin Alexander would take her shopping to Peter Jones where she would pick out her Christmas and birthday gifts for friends and family – always rather modest and often the same as last year, working through her lists. But she was now finding even this exhausting. Robin recalls being told to go out and get a taxi while Patience lay lounging 'majestically' on a double bed that was part of Peter Jones's ground-floor display, enjoying the amused stares of staff and customers.[4] Then there were the many family visits, even a revival of Sunday family lunch. She was rather basking in the prospect of Susan's second marriage to the writer Frank Delaney, and arranged to be taken to Sophie's first-year exhibition at Chelsea School of Art: Sarah Armstrong-Jones was a fellow student, Patience noted on more than one occasion in her diary. At her daughter Sarah's party to welcome in 1987, she felt surrounded by 'many people I had known throughout the MANY YEARS'.

But her relationship with Anna, who had her own health problems to endure,

Patience and Anna at Hawthorn, Summer 1982.

seemed to have almost reached breaking point. The pattern of irritation, recriminations and reconciliations had kept on building. There seemed to be 'non-stop embitterment', Patience noted just before her move, vowing to end the relationship, but then not.

On 3 February, 1987, they lunched together at the Trattoria Imperia on the Charing Cross Road, but it rapidly developed into a disaster. 'She was in a foul, cruel mood', Patience wrote in her diary, and there was a terrible public scene: 'I ended up at the entrance of the Garrick Theatre, calling her a "BITCH".' She knew she provoked Anna, who would be suddenly furious, apparently without reason: Anna would leave, crying that she had 'adamantly FINISHED WITH COMING HERE', yet then receive her again in Kent. Their relationship seemed to be receding in waves.

In December, 1986, she got a call from BBC Television. It had been over two years since Patience had had work: after *Pickwick*, there had been only a voice-over for Schweppes. Would she consider doing a week's spot on the *Five to Eleven* programme: five minutes of poetry, selected and read by her, to be broadcast each morning for a week. The director, Ralph Rolls, spent almost two hours with her discussing staging and the kinds of poems that went down well with the viewers, making her feel, she confessed to her diary, 'rather inadequate'. But in January came a further possibility: a small part in an adaptation of J. G. Farrell's *Troubles*, to be directed by Charles Sturridge for London Weekend Television. She went for the interview: the part she would play was that of the blind, elderly grandmother Mrs Rappaport in Farrell's black comedy about the last vestiges of British colonialism.

Settling to read the script at her desk, Patience marked out the bizarre Mrs Rappaport's appearance in a 'TINY, SHADOWY PART COMING INTO 18 scenes (own slippers, own specs, handbag to hang about shoulders)', calling it 'strange Anglo-Irish whimsy!' She had lost none of her organisational drive in all the hubbub about health and helpers. As February came on, she fixed the dates for make-up tests, made appointments with Cosprops and Wig Creations, while back and forth-ing with her agent, Joyce Edwards, who was negotiating the deal. She was to receive £9,500 for two episodes, and Robin Alexander would be employed by LWT to look after her during the production.

She went to the first read-through on 16 February, 1987, meeting the starry and mostly familiar cast, Michael Palin, Ian Richardson, Colin Blakely and Rachel Kempson among them. She had a 'special reclining chair' and sat among them 'almost incongruously', Palin noted in his diary of her rather frail but grand presence.[5] Filming of her scenes was set to begin a month later. But less than a week before *Troubles* was due to start, when Patience and Anna had had a particularly unpleasant set-to, Joyce Edwards rang. The news was extraordinary: a battle with the camera staff union had been lost by LWT and it was all cancelled, the whole project. 'HEART LIKE LEAD', Patience wrote in her diary.[6]

A month after the cancellation of *Troubles,* on 15 April, 1987, Patience was getting ready to be photographed by Robin Alexander for her entry in the trade directory of actors, *Spotlight.* Arrangements for *Five to Eleven* were progressing well. The director had come to discuss her clothes and set for the programme, she had chosen the poems, and they had fixed the date for recording, 23 June. But although the photography session seemed relatively easy and enjoyable from Robin's perspective, set as she preferred, in natural light, for Patience it seemed hard to get through. She fell asleep on and off all the time, she noted in her diary. She was feeling utterly exhausted, in and out of bed all day, 'more perpetually tired than I can BELIEVE! WHAT IS WRONG??' Amidst the high drama of her relationship with her current liver-in – 'drunk again' and a disappearance of cash – there had been readings at a friend's funeral, even visits to the theatre, but she was in 'too much pain to be out'. She began to explore the situation with friends and family: did she need to go into hospital or a convalescent home for a rest? She underwent a thorough medical examination.

On 6 June, she was admitted to the Churchill Clinic: her chronic condition of Raynaud's disease and a lifetime of smoking had caught up with her and she had gangrene in her toes. She seemed to be deteriorating fast: 'VERY GREAT SLEEPY PAINFUL MUDDLE', she wrote in her diary. Dazed with drugs, aware she was 'NOT EXACTLY 'WITH IT', she saw all the children during the day; there was a problem with her vein which had to be urgently dealt with at St Thomas' Hospital.

Back at the Churchill, she slept, losing track of the days. On 11 June, she recorded visits from the Alexanders and a late night visit from Joe, but this was the last entry she made herself in her diary. Others now pencilled in the various entries – her daughters, granddaughters, a nurse – and the fact that, in a horrible replay of Alice Lytton's problems, the surgeons had to amputate her leg.

Patience now had a constant stream of visitors, as the family tried to ensure she was not left alone. She was 'grand to the last', Joanna Lumley recalls. When Joanna arrived a few minutes early for her scheduled visit, Patience remained silent until 'at last she got out her massive swan's down powder puff, powdered her nose and said, "You were early."' Helen Bourne remembers her drifting in and out of consciousness: 'She was having horrible hallucinations – she was drugged, she sort of came in and out. I thought she knew it was me, and I was asked to puff that, bring my chair forward, but then these awful images she was having… horrible… ' Patience became delirious with pain and morphine, Rohan Collier recalls, and imagined Joe was her brother: 'It seemed like her way of dealing with the situation, to remove herself from it.' There was talk of the doctors having to amputate her other leg, and, now, she seemed to will herself to die, refusing all food and drink. Alec McCowen, visiting her just a few days before she died, told Sarah and Susan how he had held her hand for a little while: 'I wasn't sure if she knew me, but she smiled once.'[7]

Patience turned her face to the wall. She died on Monday, 13 July. Strangely, it was the very day on which her first *Five to Eleven* poetry reading for BBC Television had been scheduled to be broadcast.

Patience Collier (Rene Ritcher)
b. 19th August 1910, *d.* 13th July 1987

EPILOGUE

All London's theatrical world seemed to be present at Patience Collier's funeral on Monday, 20 July, 1987. The gathering at the South London crematorium read like a map of the profession, and of her acting career. Some friends and colleagues were too elderly and frail to attend; some, like Alec McCowen, could not bear to; some were otherwise engaged at rehearsals or fittings. Patience, always a stickler for professionalism, would have approved of their priorities.[1]

There were messages and condolences from family, old school friends, and from the hospital where she had died. There were huge bouquets, from theatre designers and directors, make-up artists, television producers and fellow actors. John Gielgud sent lavish white lilies: 'with my love and admiration and many happy memories'.

The ceremony opened with the haunting, sensuous strains of *Rhapsody in Blue*. There was no religion, no minister and no rabbi: instead Joe Collier introduced the tributes. Audrey Postgate led the eulogies with memories of Patience battering at the doors of Broadcasting House in the late 1940s, and transforming programmes with her ability to do half a dozen voices in the space of half an hour. Janet Suzman provoked laughter with her reading of David Copperfield's introduction to Mr Dick, recalling Patience's stellar television performance as Betsey Trotwood in 1974. She then switched moods dramatically with Edward Thomas's poem 'Lights Out': 'I have come to the borders of sleep,/The unfathomable deep/Forest where all must lose/Their way... ' Paul Scofield, his tweed jacket somehow providing a sense of reassurance to the family, chose the chorus from

T. S. Eliot's *The Family Reunion*, evoking his first performance with Patience back in 1956, under the direction of Peter Brook: 'We have suffered far more than a personal loss –/ We have lost our way in the dark.'

She would have roared at Peter Hall's opening lines, as he stood before what felt like a theatre audience: 'Is everyone sitting up straight? I see some of you are not wearing gloves. Patience would *not* have approved… ' They brought the relieved laughter of complete recognition. Patience herself would probably have wanted a touch more of the raucous – some Brendan Behan, perhaps, a sketch from a revue, a wicked trace of her ghostly part in *Fiddler on the Roof*, or even one of the limericks she was due to broadcast the very week of her death:

> *A famous theatrical actress*
> *Played best in the role of malefactress.*
> *Yet her home-life was pure,*
> *Except, to be sure,*
> *A scandal or two just for practice.*

She had been a brilliant actor, the obituaries agreed, with a 'chameleon-like quality' that enabled her to change appearance completely, building each character with total concentration and integrity, avoiding the easy tricks of the trade.[2] Her late-blooming career had spanned five decades of performance, and all four mediums: theatre, radio, television and film. She had been at the right place at the right time – for the most innovative and popular days of wireless, the height of the commercial West End, the success of Joan Littlewood, the rolling out of the Royal Shakespeare Company, then the National Theatre under Peter Hall; for the best times of television drama, the hits of British film studios. She was, they said, a complete perfectionist. The private and changing faces of Patience – her childhood and youth, friendships, marriage, family relationships, lovers, her political weavings, her quarrels, sorrows, braveries and failures – those aspects could only be hinted at, in Audrey's reference to Patience's exotic yet bleak childhood, or as recalled by her brother, Geoffrey, whose bouquet card – 'with pride and deep affection' –

Actress Grandmother

by Sophie Herxheimer

Each word heavy like her well defined amber coloured eyes
which blink slowly, and her rope of amber, hanging like a mayors
chain of office over her imposing breast in its sage cashmere
cardigan, whose drape in turn rests above a Jaeger skirt with swish.

Everything is impeccably laundered, scented, pronounced.
Do you smoke yet, Darling? Index finger holding open her
Gauloises' in my alarmed twelve year old face, as she sits before
the dramatic floor to ceiling fall of those John Piper curtains.

Later I take my rakish council flat boyfriend round
to supper there. Staring at him, she addresses me:
*Darling, he's awfully handsome, but I can't understand
a word he's saying, his diction is appalling.*

Her table, polished mahogany with lions' feet, silk lampshades
on ceramic bases (look like Ming to me, still give me shudders,
send me scuttling to Ikea) The stiffness of the unplayed piano.
Black coffee in embossed white china, a mise-en-scene.

Once egged on by an innocent friend we just call by on her
on the way back from school (as if she is a normal granny.)
She takes a while to come to the door, is furious. *Darling!
You didn't phone.* I've never seen her without her wig before.

We thought she'd like to see our Biba bargains, but no.
When she visits me in dreams it's dressed as a humble thirties
housewife in a faded floral pinny. She acts sweet, bambi lashes
down: *Darling,* she entreats, *remember me nicely. Don't be harsh.*

was addressed to the sister he still remembered as Rene. Patience had led many existences – the debutante, the leftist, the working mother, the grande dame – sequentially but also side by side, sometimes blending the professional and personal, often carefully separating them as though they belonged to different people. Each person at the funeral had their own remembrances and stories, some knew of secrets, and had the strongest of relationships with her, but no one there quite knew it all. 'I couldn't imagine anyone being truly intimate with her,' reflects Helen Taylor Robinson. 'Her acting was a release – but was it also a protective mask?'

The obituaries and tributes made no secret of her latter-day reputation for autocratic behaviour and outspokenness: her 'most salutary candour,' as Vernon Dobtcheff put it kindly.[3] Friends would be summoned to come to dinner with no excuses; we were her 'courtiers and sometimes her lackeys,' wrote Robyn Karney in her obituary in *The Independent*.[4] Dressing rooms would be altered to her requirements, lovers flaunted. She could be cruel, contrary, arbitrary, outrageous, hugely egocentric, a monster. She had been a Patience Collier who had ditched her persona as Rene Ritcher long ago, only to readopt, adapt and develop it, becoming nearly larger than life. She evokes uncomfortable memories even to this day. Over twenty-five years after her death, her granddaughter Sophie Herxheimer would write of her appearing in dreams, as if a humble thirties housewife 'in a faded floral pinny': 'Darling, she entreats, remember me nicely. Don't be harsh.'

Yet Patience had also been warmly loyal in friendship, and *funny*: 'Her turn of phrase could transform an account of a bus ride into the funniest story,' wrote Robyn Karney. Something about her inspired reciprocal loyalty and engagement. She 'beguiled us all with her autocratic ways,' an old school friend recalled. While many years after her death, some would still be remembering the Patience stories with distaste and recoil, by far the strongest feelings would be of exhilaration, laughter, affection, and love: 'She was a tyrant – but people adored her,' says Paul Alexander.[5] 'I loved Patience dearly,' wrote Peter Brook. 'I wouldn't think anyone could forget her, but I actually miss her – it's funny – actually *actively* miss her,' says Charles Kay. Her granddaughter Charlotte Herxheimer reflects on this strange contradiction: 'I think if people are naughty, [other] people love that someone else is prepared to be naughty; then they don't have to be, and can just enjoy it.'

'She was the one and only Paish,' Audrey Postgate said, concluding her funeral eulogy, 'outrageously demanding, outrageously funny.' Paul Scofield brought the ceremony to its closing stages with Prospero's epilogue from *The Tempest*. With it, the play bows out, gently breaking the ties between audience and actors: 'release me from my bands.' Emotions swelled again with *Jerusalem*; the curtains closed round her coffin. Yes, Patience might have said, as she had noted of Noël Coward's funeral back in 1973: 'Marvellous "SHOW"!'

NOTES

Abbreviations:
AP: Audrey Postgate
PC: Patience Collier
RR: Rene Ritcher
HJC/H: Harry Collier

PROLOGUE

1. Quotations from Peter Barkworth's interviews with Patience Collier in *More About Acting*, 1984.
2. Nigel Andrews, *Financial Times*, 16.10.81.

PART ONE THE ACTRESS, THE MARXIST AND CHURCHILL'S DAUGHTER

Chapter 1. The Actress

1. Audrey Postgate notes, PC archive. Henceforth referred to as AP Notes.
2. Sarah Churchill, *Keep on Dancing: An Autobiography*, ed. Paul Medlicott, 1981, p.17; Sonia Purnell, *First Lady: The Life and Wars of Clementine Churchill*, 2015, p.184.
3. RADA Diaries, 1930–1932, RADA Library.
4. *Daily Telegraph* and *RADA News*.
5. Rene attended the Villa St Monique, run by Mlle Emilie Manilève. The school was enlightened, the students well taught, and introduced to French culture. Vivien Hartley – Vivien Leigh to be – was a contemporary of RR's there as well as at RADA. Interview with Pauline Summerscale, 7.11.2014.
6. AP Notes.
7. Ibid.
8. Clementine Churchill to Winston, 12.2.1931, in *Speaking for Themselves: The Personal Letters of Winston and Clementine Churchill*, ed. Mary Soames, 1998.
9. RR's Student's Report, spring, 1932: PC archive.
10. PC recollections in AP Notes, together with Patience's much later written account of the trip, undated but perhaps 1980.
11. Maurice Browne to RR, 9.3.1934: PC archive
12. RR Diary, February, 1935; Mary Soames, *A Daughter's Tale: The memoir of Winston and Clementine Churchill's youngest child*, 2011, p.99.
13. Collin Brooks, 21.2.1935: from *Fleet Street, Press Barons and Politics: the Journals of Collin Brooks, 1932–1940*, ed. NJ Crowson, 1999; Churchill to Clementine, 23.2.1935, 2.3.1935, and 8.3.1935, *Speaking for Themselves*, op. cit.
14. Margaret Lewis to RR, 28.5.1935, PC archive.
15. Harry to RR, undated but late December, 1935.

Chapter 2. The Marxist

1. HJC's 'Spring Song', *The Silver Crescent*, Michaelmas term, 1933.
2. AP Notes.
3. Harry to RR, undated but late December, 1935.
4. Harry to RR, undated but probably January, 1936.
5. H to RR, 5.1.1936, and 24.2.1936.
6. H to RR, undated, late April, 1936.
7. RR Diary, 1.5.1936.
8. See Miranda Carter, *Anthony Blunt: His Lives*, 2001, p. 150. Harry's friends Hugh Sykes Davies and Roland Penrose were

on the English organising committee for the exhibition, while Gavin Ewart contributed to the special surrealist edition of *Contemporary Poetry* for June, 1936 which accompanied the exhibition. Ian McMillan, 'An Explosion of Geraniums: he International Surrealist Exhibition of 1936', Radio 3, 19.6.2016.

9. Willie Gallagher, Clydeside CP leader, visiting Cambridge 1934, quoted by James Klugmann in his Introduction to Jon Clark et al, *Culture and Crisis in Britain in the Thirties*, 1979.
10. Mrs Collier to RR, 3.6.1936.
11. RR to Mrs Collier, 17.6.36; Mrs C to RR, written 17.6.36 but posted 20.6.36.
12. RR to H, undated but *c.*20/21.6.36.
13. RR to H, 24.6.36.
14. *Times*, 26.6.36. Dr Bliss's trial was fully reported in *The Times*, around the country and in the *British Medical Journal.* She was found guilty of offences under the 1929 Infant Life Preservation Act and sentenced to three years' penal servitude, her nurse to twelve months' imprisonment. The case was something of a *cause célèbre* and caused considerable anxiety among medics: it was unusual for medical doctors to be prosecuted. A Metropolitan Police memorandum suggests that it was brought in the light of feminist agitation for abortion law reform and moves within the BMA itself to change the law: these were spurred on by the Bliss case. The recommendations of the Birkett Committee set up by Government following this and another landmark case involving a rape victim were shelved on the onset of war in 1939: see Barbara Brookes, *Abortion in England, 1900–1967*, 2014.
15. H to RR, 30.6.1936 and H to Mrs Collier, undated but probably also 30.6.1936.
16. One of a number of versions of 'Magna' and 'Parva Carta' – promises for R to keep – written out by both.
17. RR to H, 14.7.36.

Chapter 3. Becoming Patience

1. H to Mrs C, op. cit.; see Ch.2 note 11.
2. RR to H, 18.7.1936.
3. Ibid. For Festival Theatre, see Norman Marshall, *The Other Theatre*, 1947, and Billy J. Harbin, 'Terence Gray and the Cambridge Festival Theatre' 1926–33', *Educational Theatre Journal*, Vol. 21, no. 4 (Dec 1969), pp.392–402.
4. RR to H, 21/22.7.1936.
5. H to RR, 22 and 23.7.1936.
6. RR to H, 22.7.1936.

PART TWO COMRADES

Chapter 4. The Left

1. Quote from Brian Barton, *The Blitz: Belfast in the War Years*, 1989, p.2, which traces the city's staggering incidence of unemployment, poor housing and ill health. There had been sectarian disturbances through the summer of 1935.
2. Professor Flynn was – the Colliers must have wryly noted – the father of Errol Flynn, who was fast gaining success in Hollywood.
3. AP Notes.
4. John Hewitt Society and Northern Ireland Literary Archive websites.
5. Sir John Orr, pioneering nutritionist. His *Food, Health and Income*, 1936, showed that at least one third of the UK population could not afford a healthy diet.
6. AP Notes.
7. Barton cites, for example, two church studies of Belfast poverty conducted in 1937.
8. *Manchester Guardian*, 1936–1938; see also Michael Wolf, 'Bye Bye Blackshirt...' for *Searchlight* and Z. Yaakov Wise, 'Fascism

in Manchester' on Centre for Jewish Studies website, University of Manchester.

9. AP Notes.
10. *Broadcasting a Life: the autobiography of Olive Shapley*, 1996, pp.38–39.
11. PC quoted in Howard Goorney, *The Theatre Workshop Story*, 1981, p.18.
12. *Manchester Guardian*, 20.11.1937, *Manchester Evening News*, 25.2.1939.
13. One thing they had in common was something they may never have known about each other, the experience of abortion. Joan's termination, in contrast to Patience's, had been a back street affair like that of their mutual friend, Olive Shapley: see Peter Rankin, *Joan Littlewood, Dreams and Realities: The Official Biography*, 2014. Olive Shapley, op. cit., pp. 39–40.
14. Joan Littlewood, *Joan's Book*, 1994, p.68.
15. Goorney, op. cit.
16. Anne Dyson, quoted in Goorney, op. cit., p.19.
17. *Manchester Guardian* 13.5.1939

Chapter 5. War

1. AP Notes.
2. In Paris, Erica – Patience's old school friend – had operated 'The Press of the Hotel Sagonne' from 1938 to 1940: see 'Introduction' to Erica Marx Papers, Archives of the University of Washington Libraries. Information on Bice Summerscale, née Wilson, from interview with David and Pauline Summerscale, 1.11.2014.
3. Ben Harker, 'Mediating the 1930s: Documentary and Politics in Theatre Union's Last Edition (1940)', 2009, at univ.salford.ac.uk. Harold Lever found Littlewood and Miller a defence barrister but they were still barred by the BBC: see Peter Rankin, *Joan Littlewood*, op. cit.
4. Correspondence between PC and BBC, August-September, 1940, PC's personal file, BBC Sound Archives.
5. AP Notes; interview with Joe Collier and Sarah Campbell, November, 2012.
6. Garrick and Royal Court theatre programmes, 1942.
7. *Guardian* obituary for Harry Collier 2.9.1983; AP Notes.
8. Letters to John Burton to PC, April, 1943 to July, 1945, PC archive. Forty years later, he wrote up his experiences as a POW in *Mirador: my term as Hitler's guest*, 1986.
9. Burton to PC, 5.6.1945; see also Christabel Bielenberg, *The Past is Myself*, 1968. As we know from that memoir, Peter Bielenberg's escape from execution was almost certainly due to her stance during Gestapo interrogation and her ability to exploit Nazi assumptions about her British newspaper magnate connections.

PART THREE **VOICES IN THE AIR**

Chapter 6. Radio Time

1. Script of 'Voices in the Air', BBC Written Archives.
2. Listeners' letters re the *Jane Eyre* serial: PC's personal file, BBC Written Archives.
3. AP Notes.
4. Interview with Charles Kay, 11.2.2015; Asa Briggs, *Sound and Vision*, Vol. IV of *The History Broadcasting in the UK*, 1952; Val Gielgud, *British Radio Drama, 1922–1956: A Survey*, 1957; Jocelyn Tobin, 'My Memories of BBC Radio Drama, 1951–1957', www.suttonelms.org.uk/jocelyn-tobin.html; Olive Shapley, op. cit.
5. Postcard, 29.1.51, BBC personal file, op. cit.
6. Note written on PC's letter dated 14.11.48, personal file, BBC.
7. BBC recording of 'Jennifer's Journeys',

21.5.1950, BBC Sound Archives; PC Diary, May, 1950; Hilary Field, 'All Right on the Night', *Radio Times*, 9.9.49.

8. 'Lucy Must Be Blue', broadcast 26.9.1950, BBC Written Archives.
9. AP Notes.
11. PC's Evening Institute Notebook.
12. PC's Townswomen's Guild Notebook.
13. Interviews with Joe Collier 7.11.2012, Sarah Campbell 16.2.2014 and 16.2.2015, Sally Coles Freeman 12.1.2013 and Sophie Herxheimer 13.7.2014.

Chapter 7. New Elizabethans

1. Joanna Scott-Moncrieff, Foreword, *The Book of Woman's Hour: the words behind the voices* (London, 1953); also Kristin Skoog, 'Focus on the Housewife: the BBC and the Post-War Woman, 1945–1955', *Networking Knowledge, Journal of the MeCCSA Postgraduate Network*, Vol. 2, no. 1, 2009.
2. Script of 'My Best Holiday', BBC Written Archives.
3. Letter from Harry to solicitor, 14.5.1951 and PC Diary, January, 1951.
4. In her autobiography, Sarah Churchill wrote of the impact of sedation and repeated ECT – then often applied without muscle relaxants or anaesthetic – on her sister: 'The bright life has been rather successfully dimmed for her by various doctors' experiments.' Writing to her mother in 1955, as Diana's serious depression and aggressive treatments continued, she said, 'She has a feeling of having been greatly wronged. This is not specific, it does not relate to any one person, or even any special time in her life; but this feeling persists, accompanied by a feeling of unfulfillment and lack of recognition.' Quoted in *Keep on Dancing*, ed. Paul Medlicott, 1981, p.206.
5. Patricia Noble on Tennent's: interview with Kate Harris, Theatre Archive Project, British Library; Dominic Shellard, '1950–1954: was it a Cultural Wasteland?' in Shellard, ed., *British Theatre in the 1950s*, 2000.
6. AP Notes plus PC Diary; *Radio Times*, 25.2.1955; Profile of PC, *Theatre World*, September, 1958.
7. Quoted in Sheridan Morley, *The Authorised Biography of John Gielgud*, 2001, p.231.
8. According to Gielgud's biographer, Sheridan Morley, after the story of Gielgud's court appearance featured on the front page of the *Evening Standard*, Thorndike broke the tense atmosphere at rehearsals of N. C. Hunt's *A Day by the Sea*, with her cheerful and affectionate greeting, 'Well, John, what a very silly bugger you have been!' She arranged for hate mail to be redirected to her, and virtually compelled the Liverpool first-night audience to give him a standing ovation. (Morley, op. cit., pp.247 and 249.)
9. *Cherry Orchard* play script for the production, with amendments by Gielgud, Add. MSS, British Library.
10. Recollections, AP Notes; Gielgud's play script, op. cit; interview with Sarah Campbell, 17.2.2014.
11. AP Notes.
12. *Daily Telegraph*, London Letter, 27 May, 1954.
13. Ivor Brown in the *Observer*, 23.5.1954 and Alan Dent in the *News Chronicle*, 22.5.1954.
14. Harold Hobson, *Sunday Times*, 23 May, 1954.
15. 24 May and 26 June respectively.

PART FOUR WITH THE FIRM

Chapter 8. Three Angels

1. *Times* and *Evening Herald*, Dublin, both 25.9.1956.
2. Dominic Shellard, '1950–1954: was it a

Cultural Wasteland?' in Shellard, ed., *British Theatre in the 1950s*, 2000.

3. Tynan in Foreword to *Persona Grata, 1953, quoted in Shellard, op. cit.*

Chapter 9. Nuders

1. Letter to his mother quoted in Sheridan Morley, *John G: The Authorised Biography of John Gielgud*, 2001, p.277; to Lilian Gish, *The Letters of Noël Coward*, ed. Barry Day, 2007, p.620; to NC, ibid., p.624.
2. NC to Lesley Leonard Cole, p.621, *Letters of Noël Coward*, ed. Barry Day, 2007.
3. AP Notes; NC *Letters*, p.624; PC Diary, 30.9.1956.
4. *Times*, 25.9.1956 and *Evening Herald*, Dublin, same date.
5. *Manchester Guardian*, 9.1.1956.
6. NC to Joyce Carey, *Letters of NC*, op. cit., p. 624.Coward later wrote to Patience from New York after the play's opening there where the critics' response was similar: 'But just as in London, they pack the theatre to the roof every night and then raise it to boot, so who cares about the silly old critics?' 21.11.1957, PC archive.
7. JG to NC, *Letters of NC*, p.625.
8. *Observer*, 11.11.56. Tynan was requoting Cyril Connolly.
9. AP Notes.
10. *FT* and *Evening News* 8.6.1956, *Plays and Players*, August 1956.
11. *Observer*, 11.11.1956

Chapter 10. Television Sets

1. *The Suffragette* was produced only months after a radio programme by Jill Tweedie called *The Women's Rebellion* had outraged veteran suffragettes, particularly Annie Kenney, with its alleged bias towards the Pankhursts. The BBC had been forced to apologise and promised another production to make amends. Both Jessie and Annie Kenney were closely consulted on the script for *The Suffragette* and sent detailed amendments. See Kenney Papers, University of East Anglia Archive, and production file for *The Suffragette*, BBC Written Archives.
2. PC's 'Notes on Acting', a talk to drama students at Bede College, Durham University, March, 1971; see also Kate Dunn, *Do Not Adjust Your Set*, 2003.
3. Barry replaced Val Gielgud, who now returned to radio.
4. ITC was directed by Lew Grade. When a rival bid by Associated Development Broadcasting Company fell apart, the two companies merged to form Associated Television (ATV), with Littler as Board chairman: Laurence Marcus, 'The Armchair Theatre Effect', http://www.televisionheaven.co.uk/armchair_theatre_effect; also Lez Cooke, *British TV Drama: A History*, 2003.
5. Interview with Paul Huntley, 6.3.2014.
6. Interview with Charles Kay, 28.2.2013.
7. *Evening Standard*; *Observer*, 11.11.1956; Charles Kay, op. cit.
8. NC to PC, 15.6.1959, PC archive.

PART FIVE THE WOMAN IN THE BLACK BERET

Chapter 11. Campden Hill Road

1. Interview with Joe Collier and Sarah Campbell, 7.11.2012.
2. Interview with Sarah Campbell; interview with Robin Karney and Helen Bourne 18.5.2013.
3. Interview with Robin Karney, op. cit.
4. Memo, 17.12.59: PC's Personal File, BBC Written Archives.
5. George Rose, undated letter, ref 'Summing Up: 1959' (see Tynan's *Curtains*, 1961).
6. Joan Littlewood, *Joan's Book*, 1994, p. 538.

7. Brenda Ferris, memories of Theatre Workshop, 23.1.2018.
8. *Joan's Book*, op. cit., p.572.
9. PC to family, 2.9.1960.

Chapter 12. Off Piste

1. PC to family, 2.9.1960; AP Notes.
2. AP Notes.
3. PC quoted in Howard Goorney, *The Theatre Workshop Story*, 1981, p.156; letter home 13.9.1960.
4. PC letter home, undated but probably 22/23.9.1960.
5. All reviews, 21.9.1960; PC letter home, 2.10.1960.
6. PC letters home, 13.9. 1960 and 18.10.1960.
7. *New York Times*, 21.9.1960.
8. Ulick O'Connor, *Brendan Behan*, 1970; Black Swan edition, pp.208–209.
9. Bill Slocum, *Journal American*, quoted in O'Connor, op. cit.
10. PC letters home, 2.9.1960 and 13.9.1960.
11. AP Notes and interview with Pat and Peter Rice, 12.3.2013.
12. PC letter home, 30.10.1960.
13. Letters home.
14. Letters home, 9.10.1960, 18.10.1960 and 6.11.1960, and interview with Vernon Dobtcheff, 16.2.2015.
15. Letter home, 2.10.1960.
16. Letters home 2.10.1960 and 27.12.1960.
17. Letter home 6.12.1960.
18. 'Peter Hall's first Stratford Season', originally written for *Go* magazine, and reproduced in the RSC's souvenir programme for 1960, which accompanied a special comedy season. The programme's illustrators included Felix Topolski and Ronald Searle, and Anthony Armstrong-Jones was among the photographers.

PART SIX **O SWEET MR SHAKESPEARE!**

Chapter 13. Rivalry

1. Interview with Paul Greenhalgh, 10.9.2013.
2. Interview with Peter Rice, 12.3.2013; AP Notes.
3. 'W.T.' in *Guardian*, 19.7.1962 and J. C. Trewin, *Illustrated London News*, 28.7.1962 respectively.
4. *Guardian*, 20.12.1962 and the *New Daily*, 27.12.1962 respectively.
5. Ken Tynan's review reprinted in *A View of the English Stage, 1944–1963* (London, 1975); Peter Brook in conversation with Peter Roberts, *Plays and Players*, December, 1962.
6. Peter Brook, *The Empty Stage* (London, 1968), p.118.
7. Interview with Ken Lintott, 12.8.2014.
8. AP Notes.
9. Interview with Susan Engel, 1.8.2014.
10. Interview with Alec McCowen, 17.10.2013; AP Notes.
11. Interview with Paul Greenhalgh, op. cit.
12. Brook, *Plays and Players*, op. cit.
13. Robert Kee, *Queen*, January, 1963; *Guardian* obituary of Worth, 12.3.2002.
14. 16.12.1962; PC undated.
15. Sally Beauman, *The RSC: A History of Ten Decades* (Oxford, 1982); Ken Tynan, *Observer* review, 1962 reprinted in *A View of the English Stage, 1944–1963*, op. cit.
16. Greenhalgh, op. cit.

Chapter 14. Death and Scandal

1. Interviews with Sarah Campbell 16.2.2014 and Rohan Collier 12.2.2015.

2. Richard Davenport-Hines, *An English Affair: Sex, Class and Power in the Age of Profumo*, 2013; David Profumo, *Bringing the House Down: A Family Memoir*, 2006.
3. *Shields Gazette*, 22.7.1963.
4. *Times, 25.10.1963.*

Chapter 15. A Company It Is

1. Interviews with Alec McCowen, 17.10.2013 and Charles Kay, 28.2.2013.
2. Interview with Paul Greenhalgh, op. cit.
3. Alec McCowen interview, op. cit.
4 Interviews with Timothy West, 28.2.2013, Ruth Schachter, 10.9.2013, Robyn Karney, and Helen Bourne, 18.5.2013.
5. Interview with Vernon Dobtcheff, 25.3.2013.
6. Interview with Auriol Stevens, 'Guardian Women', *Guardian*, March, 1969.
7. Interviews, op. cit.
8. Peter Hall, *Shakespeare's Advice to the Players*, 2003.
9. Interviews with Alec McCowen, op. cit., Ken Lintott 13.8.2014, Reg Samuel, 2.10.2014. PC Recollections, AP Notes.
10. Interviews with Robyn Karney and Helen Bourne, Ken Lintott, op. cit.
11. Scrapbooks for *Richard II, Henry IV Parts 1 & 2*, and *Henry V*, PC archive; Hugh Griffiths 16.4.1964; Peter Hall 15.4.1964 – others undated.
12. *Leamington Spa Courier*, 24.4.64, *Queen* 17.6.64, *Tatler*, 6.5.64 and *Theatre World*, May, 1964.
13. Note from Peter Hall to PC, op. cit.
14. AP Notes.
15. AP Notes; Alec McCowen interview, op. cit.
16. Catering Committee papers, PC archive.
17. Paul Greenhalgh interview, op. cit.
18. Charles Kay interview, 28.2.2013.

Chapter 16. What's It All About, Slawomir?

1. Erna Hannan's own account of her life, 1971; letter to PC July, 1964; both PC archive.
2. Letters from John Bury to Harry and Patience, 16 January, 1963.
3. Interviews with Ken Lintott, op. cit, and Timothy West, op. cit, respectively.
4. 12.2.65, 5.2.65, 12.2.65 and 5.2.65 respectively.
5. *Evening News*, 5.2.65, *Stratford up Avon Herald*, op. cit; John Krish to PC, 28.2.65.
6. PC Diary, interview with Alec McCowen, op. cit.
7. BBC memo from Patrick Garland, 15.4.1965, BBC Written Archives.
8. Interview with Rosemary Beattie, 5.1.2015.
9. J.C. Trewin, *Illustrated London News*, 31.7.1965.
10. Alan Brien in the *Sunday Telegraph*.
11. 26.5.1966; PC Diary, May, 1966.
12. Montague Haltrecht, *Queen*, 18.8.1966.
13. Charles Causley's memories of Erica in *The Author*, Autumn, 1985. Causley's first collection was published as one of Erica Marx's *Poems in Pamphlet* series.
14. Interview with Sarah Campbell, op. cit.

PART SEVEN **JUST WAITING TO PLAY BARBRA STREISAND'S MOTHER...**

Chapter 17. It's *Ritcher*, Not Ritscher

1. Interview with Charlotte Herxheimer, 10.5.2013.
2. *The Times*, 9.3.1934; AP Notes.
3. AP Notes.
4. *Guardian*, March, 1969.
5. AP Notes.

6. According to Patience, it was actually Eva's brother Samuel – 'so good at reading Shakespeare' – for whom the little theatre was made: see Recollections.

7. Albums of Eva and Paul Ritscher's wedding, with its innumerable cuttings, primarily from the Jewish press: PC archive.

8. Louis Spitzel naturalisation papers, National Archives; obituaries in *Jewish Chronicle* and *Jewish World*, 7.9.1906; census 1881, 1891, 1901; *Fielding Star*, 19.1.1907 and *Advertiser*, Adelaide, 9.11.1907.

9. Elkan Levy, 'The New West End Synagogue, 1879–2004', 11.7.2004, www.newwestend.org.uk.

10. Louis Spitzel's will; *The Times* 28.3.1907, 6.4.1907 and 10.5.1908; (Melbourne) *Evening Post*, 16.1.1908; Census, 1911.

11. See: *Argus*, Melbourne, 29.4.1890, *South Australian Register*, 15.5.1890, *London Gazette*, 30.5.1890, *Times* 20.3.1899 and 7.6.1901; Old Bailey Proceedings, Central Criminal Court, 14.9.1891; also *The Correspondence of G. E. Morrison, 1895–1912*, 1976; Paul French, *Through the Looking Glass: China's foreign correspondents from opium wars to Mao*, 2009; Cyril Pearl, *Morrison of Peking*, 1967; Stanley Spector, *Li Hung-chang and the Huai Army: a study in nineteenth-century regionalism*, 1964.

12. *Jewish World*, 4.9.1906.

13. AP notes.

14. AP notes.

15. AP notes. For Arthur Davis, see Interviews with Ann Davis Thomas, 29.11.2004 and 1.11.05, University of Nebraska; Oxford DNB; Sir Charles Reilly, *Representative British Architects of the Present Day*, 1931.

16. Paul Ritscher's naturalisation papers, National Archives; List of Members of the Stock Exchange, Guildhall Library. Also Elizabeth Hennessy, *Coffee House to Cyber Market: 200 Years of the London Stock Exchange*, 2001; Alan Jenkins, *The Stock Exchange Story*, 1973, Ronald Michie, *The London Stock Exchange: A History*, 1999, and Larry Neal and Lance Davis, 'Why the London Stock Exchange dominated the first age of globalization, 1901–1914', CEPR Conference, Vienna, 2005.

17. Panikos Panayi, 'Anti-German Riots in London during the First World War', *German History*, 1989, vol.7, no.2, pp.184–203.

18. Annual lists of members of the Stock Exchange, op.cit. However, Paul was required to cite his previous identity in listings throughout the war. See also Ronald Michie, op. cit.

19. PC Recollections; Dictionary of Scottish Architects. Dr Rivers' most famous patient at Craiglockhart was, of course, Siegfried Sassoon.

Chapter 18. Eva

1. AP notes.

2. AP notes and Ruth Howard, condolence letter to family, July, 1987.

3. Sometimes spelt 'Cavalle'.

4. Interviews with Sarah Campbell, op. cit. Eva's book was first published in 1950, and went through a number of editions. She was as adept at self-promotion as her daughter, obtaining reviews and features in all the best papers and magazines, including *Vanity Fair*, *Vogue*, *Tatler* and *Good Housekeeping*, and frequent press coverage: cuttings in PC archive.

Chapter 19. Good Mothers Are Hard to Play

1. Arthur Miller, *Time Bends: a life*, 1987, pp. 228 and 182.

2. Nicholas de Jongh, *Guardian*, 28.9.1971. The staging of the play coincided with publication of Gerald Clifford Weales' biography of Odets, which Patience ordered from New York (Diary).

3. Frank Marcus, *Sunday Telegraph*, 3.10.1971; *Daily Mail*, 28.9.1971.

4. Marcus, op.cit.
5. Simon Callow, *My Life in Pieces: an alternative autobiography*, 2010, p.147; Diana Rigg, *Independent*, 21.6.1993.
6. Interview with Susan Engel, 1.8.2014.

PART EIGHT A PERSON WITHOUT LIMITS

Chapter 20. Moving On

1. *Manchester Evening News*, 16.2.1945; Grove's *Dictionary of Music and Musicians*, 1980; Glyndebourne website, accessed November, 2013; Charles Kay interview, op. cit.
2. Interviews with Rohan Collier and Sarah Campbell respectively, 10.12.2013 and 17.2.2014.

Chapter 21. Costume Dramas

1. Notes for lecture to drama students, Bede College, Durham University, 18.3.71, PC archive.
2. Interview with Vernon Dobtcheff, 2.3.2013.
3. For example, as autocratic French grandmother in John Guillerman's *The House of Cards* (1967) or in Ned Sherrin's *Every Home Should Have One (*1969), starring Marty Feldman and Shelly Berman, where she caught critics' attention as the pink-rinsed au pair agent.
4. The company included Jeremy Brett, Vernon Dobtcheff, Mia Farrow, Penelope Keith, Nicola Pagett, Joan Plowright, Norman Rodway and Gwen Watford. *Bernarda Alba* was the third in their first season, under the direction of Robin Phillips; Jeremy Spenser acted as Assistant to the Director.
5. Telephone interview with Penelope Keith, 1.9.2014.
6. *Financial Times*, 23.2.1973.
7. Telephone interview with John Gorrie, 8.7.2013.
8. *Daily Telegraph*, 16.12.1974.
9. *RT*, *28.11.1974*.

Chapter 22. Dressing Room Rituals

1. *Norwich Mercury* and *Eastern Evening News*, 9.5.1975.
2. PC from Hall, 24.2.1975.
3. Interviews with Rohan Collier and Sarah Campbell respectively: 10.12.2013 and 17.2.2014.
4. Telephone interview with Zoë Wanamaker, 17.1.2013.
5. Interviews with Charlotte and Sophie Herxheimer, 10.5.2013 and 29.4.2013 respectively. Poem by Sophie Herxheimer, 'Actress Grandmother'.

Chapter 23. Who Pays?

1. When the series was finally aired in the UK following release in the US, Patience found it 'hot-makingly badly directed'. Diary, 27.6.1978.
2. Michael Blakemore, *Stage Blood: Five tempestuous years in the early life of the National Theatre*, 2013, p. 271.
3. Telephone interview with Christopher Morahan, 15.7.2014.
4. Interview with Helen Taylor Robinson, 11.2.2014.
5. Interview with Helen Bourne, 16.5.2013.
6. *Tatler* and *The Times* respectively, cuttings undated.
7. The Riverside Studios production was directed by Peter Gill, with Charlotta played by Eleanor Bron. Patience, seeing it on 3 February, thought it 'brilliant and inspired'.
8. Entry for 29.9.1978; *Peter Hall's Diaries: The Story of a Dramatic Battle*, ed. John Goodwin, 1983, p.378.
9. Hall to PC, 21.11.1975.
10. *Tatler*, April, 1978 and *Morning Star*, 16.2.1978.

PART NINE LEARN TO DISAPPEAR

Chapter 24. Fifty Years – In Character Throughout

1. From Sophie Herxheimer's poem, 'Actress Grandmother'.
2. Barkworth's condolence letter on Patience's death, 19.7.1987.
3. Telephone interview with Joanna Lumley, 28.0.2012.
4. Interview with Robyn Karney, 10.5.2013.
5. Telephone interview with Daniel Collier, 28.12.2012.
6. *NYT*, 18.9.1981 and *FT* 16.10.1981.
7. Kathryn Hughes, 17.2.2013.
8. Interviews with Ken Lintott, 12.8.2014 and Daniel Collier, 28.12.2012; PC Diary.
9. Telephone interview with Paul Alexander, 30.8.2014.
10. *Scotsman*, 15.8.1982; *FT* and *Times*, 27.2.1983.
11. *Times*, 26.2.1983.

Chapter 25. Legend

1. Peter Barkworth, *More About Acting*, 1984.
2. The dramatisation was eventually broadcast in 1988 as the drama series *Christabel*, starring Elizabeth Hurley and Stephen Dillane.
3. Interview with Helen Bourne, 10.5.2013.
4. Interview with Joanna Lumley, op. cit.
5. Interview with Alec McCowen, 13.2.2013.
6. Interview with Robyn Karney, op. cit.

Chapter 26. Receding In Waves

1. Paddy was named as Harry's 'devoted companion, Paddy Dewsbery Collier' in *The Times* death announcement, 31 August, 1983.
2. In fact, as Harry's obituaries show, his career was prestigious, but it was in industry rather than academia, which he would have preferred – until the very end of his career when he became an honorary Professor of London University at Chelsea College, and set up a research unit on drug dependence. Harry was particularly known and respected for his work on aspirin, prostaglandins and drug dependence: *Times* obituary, 2.9.1983.
3. Telephone interview with Penelope Wilton, 12.3.2013.
4. Telephone interview with Robin Alexander (professional name Robin Hart) 26.10.2014.
5. Michael Palin, *Halfway to Hollywood: Diaries 1980–1988*, 2009, p. 468.
6. *Troubles* was eventually re-started later that year under Christopher Morahan's direction, and televised in 1988.
7. Condolence letter on PC's death, 14.7.1987.

Epilogue

1. Interview with Pat and Peter Rice, 19.1.12; family papers ref. death and funeral, including order of ceremony, condolence letters, cards and obituaries.
2. *Telegraph*, 16.7.1987.
3. Condolence letter, 20.7.1987.
4. Condolence letter, 17.7.1987.
5. Interview with Paul Alexander, op. cit.

BIBLIOGRAPHY

Archives, collections and documents

This book draws primarily on the large personal archive of Patience Collier, in the ownership of the Collier/Campbell family, together with the notes and papers of Audrey Postgate about Patience, lent by the Postgate family.

In addition:

BBC Written Archives
BBC Sound Archive
British Film Institute
British Library: Gielgud papers and Theatre archive project
Cambridge University Library
Guildhall Library
King's College, Cambridge
National Archives
National Theatre archive
RADA Library
Royal Shakespeare Company archive at the Shakespeare Centre, Stratford-upon-Avon
University of East Anglia archive: Kenney papers.
Wills and probate, birth, marriage and death certificates

BMD, burial records, census, criminal registers, local directories, electoral registers, land tax valuation rolls, parliamentary debates, phone books, passenger lists, service records, accessed on line, through genealogical and other websites.

Interviews

Conducted in person and by phone or email with:

Pat Albeck, Paul Alexander, Robin Alexander, Rosemary Beattie, Helen Bourne, Peter Brook, Sarah Campbell, Sally Coles, Daniel Collier, Joe Collier, Rohan Collier, Paola Dionisotti, Vernon Dobtcheff, Susan Engel, Brenda Ferris, Annie Firbank, John Gorrie, Paul Greenhalgh, Charlotte Herxheimer, Sophie Herxheimer, Kathryn Hughes, Paul Huntley, Robyn Karney, Charles Kay, Penelope Keith, Kenny Lintott, Joanna Lumley, Alec McCowen, Christopher Morahan, Caroline Morgan, Debbie Postgate, Peter Rice, Reg Samuel, Ruth Schachter, David Summerscale, Pauline Summerscale, Helen Taylor-Robinson, Louise Walker, Zoë Wanamaker, Timothy West, Penelope Wilton.

Newspapers and periodicals

The Patience Collier archive includes a very extensive collection of newspaper cuttings for all the productions in which she appeared, issues with which she was involved, obituaries etc., together with Spitzel and Ritcher family cuttings albums. Newspapers accessed in addition for the project include particularly:

- *Jewish Chronicle*
- *London Gazette*
- *Manchester Guardian*
- *Times*
- – and, for Louis Spitzel, the Australian press of 1890–1910.

Books and articles

Barker, Clive and Gale, Maggie B., eds., *British Theatre between the Wars, 1918–1939* (Cambridge, 2000).

Barkworth, Peter, *About Acting* (London, 1980).
—*More About Acting* (London, 1984).

Barnes, Kenneth, *Welcome, Good Friends: the autobiography of Kenneth Barnes*, ed. Phyllis Hartnell (London, 1958).

Barton, Brian, *The Blitz: Belfast in the war years* (Belfast, 1989).

Bassett, Kate, *In Two Minds: a biography of Jonathan Miller* (London, 2012).

Beauman, Sally, *The Royal Shakespeare Company: a history of ten decades* (Oxford, 1982).

Behan, Brendan, *Confessions of an Irish Rebel* (London, 1965).

Behan, Rosemary, 'New York: In Brendan Behan's Footsteps', *Telegraph*, 20.4.2011.

Best, Geoffrey, *Churchill: a study in greatness* (London, 2001).

Bielenberg, Christabel, *The Past is Myself* (London, 1968).

Bignell, Jonathan and Stephen Lacey, eds., *British Television Drama: past, present and future* (London, 2000).

Billington, Michael, *State of the Nation: British Theatre since 1945* (London, 2007).

Black, Gary, *Living Up West: Jewish life in London's West End* (London, 1994).

Blakemore, Michael, *Stage Blood: five tempestuous years in the early life of the National Theatre* (London, 2013).

Brandreth, Giles, *John Gielgud: an actor's life* (London, 1984).

Branson, Noreen, *History of the Communist Party of Great Britain, 1927–1941* (London, 1985).

Branson, Noreen and Heinemann, Margot, *Britain in the Nineteen Thirties* (London, 1971).

Braun, Edward, *The Theatre of Meyerhold: revolution on the modern stage* (London, 1979).

Bridson, D. G., *Prospero and Ariel: the rise and fall of radio: a personal recollection* (London, 1971).

Briggs, Asa, *The History of Broadcasting in the UK*, Vol. IV, *Sound and Vision* and Vol. V, *Competition* (Oxford, 1995).

Brittain, Vera, *Testament of Youth*, (London, 1933).

Brook, Peter, *The Empty Stage* (London, 1968).

Brookes, Barbara, *Abortion in England, 1900–1967* (London, 1988).

Brown, Andrew, *JD Bernal: the sage of science* (Oxford, 2005).

Browne, Maurice, *Too Late to Lament: an autobiography* (London, 1955).

Bunie, Andrew, Paul Robeson, *The Years of Promise and Achievement* (Massachusetts, 2001).

Burton, John, *Mirador: my term as Hitler's guest* (London, 1986).

Caird, John, *Theatre Craft: a director's practical companion from A to Z* (London, 2010).

Callow, Simon, *My Life in Pieces: an alternative autobiography* (London, 2010).

Carter, Miranda, *Anthony Blunt: his lives* (London, 2001).

Caughie, John, 'Before the Golden Age: Early Television Drama,' in *Popular Television in Britain, studies in cultural history*, ed. John Corner (1991).

Churchill, Sarah, *Keep on Dancing: an autobiography*, ed. Paul Medlicott (London, 1981).

Clark, Jon, Heinemann, Margot, et al, eds., *Culture and Crisis in Britain in the Thirties* (London, 1979).

Clark, Michael, *Albion and Jerusalem: the Anglo-Jewish community in the post-emancipation era* (Oxford, 2009).

Coleman, Terry, *Olivier: the authorised biography* (London, 2005).

Collins, Rose, *Coral Browne: 'this effing lady'* (London, 2007).

Comer, John, ed., *Popular Television in Britain* (London, 1991).

Coren, Michael, *Theatre Royal: 100 years of Stratford East* (London, 1984).

Cornwell, Paul, 'American Drama at the Cambridge Festival Theatre, 1928–1935', in *The Eugene O'Neill Review*, Vol. 27, 2005.

— *Only by Failure: the many faces of the*

impossible life of Terence Gray (Cromer, 2004).

Cooke, Lez, *British Television Drama: a history* (London, 2003).

Coulton, Barbara, *Louis MacNeice in the BBC* (London, 1980).

Croall, Jonathan, *Gielgud: a theatrical life* (London, 2000).

Crowson, N. J., ed., *Fleet Street, Press Barons and Politics: the journals of Collin Brooks, 1932–1940* (London, 1999).

Davenport-Hynes, Richard, *An English Affair: sex, class and power in the age of Profumo* (London, 2013).

Davis, Angela, 'Belonging and Unbelonging: Jewish Refugee and Survivor Women in 1950s Britain', *Women's History Review*, 2.1.17; 26 (1):130–146.

Day, Barry, ed., *The Letters of Noël Coward* (London, 2007).

Deacon, Richard, *The Cambridge Apostles: a history of Cambridge University's elite intellectual secret society* (New York, 1985).

Denning, Tom, *Lord Denning's Report*, London, 1963.

Duff, Charles, *The Lost Summer: the heyday of the West End theatre* (London, 1995).

Dunn, Kate, *Do Not Adjust Your Set* (London, 2003).

Elsom, John and Tomalin, Nicholas, *The History of the National Theatre* (London, 1978).

Falk, Quentin, *Mr Hitchcock* (London, 2007).

Fay, Stephen, *Power Play: the life and times of Peter Hall* (London, 1995).

Fiddick, Peter, 'Vision of Tomorrow', *RADA: The Magazine*, no.7, Autumn, 1996.

Giddings, Robert and Selby, Keith, *The Classic Serial on Television and Radio* (London, 2002).

Gielgud, John, *An Actor and His Time, 1904–2000* (London, 1979).

Gielgud, Val, *British Radio Drama, 1922–1956: a survey* (London, 1957).

Gilbert, Martin, *Winston Churchill: the wilderness years* (London, 1981).

Goldsmith, Maurice, *A Life of J. D. Bernal* (London, 1980).

Goodwin, John, ed., *Peter Hall's Diaries: the story of a dramatic battle* (London, 1983).

Goorney, Howard, *The Theatre Workshop Story* (London, 1981).

Grevatt, Wallace, *BBC Children's Hour: a celebration of those magical years* (Lewes, 1988).

Hall, Peter, *Making an Exhibition of Myself: the autobiography of Peter Hall* (London, 1993).

— *Shakespeare's Advice to the Players* (London, 2003).

Harbin, Billy J., 'Terence Gray and the Cambridge Festival Theatre, 1926–33', *Educational Theatre Journal*, Vol. 21, no. 4 (Dec 1969), pp.392–402.

Hardwick, Joan, *Clementine Churchill: the private life of a public person* (London, 1997).

Harker, Ben, 'Mediating the 1930s: Documentary and Politics in Theatre Union's Last Edition, 1940', in A. Forsyth and C. Megson, eds., *Get Real: documentary theatre past and present* (London, 2009).

Hennessy, Elizabeth, *Coffee House to Cyber Market: 200 years of the London Stock Exchange* (London, 2001).

Hobsbawm, Eric, *Interesting Times: a twentieth century life* (London, 2002).

Holdsworth, Nadine, *Joan Littlewood* (London, 2006).

Holmes, Kenneth C., 'The life of a sage', *Nature*, 440, pp.144–150, 9.3.2006.

Howarth, TEB, *Cambridge Between Two Wars* (London, 1978).

Hylton, Stuart, *A History of Manchester* (Manchester, 2003).

Ingram, Kevin, *Rebel: the short life of Esmond Romilly* (London, 1985).

Irwin, Mary, 'What Women Want on TV: Doreen Stephens and BBC TV Programmes for Women, 1953–64', www.westminster.ac.uk.

Jacobs, Jason, *The Intimate Screen: early British television drama* (Oxford, 2000).

Jenkins, Alan, *The Stock Exchange Story* (London, 1973).

Jenkins, Roy, *Churchill* (London, 2001).

Kadish, Sharman, *Jewish Heritage in England: an architectural guide* (London, 2006).

Karlin, Miriam, *Some Sort of a Life* (London, 2007).

Komisarjevsky, Theodore, *Myself and the Theatre* (London, 1927).

Kustow, Michael, *Peter Brook: a biography* (2005).

Landy, Marcia, *British Genres: cinema and society, 1930–1960* (Princeton, 1991).

Lichtenstein, Rachel, *Diamond Street: the hidden world of Hatton Garden* (London, 2012).

Littlewood, Joan, *Joan's Book: the autobiography of Joan Littlewood* (London, 2003).

Lo, Hui-Min, *The Correspondence of G. E. Morrison, 1895–1912*, 2 vols. (Cambridge, 1976 and 1978).

Lownie, Andrew, *Stalin's Englishman: the lives of Guy Burgess* (London, 2015).

McCluskey, Megan, 'Interviews with Ann Davis Thomas', University of Nebraska, at digitalcommons.unl.edu

MacColl, Ewan, 'Theatre of Action, Manchester', in Raphael Samuel, Ewan MacColl and Stuart Cosgrove, *Theatres of the Left, 1880–1935: workers' theatre movements in Britain and America* (London, 1985).
— 'Theatre Union', Working Class Movement Library, 2009, accessed at www.wcml.org.uk.
— 'Theatre Workshop', ibid.

McMillan, Ian, 'An Explosion of Geraniums: the International Surrealist Exhibition of 1936', BBC Radio 3, 19.6.2016.

Mander, Raymond and Mitchenson, Joe, *Theatrical Companion to Coward: a pictorial record of the Theatrical Works of Noël Coward* (London, 1957, 2nd edition, London, 2000).

Mangan, Richard, ed., *Gielgud's Letters* (London, 2004).

Marcus, Laurence, 'The American Theatre Effect', www.televisionheaven.co.uk/armchairtheatre.

Marshall, Norman, *The Other Theatre*, (London, 1947).

Melvin, Murray, *The Art of the Theatre Workshop* (London, 2006).

Michie, Ronald, *The London Stock Exchange: a history*, (London, 1999).

Mikhail, E. H., ed., *The Letters of Brendan Behan* (London, 1992).

Miller, Arthur, *Time Bends: a life* (London, 1987).

Miller, John, *Judi Dench: With a Crack in Her Voice: the biography* (London, 1998).

Mitford, Jessica, *Hons and Rebels* (London, 1961).

Mirren, Helen, *In the Frame: my life in words and pictures* (London, 2007).

Moran, Joe, *Armchair Nation: an intimate history of Britain in front of the TV* (London, 2013).

Morley, Sheridan, *The Authorised Biography of John Gielgud* (London, 2001).

Nathan, David, *John Hurt: an actor's progress* (London, 1986).

Neal, Larry and Davis, Lance, Why the London

Stock Exchange dominated the first age of globalism, 1801–1914, 'Past, Present and Policy', CEPR Conference, Vienna, 2005.

Neavill, Gordon B., 'Victor Gollancz and the Left Book Club', *Library Quarterly*, 1971, 41(3), pp.97–215.

O'Connor, *A Life of Peggy Ashcroft: the secret woman* (London, 1997).

O'Connor, Ulick, *Brendan Behan* (London, 1970).

Olivier, Laurence, *Confessions of an Actor* (London, 1982).

Palin, Michael, *Halfway to Hollywood: diaries, 1980–1988* (London, 2009).

Panayi, Panikos, 'Anti-German Riots in London during the First World War', *German History* (1989), Vol. 7, no. 2, pp.184–203.

Pearson, John, *The Private Lives of Winston Churchill* (London, 1991).

Penrose, Barrie and Freeman, Simon, *Conspiracy of Silence: the secret life of Anthony Blunt* (London, 1986).

Priestley, *Theatre Outlook* (London, 1947).

Profumo, David, *Bringing the House Down: a family memoir* (London, 2006).

Purnell, Sonia, *First Lady: the life and wars of Clementine Churchill* (London, 2015).

Purvis, Stewart and Hulbert, Jeff, *Guy Burgess: the spy who knew everyone* (London, 2016).

Rankin, Peter, *Joan Littlewood: Dreams and Realities: the official biography* (London, 2014).

Rebellato, Dan, *1956 and All That: the making of modern British drama* (London, 1999).

Richards, Jeffrey and Aldgate, Anthony, *Best of British: cinema and society 1930–1970* (London, 1983).

Ritcher, Eva, *The A.B.C. of Millinery* (London, 1950).

Roberts, Peter, ed., *The Best of Plays and Players* (London, 1988).

Romilly, Giles and Esmond, *Out of Bounds* (London, 1933).

Scott-Moncrieff, Joanna, *The Book of Woman's Hour: the words behind the voices* (London, 1953).

Shapley, Olive, *Broadcasting a Life: the autobiography of Olive Shapley* (London, 1996).

Shellard, Dominic, ed., *British Theatre in the 1950s* (Sheffield, 2000).

Shisler, Rev. Geoffrey L., 'The Life of the Rev Simeon Singer', lecture at NWE synagogue, 28.3.2004, available at www.newwestend.org.uk.

Shubik, Irene, *Play for Today: the evolution of television drama* (Manchester, 1975).

Sinclair, Andrew, *Arts and Culture: the history of the 50 years of the Arts Council of Great Britain* (London, 1995).

Skoog, Kristin, 'Focus on the Housewife: The BBC and the Post-War Woman, 1945–1955', in *Networking Knowledge, Journal of the MeCCSA Postgraduate Network*, Vol. 2, no. 1, 2009.

Soames, Mary, *A Daughter's Tale: the memoir of Winston and Clementine Churchill's youngest child* (London, 2011).

Soames, Mary, ed., *Speaking for Themselves: the personal letters of Winston and Clementine Churchill* (London, 1998).

Spenser, David, 'Radio Memories', at www.suttonelms.org.uk.

Swann, Brenda and Aprahamian, Francis, *J. D. Bernal: a life in science and politics* (London, 1999).

Taylor, D. J., *Bright Young People: the rise and fall of a generation, 1918–1940* (London, 2007).

Tobin, Jocelyne, 'My Memories of BC Radio Drama, 1951–1957', at www.suttonelms.org.uk.

Toynbee, Philip, *Friends Apart: a memoir of*

Esmond Romilly and Jasper Ridley in the thirties (London, 1954).

Tynan, Kathleen, *The Life of Kenneth Tynan* (London, 1987).

Tynan, Kenneth, *Curtains: Selections from the Drama Criticism and Related Writings* (London, 1961).

— *A View of the English Stage, 1944–1963* (London, 1975).

Wesker, Arnold, *The Birth of Shylock and the Death of Zero Mostel* (London, 1997).

— 'What is it to be Jewish?', *Jewish Chronicle*, 10.5.12.

Wilcher, Robert, *Understanding Arnold Wesker* (Columbia, SC, 1991).

Williams, Bill, *'Jews and other Foreigners': Manchester and the rescue of the victims of European fascism, 1933–40* (Manchester, 2011).

Wolf, Michael, 'Bye Bye Blackshirt: Oswald Mosley defeated at Belle Vue', *Searchlight*, 7.1.2010.

Worley, Matthew, *Labour's Grass Roots: essays on the activities and experience of local Labour parties and members, 1918–1945* (London, 2005).

Yaakov Wise, Z., 'Fascism in Manchester', Centre for Jewish Studies, University of Manchester, www.manchesterjewishstudies.org.

Zarhy-Levo, Yael, *The Making of Theatrical Reputations: studies from the modern London theatre* (Iowa, 2008).

Reference

Barnes, Philip, *A Companion to Post-War British Theatre* (London, 1996).

Dictionary of Literary Biography (online).

Dictionary of Ulster Biography (online).

Hartnoll, Phyllis and Found, Peter, eds., *Concise Oxford Companion to the Theatre*, 2nd ed., (Oxford, 1996 and online, 2012).

Herbert, Ian, ed., *Who's Who in the Theatre: a biographical record of the contemporary stage*, 16th edition London, 1978.

Kennedy, Dennis, ed., *Oxford Encyclopaedia of Theatre and Performance* (Oxford, 2005 and online).

Oxford Dictionary of National Biography (online).

PICTURE CREDITS

Note: many of the illustrations are from Patience Collier's personal archive and are included by kind permission of her family.

2 Portrait of Patience Collier by Frank Freeman, c.1950; dress fabric by Pamela Freeman. Reproduced by kind permission of Sally Coles **9** Page from one of Patience's diaries. Photo by Alastair Campbell **14** Audrey Postgate at the BBC, reproduced with kind permission of the Postgate family **16** Items from Patience's archive. Photo by Alastair Campbell **18** Rene Ritcher *c.*1932 by Walter Bird **21** Diana Churchill *c.*1930 ©Mme Yevonde/Mary Evans Picture Library **22** Vivien Leigh, nee Hartley, Photo Repro Co 1929 **36** Paul's gambling chips. Photo by Sarah Campbell **38** Rene's sketch of Anthony Quayle for Louis Golding's *Magnolia Street*, directed by Komisarjevsky, 1934 **40** Rene in *Roulette*, 1935, with photographer Walter Bird **47** Sage Bernal, 1933, Ramsay and Muspratt, © Peter Lofts Photography/ National Portrait Gallery, London **52** Poster for International Surrealist Exhibition, 1936, by Max Ernst, Sherwin Collection, Leeds, UK/Bridgeman Images; ©ADAGP, Paris, and DACS, London, 2019 **61** Portrait of Rene by Margot Lewis **63** Rene Ritcher by Jack Teller, 1935/6. **64** Rene, 1936, by Ramsay & Muspratt, Cambridge **70** USER diagrams, 1937, *Ulster Medical Journal*, 1 April 1937, by kind permission of the Ulster Medical Society **73** Olive Shapley interviewing: BBC Photo Library **75** Joan Littlewood, in Theatre Union's production of *Fuente Ovejuna (The Sheepwell), 1939*, by kind permission of Theatre Royal Stratford East Archives collection **90** Patience, *c.*1950, at the BBC: BBC Photo Library **97** David Davis, 1950: BBC Photo Library **98** BBC Broadcasting House: Tony Baggett/Adobe Stock **110** (top) Patience as Charlotta in *The Cherry Orchard,* Tennent Productions Ltd, 1954. © Houston Rogers/ Victoria and Albert Museum, London **112** (bottom) John Gielgud's version of *The Cherry Orchard* gifted to Patience with inscription. Photo by Alastair Campbell **117** Rene and her father at first night of *Cavalcade*, 1931, Associated Press **118** Binkie Beaumont, Angela Baddeley and Emyln Williams by Angus McBean ©Harvard Theatre Collection, Houghton Library, Harvard University **120** Patience Collier with Ronald Shiner in *My Three Angels*, 1955, by Angus McBean ©Harvard Theatre Collection, Houghton Library, Harvard University **125** (top) Patience with John Gielgud in Coward's *Nude with Violin*, 1956/7, by Angus McBean © Harvard Theatre Collection, Houghton Library, Harvard University **125** (bottom) Cigarette case and Balkan Sobranie photo by Alastair Campbell **128** Patience as Maria in *The Power and the Glory*, 1956, directed by Peter Brook, photographed by John Brown, London **140** Patience in New York, 1960. Publicity shot for Theatre Workshop's New York production of *The Hostage*, directed by Joan Littlewood **142** From *Tatler* cartoon of Patience in *Living for Pleasure*, 1959 **144** Susan Collier's family Christmas card, 1958 **146** Jeremy Spenser, still from *The Roman Spring of Mrs Stone*, directed Jose Quintero, 1961: Coral Browne Collection/Collection Christophel/ArenaPAL **149** Patience Collier with Dora Bryan in Living for Pleasure, 1958/9: Angus McBean © Harvard Theatre Collection, Houghton Library, Harvard University **152** Joan Littlewood, 1963 © Daniel Farson/National Portrait Gallery, London **155** Patience as Miss Gilchrist with Aubrey Morris (Mr Mulleady) and Avis Bunnage (Meg). in The Hostage, 1960. Photo by Friedmann-Abeles, © The New York Public Library for Performing Arts **158** Brendan Behan by Sam Shaw **166** Patience by Christian Woodgate,

1960 **171** Irene Worth as Goneril and Patience as Regan in Peter Brook's *Lear*, RSC, 1962. Photo by Angus McBean, © Royal Shakespeare Company **174** Patience with Jean-Louis Barrault, Director of the Odeon Theatre, and Paul Scofield, photographed by Zoe Dominic for *The Sunday Times* during the Paris tour of *Lear*, May, 1963: Zoe Dominic/ArenaPAL **177** Barry Justice by Gordon Goode, Stratford **179** Patience as Mrs Traipes with Ronald Radd as Peachum and Tony Church as Lockit, in Peter Wood's *The Beggar's Opera*, RSC, 1963. Photo by Zoe Dominic for RSC: Zoe Dominic/ArenaPAL **188** 'O sweet Mr Shakespeare!' Good luck card by Sarah Collier, 1962 **190–191** 'All hands on deck for our Regan!' Good luck card sent by 'Jerry and the boys in the props department,' 1963, probably Gerry Watts, Property Shop Manager at Stratford in 1960s **197** Good luck messages for *The Governor's Lady*, also from Jerry and the boys – see above – and Timothy West **201** Make-up diagram for the role of Anna Andreyevna in *The Government Inspector*, directed by Peter Hall, RSC, 1966 **204** Poster for the RSC's *The Revenger's Tragedy*, directed by Trevor Nunn: © RSC **206** 'Tevye's Dream', showing Patience as Fruma Sarah with Topol in *Fiddler on the Roof*, 1971, directed by Norman Jewison, Mirisch Production Company/United Artists: Peforming Arts Images/ArenaPAL **214** Interior of Inverness House – now the Grand Royale Hotel: Spitzel album, c.1905 **215** New West End Synagogue, interior, St Petersburgh Place: GLA 17.3.2009, © Historic England **220** Arthur Davis's birthday card to Rene, 1921, using one of Mewes and Davis's designs probably for the RAC Club, Pall Mall, completed 1911 **226** Eva as 'Eva Cavalle', 1927, by Hugh Cecil **228** 'Mme Ritcher': the frontispiece to Eva Ritcher's *The A.B.C. of Millinery*, 1961, published by Skeffington and Son **234** Print of the Sabbath dinner, Arnold Wesker's gift to Patience, with note **239** Anna Pollak in Lennox Berkeley's *Ruth*, with Peter Pears, Scala Theatre, 1956 **248** Patience as Betsey Trotwood with Jonathan Kahn as Davey, in *David Copperfield*, directed by Joan Craft for BBC Television, 1974: BBC Photo Library **251** Sarah Campbell's good luck card **253** Patience as Nurse Guinness with Colin Blakeley as Captain Shooter in *Heartbreak House*, directed by John Schlesinger ,National Theatre, 1975: photo by Michael Childers **257** (bottom) Patience rehearsing with Tom Conti for *The Devil's Disciple*, directed by Jack Gold, RSC, 1976: Sophie Baker/ArenaPAL **260** Patience with her grandson Louis, 1978. Photo by Alastair Campbell **262** Patience as Elizabeth I in *The Life of Shakespeare* series, directed by Robert Knights, ATV, 1976–7 **264** Patience as Katerina Matakis in Who Pays the Ferryman, BBC, 1977, produced by William Slater: BBC Photo Library **270** Patience as Mrs Poulteney in *The French Lieutenant's Woman*, directed by Karel Reisz, United Artists, 1980. Still © Frank Connor **277** Patience as Queen Victoria at the Brackenbury Primary School centenary, 1979 **278** Drawing from *Beau Brummel* playbill, devised and performed by Paul Alexander, and directed by Patience Collier, 1981–82 **287** (top) Jeremy Brett with Alice Lytton at 23 Campden Hill Rd, 1970. Photo by Roger Pring **290** Patience at N° 23 Campden Hill Rd, 1982 by Kenny Lintott **297** Patience Collier by Robin Alexander, 1987 by kind permission of the photographer. **303** Rene Ritcher before she became Patience Collier, photographed by Walter Bird, c.1932.

ACKNOWLEDGEMENTS

This project could never have progressed without the generous support of Patience Collier's daughter, the designer Sarah Campbell, who gave me complete access to the personal archive on behalf of the family. She helped secure interviews with her mother's former colleagues, provided her own memories and observations, and assisted with its production, without ever wishing to influence the approach I was taking. My warm thanks too for the interest, commitment and support of Patience's son, Joe, his wife, Rohan, and Patience's grandchildren, Charlotte and Sophie Herxheimer and Daniel Collier. My gratitude too to the Postgate family, who so kindly lent their mother's notes and gave me complete freedom to use them.

The book depends on the lively memories of those who knew Patience, and it has been a fascinating journey to hear her being recreated through their stories. Pat Albeck, Robin Alexander, Paul Alexander, Rosemary Beattie, Helen Bourne, Peter Brook, Sarah Campbell, Sally Coles, Joe Collier, Daniel Collier, Rohan Collier, Vernon Dobtcheff, Paola Dionisotti, Susan Engel, Brenda Ferris, John Gorrie, Paul Greenhalgh, Charlotte Herxheimer, Sophie Herxheimer, Kathryn Hughes, Paul Huntley, Robyn Karney, Charles Kay, Penelope Keith, Kenny Lintott, Joanna Lumley, Alec McCowen, Caroline Morgan, Christopher Morahan, Debbie Postgate, Peter Rice, Reg Samuel, Ruth Schachter, David Summerscale, Pauline Summerscale, Helen Taylor-Robinson, Louise Walker, Zoë Wanamaker, Timothy West, Penelope Wilton: I would like to thank you all for your generosity with your time and recollections, for your hospitality and most helpful introductions to other colleagues.

I would also like to thank archivists and librarians for their help at the BBC Sound Archive and Photo Library, the British Film Institute, the British Library, the Cambridge University Library, the Guildhall Library, the archives at King's

College, Cambridge, the Houghton Library at Harvard, the National Archives, the National Portrait Gallery, the National Theatre archive, the New York Public Library, the RADA Library, the Royal Shakespeare Company archive, and at the University of East Anglia archives. I would particularly like to express appreciation for the help of archivists at the BBC Written Archive over successive visits and Biddy Hayward at ArenaPAL Ltd.

My thanks to those who have most kindly allowed me to use particular images - the archives referred to above, but especially, Robin Alexander, Debbie Postgate and Sally Coles, and of course the Collier family. I would also like to thank Sophie Herxheimer for permission to use in full her poem, 'Actress Grandmother.'

My appreciation too of The Literary Consultancy, which gave a 'Free Read' critique early on, and to staff and tutors at the national Writer's Centre based here in Norwich. I would particularly like to thank the writer Keiron Pim, for his advice, mentoring and kind encouragement.

Thanks also goes to my copyeditor, Sue Lascelles, for her invaluable help.

Very special appreciation goes to Alastair Campbell for his brilliant design of the book, with my warm thanks for all his invaluable help.

Some of the people who contributed their memories have sadly died before this project could be completed: the actor Alec McCowen, who so kindly entertained me with tea, stories and videos of Patience, the designer Pat Albeck and theatre designer Peter Rice, who were my first interviewees, each with a different take on Patience, and Daniel Collier, Patience's grandson, keen to tell me about his experience of Patience as an extraordinary actress grandmother. I would like to pay tribute to them. I would like also to specially remember Patience's eldest daughter, the designer Susan Collier, who with her sister first told me about their mother's personal archive. She died in 2011, before the project could begin.

And finally my special appreciation of the support and endurance of my husband, Sam, who has put up with the ups and downs of this long project and acted as a most supportive critical reader.

INDEX

Entries in italics indicate images

A

B

C

S

ABOUT THE AUTHOR

Vanessa Morton is a graduate of the Life-Writing MA, part of the celebrated Creative Writing school at the University of East Anglia. She won the Lorna Sage Memorial Prize and a distinction for her achievement there in 2010. With a doctorate too in social history, she has taught literature and social history with the University of Colorado, the Open University and the University of East Anglia.

She has been involved in local and community politics, served as a city councillor, and has worked at senior level for local government.

Her writing has appeared in anthologies and, in 2012, her first book, *Travelling Towards War*, was shortlisted for the East Anglian Book Awards. An early draft for *The Performer's Tale* won her a 'Free Read' in 2014, under the national scheme with The Literary Consultancy. In 2018 she collaborated with her husband on a book of memoir and social history, *Taking the Boy Out of Ballymena*. She lives in Norwich.

By the same author

'The Sitters' in *UEA Creative Writing Anthology*, 2010 (Egg Box Publishing)
Travelling Towards War, 2011 (Matador)
'Earlham Hall Unwrapped' in *Ziggurat*, 2014/15 (UEA)
Taking the Boy Out of Ballymena (ed.), 2018